# Acknowledgements

# There are so many people to thank for their help

I really don't know where to begin. Probably the first person I need to thank is my cousin, Deann's daughter, Rachel Harrison. Without her help and expertise, this book would not have been completed, at least not in its present form. I cannot thank her enough for all the pictures she helped me with and to do it without strangling me shows maturity far beyond her years. If the book has any redeeming qualities, it is definitely because of the pictures.

After my retirement from First Security at the end of 2001, they allowed me to keep my office and use their computer to write this book. I cannot thank them enough for this kind gesture. It has certainly helped me, because I found that I could not work on the book at home. Thanks to Sid Halma and the Catawba County Museum of History for allowing me to use their pictures of the Flood of 1940. They worked beautifully with the pictures I had. I need to thank them also for their encouragement.

Two beautiful ninety year old women are also to be greatly thanked. Lillian Holsclaw and Lil Stepp have been a Godsend for me. They both have an extensive collection of pictures pertaining to Brookford. So many of the pictures used in this book are from their collections. I know at times I had to be a pest, but their patience and encouragement were a great help to me. The book would not be complete without their efforts.

Of course, I need to thank Ann Pope Little and Joe Thomas Elders for allowing me to include their writings on Pope Hill and on Living in Brookford. Their contributions only made the book better. There are so many others to thank and I certainly hope I do not leave anyone out. I could use the easy way out and say thanks to all of the people with Brookford connections, but I choose not to do so because many need to be thanked individually. It was a joy to get the information from Babe Thompson for the articles on her and Chop and on Seth and Kate Miller and on her dad and mom. Babe has always been one of my favorite people ever since she took us to the play in the branch. Naomi Bolick Taylor was a tremendous help on the article on her dad and mom and her grandmother, Mother Bolick. She also furnished some much needed pictures. She helped in guiding me about some of the historical facts about Brookford. She remembers better than I do. She should have been the one to write the book. Ruth Hollar graciously help me on the article about her and Pete. She is another beautiful ninety year old woman. I do believe Brookford leads the league in beautiful ninety year old women.

Leoma Melton Hamby and Buck Melton provided so much information on their dad and mom that the article wrote itself. Their dad and mom were two wonderful people and added so much to my life. Thanks to Mildred Deal for her help on the article about her daughter, Tenita. Forest Gaines, Margie Helton, Bruce Bishop, Sue Helton Griffin, Carol Robinson, and Mary Burns are to be mentioned for their contributions.

Annie, Max and David Crump were so cooperative in helping put the article together on Annie and Baxter. Hillside Baptist Church ever stands as a living monument to the faith of Annie and Baxter. Reba Foster Poovey and David Foster brought back so many memories of their dad and mom, Bertha and Jerm. David's daughters, Debbie and Theresa are also to be thanked. Jerm and

Bertha are one of the beautiful love stories of Brookford. Viola Wallace Mitchell provided much information and pictures on her mom and dad. Shilda Berry Burns gave me insight on the article about the Summer of 1944 as well as some of the best pictures used in the book. Annie Berry Barlow and Jennie Berry Lewis offered a number of pictures as well as encouragement. Bruce Bishop gave much help about the polio camp at Lake Hickory.

Jerry Copas provided much information on the Brookford Mills Basketball Team. Babe Thompson's daughter, Carolyn found prize pictures of the boarding house and the Union Hall Building. Boots Milam came up with a real find in her grandmother's scrapbook of Brookford people serving in World War II. Lamar Hunt had some wonderful pictures that he shared with us. Carroll Bartholomew gave us pictures of Dugaloo and the arrest paper of Brookford's Calaboose.

Betty Lafone gave much insight and information on Grandview School on Windy Hill, a school I had not heard of until I started this book. She has been one of my staunchest supporters and one anxiously awaiting this book. I just hope it is worth the wait. My daughter, Kelley took the time to make copies of all deeds used in this book as well as the plats. Myrtle Laney Franklin was a great help to me on the article on her mom and dad. Chris Revis, my neighbor down the street, allowed us to use the lyrics to his song, "Mill House Dream." Now if he can just find someone to write the music, we may be singing his song one day.

Last but certainly not least I need to thank my daughter, Amy and her husband, Nap. I literally could not have done the book without them for they served as my editors and my publishers. I am eternally indebted to them. I am sure that with all the names mentioned I still have left some people out, but one of the benefits of having attained the age of sixty eight years is that you can always claim senility. Unfortunately that is too close to the truth to be funny. I close these acknowledgments on a note of sadness because five of the people who helped me with this book are no longer with us. Tom Workman, Aileen Wilson, Stella Grubb, Ralph Reinhardt and Nelda Elrod Campbell all passed away before this book could be completed. Each one of them was a great help and inspiration to me and I regret deeply that I will never have the opportunity to give them one of the books. The last time my wife, Jackie, saw Tom at the doctor's office, he said to her, "I'm waiting."

## Tribute
___

This is a tribute to the two people who raised me, my mom, Maggie Lee Little and my granny, Essie Louiza Price Little. A person is indeed blessed to be born into a loving and supportive family. I certainly am most fortunate to be raised by these two wonderful women and I am proud to write this tribute to them.

My granny was born May 20, 1882 in the Newton area of Catawba County. At age 15, she married John Riggs and this marriage produced a son also named John. Not long after the birth of her son, her husband died, leaving her a widow with a small baby. In 1900, my granny married George Little and this marriage produced five living children.

Not long after the birth of Russell, my grandfather abandoned his family. So now my granny was a single mother with six children. My grandfather never became a part of this family again.

In order to survive, she took a job at Brookford Mills and my mom, Maggie, who was eight years old, had to quit school to look after Russell. My granny and my mom never talked much about this time in their lives, but I know life had to be extremely difficult for them. But I believe the hardships they had to endure only made both of them stronger and more determined. They never allowed their harsh life to grind them down.

By the time I came along in 1935 the roles for my granny and my mom were reversed. Now Granny looked after me while Mom worked in the mill. And look after me she did.

Some of my earliest memories are of being at home with Granny while Mom was at work. She would send me to the Company Store to get three of the things she enjoyed the most - her Tube Rose Snuff, Coca Cola and a Goody's headache powder. She usually produced a nickel for me to get some candy.

She also allowed me to walk down to the steps leading to the mill to wait for my mom getting off from work. This was the highlight of my day! I can still hear that two o'clock whistle blow and see all of the first shift people coming out of the mill after a hard day at work. My mom walking up the sidewalk was a sight for me to behold. Some times in my mind, I am still that little boy waiting for my mom to get off work.

Essie Louiza Price Little with her son, Russell.

> "Perhaps the person had been sick or just needed to talk and granny was there. These visits happened often and mom threatened to send me after her a time or two. But granny was right–that person needed a visit from her."

Everybody on the mill hill called her Granny Little, too, and as she got older, she became the Mill Hill's unofficial "Good Will" ambassador. She would announce to my mom and me, "I have to visit so and so." and off she would go to spend the better part of the afternoon visiting this person. How she knew that they needed a visit, I don't know, but she knew. Perhaps the person had been sick or just needed to talk and granny was there. These visits happened often and mom threatened to send me after her a time or two. But granny was right - that person needed a visit from her.

She also liked to visit some of her relatives in Newton from time to time and ever so often she would take me along with her. The first train ride I ever had was on one such visit. It's sad that I can't remember any of the names of the relatives. I do remember they were always glad to see Granny. Going with her was such fun.

How far granny got in school, I have no idea. In her day most people did not get very much education. Granny could read and I know she could write her name. But how she acquired her wisdom I do not know. She and my mom were two of the wisest people I have ever known. You are supposed to learn through your experiences and life had dealt both my granny and my mom some hard lessons.

In 1952 my granny suffered a stroke from which she never recovered. She was bed-ridden for almost a year before she passed away April 18, 1953. No one ever had a stronger spirit or loved to visit or be a friend than my granny. She taught me so much about life and about love and I miss her to this day. I'm sure she's finding someone that needs a visit and off she goes.

My mom, Maggie Lee Little, was born June 16, 1907 in Catawba County. I know everyone likes to think his mom is the greatest mom in the whole world. I am no exception, but it has taken me the better part of my lifetime to realize just how very special she was.

This is not to imply my mom was perfect. In a time when having a child outside of wedlock was just not done, she had two illegitimate sons. Both of the dads were married men. In the minds of most people this was the worst sin that you could commit. My harshest feeling against my mom was because I was illegitimate. In my teen years this fact was overwhelming to me and it caused a rift between Mom and me. The person I loved the most in my life was also the person I hated the most. It took me a long time to get over these feelings.

Gradually I came to realize that the desire to have a family was the overwhelming reason my mom put herself and my brother Jerry and me through this ordeal. I think the reason she chose to have children with a married man is because she could have the child, but did not have to have a man in her life. And I believe this all goes back to having her dad desert her and her family at such an early age. I never discussed this with my mom, but I arrived at this conclusion on my own.

To the credit of the people of Brookford, the fact that I was illegitimate was never mentioned to me and I'm sure everyone knew about our situation. I suppose there is no lower level in society than being the second illegitimate son of a cotton mill worker. But thanks goes to the people in Brookford for making me feel that I was a part of their community and that I was loved and accepted.

Mom spent most of her life working in the card room at Brookford Mills. I know very little about mill work, but people tell me that the card room is one of the toughest jobs in the mill. I never heard her complain about the work; she was grateful to have a job. And work hard she did. When the mill closed in 1957, my mom was 50 years old and all she knew was card room work. Cotton mills no longer hired women for their card rooms because it was such strenuous work. Mom never worked in a cotton mill again.

In 1961 she sold her beloved home in Brookford and came to live with my family. She soon had a reputation as a baby sitter. Many people in the Hickory area would think nothing of leaving their children in Mom's expert care for days and weeks at a time. They all knew that their children would be looked after and cared for. Some of the children were thrilled to see Mom, because they knew they would get some of her wonderful biscuits and cooking. I know of no better cook than my mom and she never used any recipes. All the food was prepared from her memory. She had quite a baby sitting business going for her up until the time of her death.

My mom loved her family, especially the grandchildren. When my brother Jerry moved to New Jersey in 1955, it almost broke Mom's heart because she would be so far away from Jerry's four daughters. I know she always missed them and was thrilled whenever

> "She always looked for the good in each person she met and if Mag Little was your friend then you were truly blessed."

**My mom Mag Little.**

they came down. She loved my children and seemed happy to be living with us, but it was still not Brookford.

In 1970 my mom had a stroke and was taken to the hospital on a Saturday. She never spoke another word and passed away the next Saturday, October 3, 1970 at the age of 63. They say you never get over losing your mom. It has now been over 33 years since she died and sometime the pain of losing her is as great as the day she died. There are so many things that I wish I had told her. I'm sure she knows about the things I needed to say. But I still regret not having said them.

The longer I live the more I realize how very special my mom was, not only to me, but to everyone whose life she touched. She was filled with unconditional love. She loved her family, her friends and neighbors and always looked for ways to help other people. She always looked for the good in each person she met and if Mag Little was your friend then you were truly blessed.

# Introduction

Any time you get at least two Brookford people together, it is not long before the subject of growing up in Brookford is brought up. Everyone I talked to seems to have only wonderful memories of their childhood in Brookford. I have often thought about this phenomenon. Why do we have this compulsion to talk about Brookford back when? Surely growing up in Brookford couldn't be as wonderful as we remember it. Or could it?

When I made the decision to put together a book on Brookford, I started to recall events of my childhood and I could only remember good feelings about Brookford. I'm sure part of it was selective memory and part of it was the times. I was born in 1935 and started school in 1941. The Depression was over, but World War II was starting. This was a time when we all felt closer to each other. The whole country was behind the war effort. We didn't mind doing without if it helped us to win the war. The only visual news we got of the war was the newsreels at the movies. The war seemed far away and strangely glamorous to a young boy. We kids really had no idea of the horrors of war.

Back then the pace of life was slower and people had more time for each other. Most of us on the mill hill were poor, but we didn't know it. We all felt rich. We had games to play, the woods were just a short distance away, the river was close at hand to fish or swim, the swimming pool would be open in the summer and the school wouldn't be. We had all kinds of ball fields. What more could a kid want? Besides we had all of these wonderful people who made my childhood and the childhood of so many others such a wonderful experience. They made all of us feel looked after and cared for and loved. It was the people of Brookford who made our childhood such a wonderful experience How in the world can we ever thank all of these people who gave us a childhood we are forever talking about? There is really no way to thank them. But in writing about them in this book we can remember all of them again so that they can live on in us and in the lives of our children and in the lives of their children.

The Brookford I knew as a young boy is no longer. The mill stands idle, the Company Store is gone. Not many people even remember Will Pitt's and Fletch Holland's stores. The boarding house, the service station, the swimming pool and the Swinging Bridge are all long gone. The back row of Red Hill was the victim of the state highway department and the rerouting of Highway #127 took care of the Weaver house, the Fisher house and most of the front row of Red Hill. The school building has not had classes since the '60's. Reinhardt Grocery is now the Bo-Peep Restauant and the service station there is now a beauty salon. The baseball field of so many childhood memories is now a softball field. Softball?

The Henry Fork River still flows through Brookford, but the gates of the dam are kept open and the great Henry Fork River of my childhood is now only a little stream. The banks of the river are so overgrown that you can hardly see the river from the road. I doubt if much swimming or fishing is done there now. One of my saddest experiences in compiling the information for the book is my trip to the woods we played in as kids. The field where we played cow pasture ball is nothing but bushes and trees. You can't walk through it much less have a ball game. It was almost impossible to recognize any part of the woods. The branch is still there and minnows are in abundance. (Do you still have the seine, Buck?). I did recognize the clay bank where the branch makes a U-turn near Pope Hill. Back when we played in the woods you could always count on Kingfishers having nests in the bank.

The woods were also a casualty of the rerouting of Highway #127. The scout pond dam was taken along with the Union Hall Building. There is a For Sale sign there for 18 acres and it has a telephone number. Wonder what the going price is for memories. Maybe Thomas Wolfe was right after all. You really can't go home again.

But the Brookford of my memory is still there. In my mind, I can hear the two o'clock whistle blow and see the first shift leaving the mill after a hard day's work. I can still hear the laughter of the kids in the swimming pool. I can see in my mind's eye all the kids coming for that first day of a new school year. I can still feel the love that surrounded all of us kids on the mill hill.

To properly write this book I would need to write about every family that lived in Brookford when I was growing up. Even I realize this is an impossible task. And so I have selected a number of families that had a great influence on my life and life in Brookford, but this does not diminish the influence of families not written about. All the people were important to make Brookford the special place it was in my childhood. Perhaps this book will inspire others to write about the people who had great influences on their lives. If this happens then it will have made all of my efforts and the efforts of the many people who have greatly helped me in this endeavor worthwhile. My only regret in writing this book is that I did not do it sooner, before so many of the people I'm writing about have passed from this life.

# Childhood Memories

## My First Dog

The first dog I ever owned was a small mixed breed dog named Skippy. I had him when I was about five or so. I don't know what it is about kids and dogs, but they seem to understand each other. It was that way with Skippy and me. I can remember this as if it happened yesterday. Granny needed some things from the Company Store. I'm sure a Coca Cola or a Goody's powder or a box of Tube Rose Snuff was included. But she also wanted some ground beef or stewing beef. She gave me a nickel to get some candy. Skippy always came along with me to the store.

With all the things I bought, I could not carry all of them, so I persuaded Skippy to carry something. I knew enough not to trust him with the meat. That would be too much a temptation even for Skippy, not to mention unsanitary. But he could carry the candy I bought. It was taffy candy in a little traveling case with a handle. There we went up the hill from the store. Me with a bag of groceries, and Skippy with the candy case in his mouth. He knew exactly what I wanted and it seemed perfectly natural for him to be doing this for me. When we got home, he gave me the candy. Whether I shared my candy with Skippy, I don't remember. I should have and probably did.

Skippy was the most gentle dog I have ever seen and he really looked after me. Granny should have paid him for baby sitting. It is a shame that I can't remember what happened to Skippy. He probably was run over by a car and my young mind just blocked it out. I have never had another dog quite like Skippy.

## Scottie and Pepper

**Me holding Pepper, with Boo Boo, Pepper's best friend**

This is a picture of me about age 10 holding my dog, Pepper. The other dog licking himself is Rose Wallace's dog, Boo Boo. Pepper and Boo Boo were the best of friends. They played together all the time. In fact, they were playing around on Rose's back porch when Pepper fell off the porch and I suppose he broke his right hind leg. We didn't take him to the vet because we didn't know what a vet was and even if we did, we couldn't afford it. From that day on, I had the only three legged dog on the hill. Pepper got along fine, but he never used that leg again.

Boo Boo was not the friendliest dog around. He probably bit half the people living on our hill. But Rose loved him despite his shortcomings and he was always good for Pepper. He never bit me, I guess because I belonged to Pepper.

How I came to acquire Pepper is a story in itself. The Guins across the way from us had a female Boston Terrier, who had a litter of puppies. They evidently knew more about breeding than most of us on the Mill Hill, because the pups were all beautiful, except for

Pepper. He was the runt of the litter and was downright homely. Anyway the Guins sold off the whole litter except Pepper. My Uncle Neal and Aunt Margaret bought one and named him Skipper. He was a beautiful dog. But the Guins still hadn't sold Pepper.

I had gone over to see the puppies when they were born. I had a keen interest, because I had witnessed the mother of the puppies get hit by a car across from Reinhardt's Grocery Store. She was carrying the puppies then and we all thought she was dead, but she was just knocked unconscious. She recovered and had no trouble delivering the pups, so when the puppies were born I was one of the first to visit. I thought all of the puppies were beautiful, but I was especially drawn to the runt of the litter. I knew my mom could not afford to buy one of the puppies and besides I already had Scottie and two dogs were one too many.

One day some of Guins' kids showed up at my house carrying that runt of the litter. They hadn't sold that dog (maybe they weren't trying too hard). They told my mom that the dog was mine free of charge. How could my mom tell them that I already had a dog and we certainly did not need another one? Besides I'm sure she saw in my eyes how much I wanted that puppy. I probably had not talked about anything but that puppy for days. I'm also sure the Guins saw how much I was smitten by Pepper. Getting Pepper was one of the happiest days of my life.

Scottie and Pepper got along just fine, but both of them had one glaring fault. They loved to fight other dogs. It didn't matter how big or how mean the other dog was, they would light into him. Sort of a tag team, before tag teams were popular. Ed Isenhour's family had a big dog and every time they met they got into a fight. Scottie took the dog head on, while Pepper got under the dog and bit him on the belly. I about never got those dogs separated.

One day Mom had some friends visit from Lexington. I don't know if they and Mom concocted this story or not, but they approached me about buying Scottie because, supposedly, they lived out from Lexington and needed a good watch dog. They finally got me to agree to sell them Scottie. I could see that having two dogs was kind of wearing on Mom. They paid me $1 for him and as they drove away, I felt like Judas Iscariot. Sure Scottie was a pain in the backside sometimes, but he belonged to me and I had betrayed him by selling him to strangers. What remorse I felt that day. The news from Lexington that Mom's friends had stopped at a service station along the way and Scottie bolted from the car didn't make me feel any better. Except that I had hopes he would find his way back home. That didn't happen and I never heard anymore about Scottie. Whatever happened to the blood money I do not remember.

> "It didn't matter how big or how mean the other dog was, they would light into him. Sort of a tag team, before tag teams were popular."

So now it's just me and Pepper. He was a good dog, but he still liked to fight. It didn't matter how big the dog was, but I think Pepper forgot one important change. He didn't have Scottie as backup. He got his clock cleaned pretty often. But his zeal for a fight never waned. I guess it was just the bulldog in him.

One day, I remember it as a Sunday, a man was driving around on the hill. That was not unusual as Sunday afternoon was visiting time on mill hills. He spotted Pepper and stopped. He asked me if that was my dog and I told him it was. He asked me if I would sell the dog to him. I had already been through that one time and I certainly wasn't going to put myself through that agony again. Besides, Pepper wasn't for sale, and I told the man as much. Later that afternoon I went looking for Pepper to feed him and I could not find him anywhere. I thought he might be playing with Boo-Boo behind Rose's house. I found Boo-Boo but Pepper was not around. I called and called, but he didn't come. Then I remembered the conversation I had with the man in the car. To my way of thinking it was unthinkable that a person would steal another person's dog, but evidently that is exactly what happened. That man stole my dog! After that, I lost all desire to have a dog. It was just too heart breaking . I never owned another dog after Pepper until I was married and our kids wanted to have a dog. I was never able to attach myself to another dog. After all, growing up, I had three of the best dogs in the world, Scottie and Pepper and Skippy.

It just occurred to me that I'm supposed to be writing about Brookford and here I am boring everyone about my three wonderful dogs. But dogs were a lot about our growing up in Brookford. They were allowed to roam free back then, the way dogs are meant to be.

Sure, it made for a lot of dog fights and a kid getting bit now and then and maybe a chicken disappearing, but it was all worth it. I'm sure that everyone who grew up on a mill hill has a favorite dog story. It was just a part of mill hill life.

## The Woods

If the river was the favorite place for kids to play in the summer, the woods ran a close second and you could play in the woods all year round. The woods I'm talking about ran from Pope Hill down to the scout pond behind the Company Store. The games you could play there were only limited by your imagination.

Part of the woods also served as a cow pasture. I can't remember anybody having any cows except for Ode Hunt and Buck Melton's dad, Lee. The cow pasture had a flat piece of land near the Gaines' and it made a perfect ball field. It only had two drawbacks. A foul ball to the right might end up in the branch, and you had to be sure you stepped on the base and not a cow patty. We had a lot of good games down there. Talk about cow pasture ball.

Today that cow pasture is overrun with trees, or it was. The new Highway #127 has taken not only the scout pond, but also many of the trees. I suppose that is called progress. One thing is sure - you couldn't play a game of cow pasture ball there today.

By the time I came along, the scout pond was no longer a pond. The dam leaked and the water was no deeper there than the rest of the branch. My brother Jerry told me that he first learned to swim in the scout pond. I would love to have seen it when the dam worked. But there were so many other things you

Cow pasture where we once played ball. Now so overgrown you cannot walk through it.

could do at the branch You could dam it up with sand to make a mini wading pool. The pool didn't last that long because the water eventually burst the dam.

We must have seined the branch dozens of times all the way from the scout pond up close to Pope Hill. We were practically on a first name basis with about every minnow there. We usually put them all back into the water. The bait of choice for us when we fished was usually worms; besides there was just a limited number of minnows in the branch and we wanted to keep on seining.

Looking for crawfish was another activity for us. The branch had lots of rocks in it and we found quite a few crawfish. Of course we didn't keep them. What could you do with a crawfish?

Seth Miller once had a cable hung from a large tree at the branch near our ball field. You could swing out over this mighty expanse of water (maybe 6 feet wide) and back. I don't think anyone ever tried to drop to the other side. It was just too risky. Carolyn Thompson said the cable was still there when the tree came down. She also remembered that she regularly dropped from the swing onto the other side. Just like a girl to upstage us boys. Anyway the swing kept us occupied for a long time, which might have been Seth's intention all along.

The best game we played in the woods was war. This was during World War II and the woods were the perfect place to wage war. It seemed like every day at school during assembly we sang "Let's Remember Pearl Harbor". By the time school let out, we were at a fever pitch to do battle. Down to the woods we went with our guns and our helmets to play war. Most of the time we fought the Japs. With a little imagination, the woods resembled the jungles we saw in the movies and everybody saw himself as John Wayne. I can truthfully say that we never lost a battle down in the woods.

Every now and then we persuaded Paul Pope to play war with us. He was a little older than the rest of us. He was blond headed and had blue eyes and most importantly, he owned a German Luger. When he played we fought the Germans and he played the part of the German officer to perfection. We always killed him at the end of battle and Paul died better than anybody else. It took him a good ten minutes to die. What a glorious day it was for the Allied Forces when he finally died.

One time Jim Mitchell decided that in order to be authentic soldiers we needed to wear stripes. He sent my cousin Joe and me home to have Granny sew on our stripes. Both of us were to be privates (I'll bet Jim didn't give himself any private stripe – most likely he had Master Sergeant stripes). When we came back to Jim's house after lunch with our stripes sewed on, he took one look at us and said, "Granny sewed those stripes on upside down. You guys will just have to be in the Air Force." That pretty well ended the stripes business. Anyway I liked the infantry better.

Once we decided that you couldn't fight a war properly without foxholes. We selected the perfect spot for ours. They were on high ground (we paid attention to detail in the war movies) and they worked perfectly. The enemy could hardly get across the branch, much less take the high ground. We all patted ourselves on the back about the brilliant idea of foxholes. That is until the next day, when Ode Hunt informed us that we would have to fill them in. His cows could step into one of them and break a leg. We did what he told us to do reluctantly. Some people just never understood "war".

It's strange, but the whole time we played in the woods, we never played Cowboys and Indians. We always played war because it was always on our minds. You would have had to have lived during that time in history to fully understand the mood of the country. Everybody was behind the war effort. I can still see in my mind the huge pile of scrap metal we all collected. I think everyone on the Mill Hill added to it. Oh, what I would give

**The branch where we played.**

> *"When the war was finally over, what a wonderful feeling it was for all of us. Words are inadequate to describe the feeling. We knew all of our guys would be coming home."*

to have a picture of that pile. I'm sure it was not as big as I remember it. But every one of us was proud of what we had done.

It was considered unpatriotic to complain about the hardship we were enduing here. All we had to do was see the news reels of how bad our fighting forces had it in Europe and in the Far East The rationing and doing without was just a minor inconvenience compared to what they were going through. All because a few jerks (Hitler, Tojo, and Mussolini) decided they wanted more. Never has a country been more behind a war effort than our country was during World War II.

When the war was finally over, what a wonderful feeling it was for all of us. Words are inadequate to describe the feeling. We knew all of our guys would be coming home. There was a song during the war that was popular. The title to the song as I remember it was, "The White Cliffs of Dover." In the song there is a line "There'll be love and laughter and peace ever after, tomorrow just you wait and see". Tomorrow was here!

And our battles down in the woods kinda died out after the war ended. All in all, it was great fun for us, but like the real soldiers, we were all tired of fighting. It was time to get on with our lives.

But the woods were still there and they were meant to be played in. Buck Melton and I got into the questionable practice of riding trees down. Young pine trees were great to ride down. What you did was climb to the top of the tree and then swing your weight out. The tree would bend over and slowly let you down to the ground. It was a great ride.

Unfortunately one day I decided to ride down a young poplar tree. I climbed to the top and swung my weight out. I learned too late that poplar trees don't bend, they break. The tree broke when I was about 12 to 15 feet off the ground and deposited me on my backside. That's about the time my love for tree riding cooled down.

If you didn't have anything else to do on the hill, you could always take your slingshot down to the woods. Buck Melton had a state of the art slingshot and he was an excellent shot. I couldn't hit the side of a barn with my puny slingshot.

We had a variety of targets, such as rabbits and squirrels and birds also I'm sad to say. I never hit a living thing with my slingshot. One day I was shooting at a bird in a tree. I missed the bird, but nearly knocked the whole tree down. Buck never let me live that down.

As we got older, both of us graduated to BB guns. The gun helped my accuracy some, but not much. One of our favorite targets was an insect Buck called a snake feeder. How that name came about is beyond me. Buck will have to explain that to you. But every time we saw a snake feeder we knew there was a snake lurking about and that insect was gonna feed it. I always had a semi-desire to see that procedure. Buck could pick off the snake feeders easily. I don't think I ever hit one, although I did kill a few throwing sand at them. Let them snakes go hungry.

One day I was down in the woods by myself with my BB gun. When I'm alone I'm in bad company, but I didn't know how disastrous this day was gonna be. I'm walking up the path toward Pope Hill and I see a bird in the top of a tree. It must have been 75 yards from me. What possessed me to shoot my BB gun in that direction escapes me. Annie Oakley could not have hit that bird from that distance, but I did. That bird toppled out of the tree to the ground, dead as four o'clock.

The remorse I felt at that instant was overwhelming. I thought God would strike me dead for killing one of His creatures. If only I could take that shot back, I would give anything. But I did give that beautiful bird a proper burial down by the branch and I never aimed that BB gun at another living creature again.

The woods provided so many wonderful times for all of us on the Mill Hill. Our parents never worried about us if we were playing down in the woods. How sad it is that kids today do not have the freedom of the woods. I can still hear my granny standing on the front porch yelling "**Dyykieee**, come to dinner". We would all head for the house to eat.

Thank you for the woods, Lord.

## Nicknames

It seems that mill hills were always full of nicknames and Brookford was the best or worst for nicknames, according to your point of view. We had nicknames for people, places and things, and sometimes we had nicknames for nicknames.

A good illustration of this is in a conversation I had with a woman not too many years ago. She was telling me that her daughter, who lived in Greensboro, was dating a guy that grew up with me in Brookford. I asked who the guy was and she answered "Lewis Fisher". I thought and thought, but I couldn't remember a Lewis Fisher from Brookford and told her so. She was sure that he knew me and that we grew up together. Finally it dawned on me. "Oh, you mean "Cooter" Fisher", I said. She looked at me disgustedly and said, "You people from Brookford are all alike. You give nicknames to everybody!" Well, maybe we did.

In other articles I have mentioned other nicknames such as "dugaloo" for Scrip Money, "Bad Eye" Starnes for Earl Starnes, "Pigeon" Weaver for Howard Weaver and "Unk" Keller for Arthur Keller.

Perhaps the cleverest nickname was for a man named William Schildnecht, who lived over in the country. He came to the U.S. from Germany, and he had a thick German accent that was barely understood by us flat talking locals. He worked in the maintenance department at the mill and was married to the sister of my seventh grade teacher, Mrs. Brooks.

His main distinction, besides his accent, was a very long neck. The people of Brookford could never pronounce Schildnechkt, but it sounded like "Short Neck" and that is what everybody called him.

He was such a kind and gentle man, and he always responded to "Short Neck". I guess he saw it was useless to try to correct us. He was a real asset to the mill. He could repair just about anything and was always good natured.

I've often wondered if he received any harassment during World War II. Our hatred for the Germans and the Japanese was rampant on the mill hill. I hope none of this hatred was ever directed toward him. He certainly didn't deserve it.

Later, after I was married, he was trying to sell 10 acres of his property located just off Zion Church Road. At his age, the property had probably become more than he could look after. I heard about the property and went over to look at it. He showed me the property lines and it would have been an ideal place for a home. He was asking $750 for the 10 acres and that was more than a fair price, but back then, $750 was a lot of money and I finally told him that I couldn't afford it. He looked at me and said, "You'll regret not buying this land." Little did I know how much I would regret it. Years later the new part of Highway #321 came right by this property. It's like my mom always said, "If it was raining silver dollars, us Littles would be out there with pitchforks." But I digress. I'm supposed to be writing about nicknames.

In my writings, I have often referred to "Buck" Melton. How he came to have that nickname is kinda an evolvement. His given name was Paul Othneal Melton and he went by the name Othneal. To his brothers and his sisters, Othneal sounded an awful much like "Oatmeal" and that's what they called him for awhile. "Oatmeal" didn't quite do it, so they started calling him "Buckwheat" (another cereal?) Eventually this was shortened to "Buck", and to most of the people in Brookford he's still known as "Buck" Melton.

I'm also going to include a nickname for Buck's sister, Leoma, in hopes that she won't blue pencil it. When Leoma entered puberty, she became extremely healthy in the chest area. This sudden development did not go unnoticed by her brothers and sisters. So naturally her nickname became "Bump". We'll just have to see if she'll let me keep it in, and if she does, will she still respond to the name "Bump"? Good news! I talked to Leoma while getting the information on the book and she had no objection at all. In fact, she still responds to the nickname, Bump.

Even the fact that you couldn't put any meat on your bones could earn you a nickname. My cousin, Charles Mitchell, was one such kid growing up and "Runt" became his nickname. Charles was always a favorite with Ruth and Lee Melton and when their last son was born, they named him Charles. Of course, his nickname became "Runt" also. Sort of a semi-second generation nickname.

The best nickname for a place has to be "Mexico", a part of the mill hill located just east of the mill near Frank's hosiery. I asked someone why they called it "Mexico" and the explanation he gave me was that part of the mill hill was stuck over there by itself and wasn't considered part of the continental USA; i.e. the rest of the mill hill. Explained that way it makes sense.

Left: Charles "Runt" and Bobbie Mitchell on back of their dad's car.

Right: Edwin "Tight" Warren after working on his car.

The second best nick-name for a place has to be "Possum Holler". It was the row of houses just below "Mexico". Today there are just two houses there, but growing up I remember more houses. Maybe it was just my imagination.

An area down from the mill hill on Sub Station Road was called "Shanty Town". It was not called that because of all the fine homes there. It wasn't actually a part of the mill hill, but that didn't stop us from bad-mouthing it.

How "Red Hill" got to be called that I'm not sure. The first ball field was located there and I suppose the red dirt and the dust earned it that nickname. The ball field was long gone before I was born, but "Red Hill" is still there, or at least part of it is. The state highway department keeps taking parts of it. The whole back row was taken when I-40 was completed and the new route for Highway #127 has just taken a few more houses on "Red Hill", as well as the Company Store and the old Fisher and Weaver homes.

When you tell someone you came from Brookford they almost always ask if you lived on "Red Hill". The stock answer is "No, I lived on the other hill". I was born and raised on the other hill. It didn't have a name unless you consider "the other hill" a name.

Unk Keller's family probably had the most nicknames. Besides Unk (Arthur) there were Buck (Marshall), Droop (Marvin), Sphynx (Hildred), and Chick (Margaret).

My cousin, Jim Mitchell, tells me we spent quite a bit of time down at the porch area at the Company Store picking up "Ducks" for Paul Pope. I don't remember doing this, but if Jim says so I guess we did. What is a Duck? It's the part of the cigarette the smoker throws away after he's finished. And the area at the Company Store was the best place to find them. I suppose we did this for Paul in hopes he would play war with us in the woods.

"Ducks" was also what you said when anyone was drinking a bottled drink around you. They were legally and morally obligated to leave some of the drink for you.

**Red Hill school students.**

A good long while after I had completed the first draft of this article, I was in Clark Tire and I saw this man that I knew had to be from Brookford. I walked up to him and said, "I know your face is very familiar and it has Brookford written all over it, but I can't come up with a name. I'm Dyke Little, and I grew up on the mill hill." He looked at me a long time and finally said, "I'm Doughbelly Newton and it's probably been fifty years since I've seen you." I mention this conversation to point out how important nicknames are to Brookford people. He didn't identify himself as Charles Newton, but as Doughbelly Newton. He knew I would remember his nickname.

This article on nicknames has a life all its own. Recently my son, Jon, was in Flat Rock, North Carolina and stopped in a bakery there. The place was owned by a husband and wife. During the conversation, Jon mentioned that he grew up in Hickory and the lady said that she had a Hickory connection. She said that her father grew up on a mill hill not far from Hickory. Jon said "It couldn't by any chance be Brookford?" The lady's name is Alexis and she is the oldest grandchild of Mildred Deal and the late Ed Deal. Jon thought she told him that her father's name is Eddie. I called Mildred to tell about my son's conversation with her granddaughter and tell her what a small world it really is. Mildred said, "Her father's name is Norman not Eddie". Eddie's name I could remember, but I didn't remember the name "Norman". Mildred said "You may remember him by his nickname "Cooch". Cooch I remember.

# The Playing Fields

The Mill Hill offered an unlimited number of places to have a ball game. The only limitations were getting enough people to play and your own imagination. The ball field in the cow pasture has already been mentioned and it was a great place to play ball, but then almost any place on the Mill Hill could be a ball field.

Of course, the very best place was the ball field up at the school. As mentioned before, the field was built with WPA money during the Depression. The government provided the money and the mill provided the labor. It was as good as any ball field in the area, with the possible exception of College field.

The field had a wooden fence around it and it was wonderful to see the guys on the mill team hit one out. Unfortunately by 1946 or so the fence had become so shabby that the mill had to take it down. It definitely took away some of the charm of the field, but it didn't change the field as a place to have a ball game. Besides none of us guys could hit one out anyway.

During the warm months, there was almost a perpetual game in the field near the swimming pool. There was a least one of the Weavers in the game as their house was located in left field. And you could usually count on Ray Fisher being there. His house was located across the road at the Company Store.

The rules of the game were pretty much the same as regular baseball except the game could last all day. The players would change from time to time as somebody would quit to go swimming or go home to eat. How we remembered who was ahead is beyond me.

But one rule remained constant. A ball hit up on top of the bank at the first row of houses on Red Hill was a home run. I never had the power to reach the top of the bank, but there were some guys who reached it regularly. If the ball hit the bank, then it was all you could get. There was an awful lot of fun to be had in those games.

Once when I was a small and gullible tyke, I was in a game in the road behind my house. Back then, you could get away with playing in the road because there was hardly any traffic. The Stepp's lived just across the road from my house. They had a fenced in back yard and a dog named Nap.

> *What is a Duck? It's the part of the cigarette the smoker throws away after he's finished. And the area at the Company Store was the best place to find them.*

During the course of the game, someone fouled a ball over the Stepp's fence, The other players decided that I was the one to retrieve the ball. They could lift me over the fence because I was the lightest (also the dumbest). Well, I found out real quickly why the Stepp's named that dog Nap. He chewed on me pretty good until one of the guys rescued me. I never went back inside that fence as long as Nap was alive.

Probably the shortest lived playing field has to be the field beside my cousin Jim Mitchell's house. Jim decided this field would be a great place for a ball field. I helped him clear it off, but it had one glaring drawback. The field sloped severely from home plate down to left field. Sure, you could hit the long ball - particularly to left field - and you could go from home to second in no time flat. But going from second to home took forever, because you were running uphill. I don't think we ever had but that one game there. Jim must have been blinded by the long ball.

Believe it or not, our favorite place to play on our hill was Mrs. Sprouse's front yard. She was a widow with grown children, but her yard was where we chose to play. She had to know that we were out there playing ball with all the noise we were making and besides the corner of her house was third base. I can never remember her coming out and telling us kids to find another place to play. To me, this personifies what Brookford was all about in those days. We were all family and the whole Mill Hill was our playground. Try doing this in today's world.

If you could not get enough to play a regular game of ball, you always play rolly-bat. You needed at least three players - the batter, the pitcher and the fielder. You could play with more players-the more the merrier. The rules of the game were pretty simple. The batter hit the ball. If the fielder or pitcher caught it in the air or on the first bounce he became the batter. If you caught a ground ball, the batter laid down his bat and you tried to hit the bat with the ball. Hit the bat and you got to be the hitter. About the only arguments were did

**Brookford Ball Field is now a softball field.**

you catch the ball on the first bounce or did the rolled ball hit the bat. There wasn't a lot of strategy in the game except try to hit the ball over everybody's head or hit a lot of ground balls. This game could go on for hours and sometimes we allowed girls in the game. Do kids today still play rolly-bat?

Another game we played was pepper. Major leaguers still play pepper sometimes before a game. It sharpens up their fielding. Danny Thompson and I played pepper when we couldn't get a regular game or a game of rolly-bat. Danny always wanted to be the fielder and I would hit to him. I believe our games of pepper helped Danny to become an outstanding fielder. He went on be captain of the Lenoir Rhyne baseball team his senior year and had an outstanding career there. I also believe it's the reason I'm a good pepper hitter and not much good at anything else in baseball.

Over the years, I played in a lot of games – high school, legion and college, but none could compare to the pickup games down on the Mill Hill.

## Little League Baseball?

When we were the age for Little League Baseball, no such league existed. Sure, the Hickory Recreation Department sent people to the various schools to have summer programs for the kids. The recreation people mainly supervised horseshoe games, volleyball and dodge ball, and made sure we didn't tear up the school or kill anybody.

But baseball games were pretty much left up to the kids. We had to schedule games and get the team together. All of the games were played in the morning. I don't remember ever having any adults around. Most of the parents were either working in the mill or looking after small kids at home.

The year I was 11 years old, we had probably our best team. Joe Elders tells me that we had 6 wins and 1 loss for the summer. Joe remembers more about this than I do. He should be the one writing this article. But I do remember we had some pretty good ball players on that team. Joe was the catcher because he was the only one with a mitt. Paul Reinhardt had given him one of his old mitts. Chad Mitchell was on the team. He could hit the ball a long way as could Richard Laney. Jim Simpson was our best all around player. Bob Newton was an important member of the team, although we had to go get him out of bed to play. He could flat throw a baseball. In one game he almost threw the runner out at first on a ground ball hit to left field.

About the only game that really sticks out in my mind was our game with the Cosmic Bombers. The Bombers were kids from the Oakwood area and we dearly loved to beat kids from Oakwood. The game was held at the Brookford field and the final score was Brookford 44, Cosmic Bombers 4. So much for the Cosmic Bombers.

All in all, we had a successful summer in baseball without all the baggage of adult supervision or parents. We played for the sheer joy of the game. That is probably the way Little League Baseball should be played today. I might add the fields we played on were all adult fields. The bases were 90 feet apart and the pitcher's mound was 60 feet, 6 inches.

# Bottle Cap Baseball

The title might seem strange to someone who has never seen a bottle cap baseball game, but yes we did play bottle cap baseball down on the mill hill. If you couldn't get enough to play a regular game or even to play rolly bat, then bottle cap baseball was the way to go. All you needed was a pitcher and a batter and a broom stick and lots of bottle caps.

The rules of the game were pretty simple. Boundary lines were made. Any ball (cap) that was not hit past the first boundary line was an out. There were second, third, and fourth lines for singles, doubles and triples. The last line was for home runs and you really had to belt one to get it past this line.

**Dyke Little, Jean Ogle, and Joe Elders on a snowy day.**

Pitching bottle caps was elevated to an art. You could make those caps do about anything. You could make them float or drop or rise or curve right or left. You could even make them flutter like a dead bird. In regular baseball, the axiom is that pitching was 75% of the game. In bottle cap baseball it edged closer to 100%. With all you could do with the caps, strikeouts were not uncommon. I hate to keep bringing up Ray Fisher, but he was one of the best at pitching bottle caps.

The game could be played anywhere, even in your own yard (if you picked up the bottle caps afterwards). The best place to play was behind the Company Store at the garages. It was almost like the field was already marked off for us. Just as in our perpetual game at the swimming pool, a home run had to be hit on top of the hill. I can't remember if you got any special recognition should you hit one in the trash bin.

The game could last for hours. If there were a lot of people wanting to play, then you had a round robin tournament in which the player to score a designated number of runs first won the game. The number could be anywhere from 5 to 21, depending on how hostile the crowd was. With this format, everybody got to play, although Ray Fisher got to play an awfully lot – he usually won. Bottle cap baseball provided hours of entertainment for us kids. I doubt you could interest kids today in playing it. Besides where are you gonna find the bottle caps?

# Dugaloo

For a long time, Brookford Mills had a program where if workers needed money to buy food during the week, they could get an advance on their salary. The mill always paid off on Friday so that if you needed to buy food for your family in the middle of the week, you could go and get a token from the office. This token was called scrip money and could only be cashed at the mill owned Company Store. I understand the tokens were in dollars, fifty cents, quarters, dimes, and nickels and you could get about three-fourths of your weekly salary in advance.

But Brookford being Brookford, scrip money was too mundane a description. Everybody there called it "Dugaloo". I'm not sure it was spelled that way. I never saw it written out, but I know that's the way they pronounced it. The first part was pronounced like do and the last part like the name Lou. I'm sure that not all of the dugaloo given to the workers ended up being spent on groceries at the Company Store. Legend has it that a peg-legged bootlegger regularly bought groceries at the Company Store and paid for his purchases in dugaloo! Makes a person wonder.

Not long before he died, "Bad Eye" Starnes told me a funny story about Dugaloo. Seems a man from the Mill Hill ordered a load of wood from a man over in the country. Brookford people called anywhere across the river the "country". Evidently the man from the country didn't know anything about life on the Mill Hill, because he came on Wednesday delivering the load of wood. Anybody who knew anything about Mill Hill people knew that by Wednesday nobody had any money.

But there he was with the load of wood. The man who ordered the wood was at work, but his wife was at home and came running out of the house. She said, "I'm so glad you brought

**Left:** Initiation into secret club. David Foster, Cooter Fisher, Jerry Sigmon and Becky Austin. Becky seems a little reluctant to join.
**Right:** Letha Mae Helton and cousin, Jim Schronce. In the left side of the background is the ever-present wood pile.

**Left:** Dugaloo

**Right:** Record of advance pay to Forest Gaines from the mill.

the wood. We really need it, but I don't have any money to pay you. All I have is Dugaloo."

The man looked at her and said, "Lady, I'm a married man and I don't do anything like that." Whether he left the wood or not, I don't know, but he did leave a good story.

I was telling this story to my niece not long ago and she asked, "Why did they call him "Bad eye?". I said, "Because he had a bad eye". Brookford people called it like they saw it. I don't know if "Bad Eye" ever resented being called that, but if he did, he certainly did not show it. He worked a long time in the Company Store and was always pleasant and helpful. I was almost 30 years old before I found out that his given name was Earl.

# I'm Sorry, Carl Dugan

The Dugan family lived on the other side of the woods from my house on what was then called Sub-Station Road. The house they lived in was about a quarter of a mile from the rest of Mill Hill. How many children the Dugans had I don't remember. All of us on the Mill Hill were needy to some extent. The Dugans were one of the needier families.

Their son, Carl, was in my class at school. His brother, Earl, was a grade behind us. You would think that being so poor and needy would earn Carl and Earl just a little bit of sympathy with the rest of the kids. Unfortunately that didn't happen. They were picked on unmercifully by the other kids, myself included. Carl and Earl were in fights almost every day. How very hard their lives must have been.

When we were in the second grade, our teacher, Miss Jerome, would ask each morning if any one had a birthday today to raise their hand and everyone would sing "Happy Birthday" to them. If nobody raised a hand, Carl would raise his hand fairly often. We must have sung "Happy Birthday" to him six or seven times during the year. All we could think of was that we had to sing happy birthday to Carl Dugan again. I suppose we were too young to realize that this was a cry to be recognized or accepted. I'm sure Miss Jerome understood.

Carl went all the way to the seventh grade with us, but the acceptance never came. The bullying had stopped, mainly because Carl and Earl had learned to take care of themselves. They gave as good as they got. Being one of the gang though never happened.

And that is why I am saying "I'm sorry, Carl Dugan". Sorry that all of us missed out on the opportunity to make your life just a little bit better. All you wanted was just to be accepted. So, "Happy Birthday to you, Carl Dugan" and I hope you found it in your heart to forgive us.

Note: On October 14, 2002 I attended the funeral of Carl's oldest sister, Dorothy Dugan Sherrill. Carl's youngest brother, Tim, filled me in about Carl's life after Brookford School. The family moved to South Carolina and Carl became a champion boxer. He won several golden gloves titles. He later joined the air force and when he had served his time, he came back to live in South Carolina. He married and settled down. He became a Christian and was well liked by all the people he met, both in the workplace and in his neighborhood. In 1967 he suffered a cerebral hemorrhage and died at age 33. The hemorrhage could have been caused by all the blows to the head during his boxing career. Perhaps Carl did indeed forgive us for our treatment of him and Earl in grade school. One thing I do know, Carl found the acceptance that we were reluctant to give him at Brookford.

## Pigeon Weaver's Airplane

One year, during the war, the school got a bunch of toy airplanes and sold them to us. How they got them I have no idea. I never saw planes like these for sale in any store. The planes were made of a sturdy cardboard and resembled the P-51. All of us guys were war crazy and we all had to have one. Even a few of the girls got one. But it was mostly a male thing as they would say today.

The planes came with one little catch. You had to do some engineering on the plane to make it fly properly. You had to put just the right amount of clay on the nose. Too little clay and the plane would flutter like a dead bird. Too much clay and the plane would do a nose dive.

CARL DUGAN

We had a ready-made place to fly these planes –the bank down the left field line at the ball park. The bank was about 15-20 feet high and if you caught the wind just right (another engineering feat?) the plane would sail for a right long way. Before school, during recess and after lunch, we would all be down at the ball field sailing our planes.

Everyone thought he had the best plane. Until one day. We were all on the hill ready to fly our planes, when Pigeon Weaver threw his plane. As we would say today, all systems must have been "go." His plane started out and caught a draft. It sailed higher and higher. All of us started running after that plane, laughing and caught up in the moment. The plane sailed all the way to the road beyond right center field. It must have traveled 500 feet. From that time on, there was no argument who had the best plane, because no one ever duplicated Pigeon Weaver's historic flight.

After that day, I don't remember much about the planes. I'm sure we still sailed them some. But after Pigeon's plane everything else paled in comparison. But at least for one day, we all witnessed history.

# Brookford Home Remedies

There were a lot of home remedies down on the mill hill. You had to be almost dead before you went to the doctor. Money was scarce and a visit to the doctor was the last resort. One such home remedy was warm breast milk for the ear-ache.

When I was about six years old, I met my cousin Joe and his mom coming down the road. Joe had developed an earache and Aunt Chris was taking him down to Ruth Melton's. Ruth had just had a baby, Barbara Jean, I think it was. Of course I had to tag along. There was not much happening that day.

Ruth was out on her back porch. Aunt Chris told Ruth that Joe had an earache and asked if she would put some breast milk in his ear. Ruth proceeded to whip out a breast and squirt the warm milk in Joe's ear.

You talk about something making an impression on me. I was astounded. I don't think I had ever seen a woman's breast before and I know that I had never seen that procedure. The remedy must have worked because Joe

**Site of the flight of Pigeon Weaver's airplane.**

was soon over his earache.. I started thinking that maybe I ought to develop an earache.

It was not too long afterwards, Mrs. Hughes, our first grade teacher, announced that one of our class mates, Katheryn Johnson, had an earache. What an opportunity to share this vast knowledge about earaches I had just learned!

I raised my hand and said, "Mrs. Hughes, I know what we can do for Katheryn, but I will have to whisper it to you." At least I had not taken full leave of my senses. I knew that I could not say the T-word out in public, but at that time in my life, I didn't know the correct word for that part of the female anatomy was breast.

Mrs. Hughes told me to come up and tell her. I proceeded to give her more than an earful about what we could do to help Katheryn. Mrs. Hughes thanked me. I don't know how she managed to keep a straight face. But she did not give Katheryn Brookford's home remedy for the earache. I couldn't understand why because in my young mind I thought all women could produce milk on demand.

I had forgotten all about my whispering to Mrs. Hughes. Obviously she hadn't because she told her husband, Chuck, about the unusual day she had at school.

I suppose this information was too good for Chuck to keep to himself, because he told some of the people in his office at the mill about my remedy for the earache. The word finally got around to my mom. She was waiting for me when I got home from school and proceeded to wear my backside out. From then on, if anybody had an earache, they had to get over it without my help.

# Unk Keller

The first time I met Unk was my first day of school in September 1941. Our paths had not crossed until then. Unk lived on the back row of Red Hill and I lived on the Other Hill. Unk was already experienced in the first grade, having been held back by Mrs. Hughes. As I look back, I'm not sure that Unk wasn't ready for the second grade as much as Mrs. Hughes couldn't bear to let him leave. There seemed to be a special bond between them. Maybe, even then, Mrs. Hughes saw how special Unk was.

> "There were a lot of home remedies down on the mill hill. You had to be almost dead before you went to the doctor."

When we were in the seventh grade, Mrs. Hughes substituted for Mrs. Brooks. She had us do the skit about Brer Rabbit and the Tar Baby. We had done this skit a number of times when we were in the first grade and Unk always played the Tar Baby. So there we were, seventh graders giving the skit and Mrs. Hughes enjoying it more than anyone else. Don't tell me she hadn't missed Unk.

Unk's given name was Arthur, but only the teachers could call him that. If any of the kids called him Arthur, they were in great danger of a thrashing. Unk's language was best described as salty-he cussed like a sailor. And this was at a time when bad words were not spoken. It was as if Unk had two languages- his classroom language and his playground language. How he was able to keep the two separated, I do not know, but I can never remember him using his playground language in the classroom.

Unk's athletic abilities were only so-so. He could hit the long ball, but only occasionally. In the field he definitely was not an asset. When we asked him his batting average, he always answered " Oh about 1500". No one ever corrected him.

I have often wondered what made Unk so special. I believe that even at his early age, Unk was his own person. He wasn't an outstanding student, in fact, I'm not sure the teachers didn't use a little bit of creative grading as far as Unk was concerned. He certainly wasn't a class leader. But he was the best at being himself and nobody was going to change him. Think about it, a child being himself in an age where children were best seen and not heard. Talk about a major accomplishment.

Arthur "Unk" Keller

When we were in the seventh grade, Mrs. Brooks decided that we would give a play of sorts for a PTA meeting. The students in the play would dress like famous people and would have lines that more or less rhymed.

I remember I was to be Robin Hood and for the life of me I cannot remember any of my lines. But I can remember all of Unk's lines. Unk was to be Buffalo Bill Cody and the lines he was supposed to say were: "My name is Buffalo Bill Cody from the Old West. My work is with Pony Express. I carry the mail through the rain, snow and hail." Try as she might, Mrs. Brooks could never get Unk to say "I carry the mail through the rain, snow and hail." Every time Unk said it, the line always came out "I carry the mail through the rain snow and   hell!. Finally in desperation, Mrs. Brooks changed Unk's last line to "I carry the mail through the rain, snow and sleet!"

The night of the play finally came and all of these "famous people" were backstage and ready. Mrs. Brooks had us come on stage in pairs, say our lines and exit the other side. This was the cue for the next pair to come out. Unk and I were paired together and when it was our time to come from backstage, everybody in the audience started laughing. Now mind you, nobody had laughed when the other pairs came out, just when Unk and I came out. I do not know to this day if they were laughing at my skinny legs in green leotards or Unk with his Buffalo Bill Cody hat and his go-to-hell walk.

Both of us got through our lines reasonably well considering the reception we had just received. Unk remembered to say sleet instead of hell, although he did pause just a little bit after rain and snow. And I don't believe anyone in the audience noticed that Unk had the only lines in the play that did not rhyme.

I didn't see Unk after the seventh grade. So many of the people I went to school with at Brookford decided to go Mountain View School. Back then Mountain View had grades 1 through 12. All of us at Brookford had just a little bit of paranoia as far as Hickory was concerned. In fact, I thought about transferring myself, but as far as I was concerned, Mountain View had one glaring shortcoming. It didn't have a football team and I wanted to play football.

Unk decided to go to Mountain View. The books were still throwing him for a loop and there didn't appear to be a Mrs. Hughes or a Mrs. Brooks or a Mrs. Clinard to push him in the right direction scholastically. He would drop out of school for awhile, and then go back for awhile. Finally he gave school up altogether and joined the army. There is no doubt in my mind that Unk could have succeeded at school. He had a native intellect far beyond his years and whatever he wanted to do he could do it if he put his mind to it. He was a sort of modern day Huckleberry Finn.

In the service, he was stationed for a number of years in Germany. His sister, Edith tells me that as far as she knows, he never married or had children. After service, he sort of drifted through life. He came back to Brookford in the mid 70's, his body worn out from years of neglect and abuse. He died much too early in 1977 at the age of 43.

# The Summer of 1944

In the summer of 1944 a polio epidemic hit the whole country and the Catawba Valley was one of the hardest hit areas. A polio camp was set up out near the lake and the care given to the polio victims received national attention. A history of this time and the care given to these victims is well chronicled in the book "Miracle in Hickory". A monument to this special time was constructed on Union Square. The building of the polio camp was a miracle in itself. Bruce Bishop, who contracted polio, told me that when he was taken to the camp, he had to stay in one of the four Army tents set up until a unit was completed for him to moved into. They would eventually have eleven units at the camp. Besides Bruce, the kids from the Mill Hill who contracted polio were Shilda Berry and H.E. Pope. Shilda had by far the worst case. She had to be taken to Charlotte and was in the hospital for fifty one weeks before she was released.

Bruce talked with me at length about his stay at the polio camp. He was eleven years old at the time and would spend four months there. He talked about receiving the Sister Kinney treatment. Sister Kinney was an Australian who developed a treatment involving cloth hot packs. At this point in time not much was known about treatment for polio, but Bruce tells me the Sister Kinney treatment seemed to help him. A cloverleaf hot tub was designed for use in treatment also. Bruce says that he was the first in Hickory to receive this treatment. Life Magazine did a feature on the polio camp and a picture of Bruce in the cloverleaf hot tub was in the magazine. If anyone reading this book has that magazine, Bruce would certainly appreciate a copy.

All of us kids on the Mill Hill were confined to our own yards until the polio threat was over. For a boy who was used to playing in the woods, swimming in the pool, fishing in the river or playing ball wherever he could get a game up, this was the worst of times. Sure, we felt for all the polio victims. We wanted all of them to get well and for the polio threat to be over and for life to get back to the way it used to be.

Buck Melton and I got right inventive about games we could play while technically in our own yards. We played horseshoe a lot with a stake in Buck's yard and a stake in my yard. We played cards and checkers with a blanket spread across the two yards. And we did an awful lot of talking about how bored we were. Buck wasn't much for playing ball, but I did talk him into playing catch with me some.

But the summer went by ever so slowly and then one day it was announced the polio threat was over and we were no longer confined to our yards. What a great day that was! It was even a greater day when all the kids got to come home from the hospital.

I will never forget that summer of 1944 when time stood still.

**left: Hazel and Shilda Berry around late 1944 at hospital tent set up at Charlotte Memorial Hospital for Polio epidemic.**

**Right: That's me at the polio camp looking right pleased with myself. H.E. Pope is right behind me.**

# A Fishy Business

Every now and then, the mill would let the dam off. They opened the gates and took the level of the river down to where it was just a stream. Why they did this I'm not quite sure. Probably it was to clear the river of debris. The only thing I noticed was it made the Henry River muddier than ever and it was muddy enough if you left it alone.

Most of the fish could not survive the muddy water. They would come to the top and start swimming sluggishly and pretty soon they would be belly up. We always said the muddy water killed them, but I'm sure what happened is the mud depleted the oxygen in the water and this is actually what killed them. The mill could not get away with this today. The environmental people would be on their backs in a minute.

Still, letting off the dam was a major event in our young lives. During one such event, Buck Melton and I got the bright idea of taking a wash tub down to the river. We figured we would collect all those sluggish fish and take them back to Mill Hill and sell them.

We had that wash tub practically full in no time. Most of the fish were still moving when we got them, although a few might have already gone belly up. We figured with all these fish we would soon be rolling in the money.

It didn't happen. Nobody wanted those fish. They were mostly horny heads with a few perch and catfish (Buck handled the catfish). And besides, everyone knew they had let the dam off and even if some of the fish were edible they would taste like mud.

All afternoon we dragged those fish all over the Mill Hill and we did not sell a single one. We finally decided we would take them to Buck's house. Maybe his mama could use them. Buck had a big family and a fish dinner would be nice.

**Left: Buck Melton**

**Right: Ruth Pope holding unidentified boy, with son, H.E. and Maggie Little at Lake Hickory Polio Camp in 1944.**

Not only did his mama tell us in no uncertain terms that she didn't want the fish, she told us to get a shovel and take those stinking fish down to the woods and bury them. Here we are muddy, worn out, smelling like fish, digging a hole. And bury them we did. Both of us knew to listen to Buck's mama. She was one sweet woman, but when she told you to do something you did it.

Our fish business lasted less than one day and was considerably short of a success. Afterwards, we both still loved it when they let the dam off, but just for the scenic beauty.

# Miss Hickory 1960

Tenita Deal, daughter of Mildred Deal and the late Ed Deal, brought honor to Brookford in 1960, when she was chosen Miss Hickory. Tenita went on to do very well in the state competition. Perhaps we're just a little bit prejudiced in Brookford, but we still think she is the prettiest Miss Hickory ever!

After winning honors for herself and for Brookford, she moved to New York City to take dancing. While in New York, she applied for a position as a flight attendant for American Air Lines. She was accepted and spent her entire career with them - a total of thirty-nine years. She is now retired and living in Suffern, New York. In her retirement, she is a doll doctor. She repairs and restores antique dolls.

**The lovely Tenita Deal, Miss Hickory 1960.**

## Hog Killing Time

As far as Buck Melton and I were concerned, hog killing time ranked right up there with letting off the dam or the mill's Christmas party at the school. We could talk about nothing else as the time approached. Buck's dad always raised at least one hog every year and the closer the time came, the more excited we became. We were beside ourselves until it finally got cold enough to kill the hog.

We both had to have front row seats when Buck's dad put the .22 slug into the hog's head. Now I cringe just to think about it, but back then it was an event I wouldn't have missed for the world. Half the kids on the hill were watching, too. We watched all the gory details, from hoisting the hog up and dipping it into a barrel of hot water to get it ready to be scraped, to gutting the hog, to quartering. We missed nothing.

We both knew that we would eat very well that night. The fresh pork tenderloin was out of this world. The women prepared hot liver mush in a dishpan - the best liver mush I have ever eaten.

It was worth the wait for us, but I'm sure that hog had a different opinion. It's funny how your feelings change about things. Today I would probably run in the opposite direction if I saw a hog being slaughtered, but back then, at least for Buck and me, life didn't get any better.

## Wheels

Wheels were very big on the Mill Hill. I'm not talking about fancy cars. Most people in Brookford didn't even own a car. The wheels I'm taking about were wheels you used in play. Can you believe pushing an old tire was a form of entertainment back then? I was 15 before I found out you could go somewhere without pushing a tire. That's an exaggeration but not by much. Can you imagine a kid today pushing a tire? I can't either but then it seemed a natural thing to do.

> *All afternoon we dragged those fish all over the Mill Hill and we did not sell a single one. We finally decided we would take them to Buck's house.*

The best set of wheels for kids on the Mill Hill had to be a pair of skates. There were many places to skate. The porch area at the Company Store was a popular place. But the best place had to be the side walk across from the ball field all the way down to the Company Store. I'm told this was quite a ride, although I can't speak from experience. I never learned to skate. I must have been the only kid on the hill who couldn't skate. I tried to learn but Rose Wallace laughed at me for busting my backside and I gave it up. Missed a lot of fun, I'm told.

Making your own go cart was popular at one time. I never actually made one, but I did offer encouragement to Buck Melton and he let me take his cart down the hill from my house toward the Company Store. It was an exhilarating ride because the hill was very steep and the cart had no brakes. I don't know what we would have done if a car had come along. I guess the ditch would have been the only option.

The best set of wheels I ever owned had to be my first bicycle, a green and white Schwinn. I can still remember the day Mom brought it home for me. I could hardly sleep that night. The bike offered real freedom, although that freedom did not extend to Hickory. I was forbidden to ride it there.

**Left: Dr. Hunsucker in the middle of the car.**

**Bottom left: Jack Stepp with his fancy tractor.**

**Bottom right: Wally Stepp at the ball ground. What did I tell you, Wally? You're in the book.**

In gathering pictures for this book, I was amazed how many pictures involved wheels of some sort, from red wagons to play tractors to fancy cars. You'll recognize many of Brookford's leading citizens in these pages. My favorite picture is Joe Reinhardt standing proudly beside his fancy car.

Joe Reinhardt

## A Boy and a Pony

No book on Mill Hills would be complete without a picture of some kid taken on a pony in a cowboy outfit. This kid happens to be me and there is a story behind the picture. My mom tells me that after the man snapped my picture, he couldn't get me off the pony. Try as he may, I clung to the pony. I cried and cried. Finally in desperation, he bribed me. He told me I could ride that pony up to the Meltons. That is how he finally got me off the pony and the cowboy outfit off of me. This picture also reveals several things about our house and the Mill Hill, in general. Our house and the house below us were the two oldest employee houses on the hill. Both had clapboard siding, whereas the rest of the houses had regular plank siding. The stick holding up the window is typical Mill Hill…no underpinning at this time for the employees houses.

But my mom didn't say anything about riding it other places. One day, Buck and I decided to take a ride on the new highway (now Hwy #70). The highway was just being completed and was not open to traffic. It was the perfect place to ride bikes, except we didn't stay on the new highway. We got on the Old Shelby Road and rode down toward the river. Buck had heard some slot machines had been dumped into the river and we needed to check that out. As I remember it, some people were swimming in the river. They probably had heard the same rumor. They didn't find any slot machines.

By now it was getting kinda late and we were a far piece from Brookford. Buck said he knew a shortcut home, but it was almost dark before we got home. My mom was not a happy person. If she only knew…

## Dr. Charles Hunsucker

Dr. Charles Hunsucker was the mill doctor for a number of years in the 1930's and early 1940's. If the truth be known, he probably delivered most of my generation down on the Mill Hill. He was a stylishly dressed man and was described by more than one of the woman I interviewed for this book as a hand-

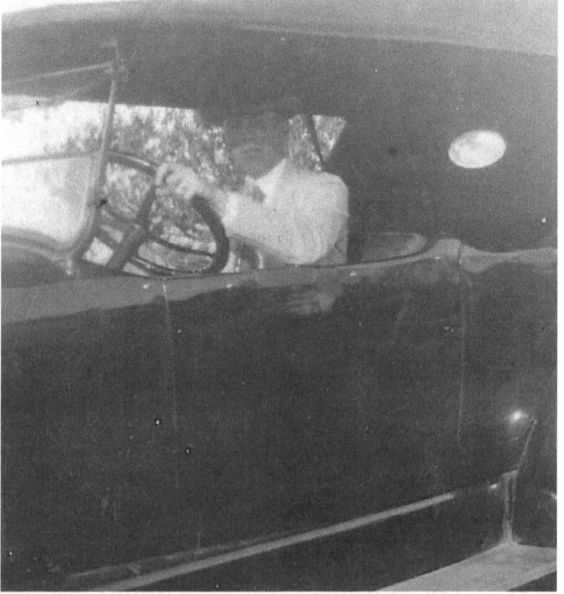

Left: Me, holding firmly to the reins.
Right Dr. Charles Hunsucker

some man. He does look quite dashing in his roadster automobile.

For a number of years, he came down to the ball park and set off fireworks every Fourth of July much to the delight of all the kids on the Mill Hill. They looked forward to the event for weeks.

## Swimming in the Beautiful Henry River

Brookford has its own river, the beautiful Henry River. Longview doesn't have a river. Highland doesn't have a river. West Hickory doesn't have a river. The town of Henry River shares the Henry River with us, but that doesn't count because Henry River is in Burke County. So there, Longview and Highland and West Hickory, eat your hearts out. Of course, now the river is known as the Henry Fork River, but to us it is still just the Henry River.

When Mr. Shuford and Mr. Holbrook decided to build the mill, they selected the site beside the river. They dammed it up and let it furnish the power to run the mill. They could not have selected a better place. Not only did the river provide the power for the mill, but it also became the favorite swimming place for the Mill Hill. No matter where you lived in Brookford you were not far from the river.

My brother Jerry and the gang he ran around with practically lived down at the river in the summertime. Brookford had a name for the kids who were forever at the river - River Rats. Some of the boys got to be right daring, jumping off the dam to the water below. This was very risky because the water wasn't that deep and you had to miss all the rocks. Jerry's gang had a tradition of jumping off the Swinging Bridge on Christmas day.

The charm of the river was lost on me. I didn't like the mud squishing between my toes and I didn't like the muddy water. If I couldn't see the bottom, I didn't want to swim in it. Besides, I knew our town poured raw sewage into the river below the dam. And if Brookford did this, what would prevent the town of Henry River or any other town up river from doing the same thing? You couldn't get away with this today, but it was done back then.

Every now and then, some of my friends would persuade me to go with them to the river. I think they liked the idea of swimming wherever they wanted to swim. At the pool you were restricted by the four sides, but in the river there was real freedom.

On one such day, they had talked me into going with them to the river. There I was in the muddy water swimming up toward the bridge when there came a dead dog floating down the river. I got out of the water right then and I looked back at that dog and said, "It's all your'n". And I never swam in the beautiful Henry River again!

## Mother Bolick

You cannot write a book on Brookford without mentioning one of its great ladies, Mother Bolick. That was how she was known on the Mill Hill, simply Mother Bolick. I doubt that many people on the mill hill knew that her given name was Mary Ollie. I know I didn't. I had to ask Paul and Stella when I was obtaining information for the book.

She was the mother of fourteen children, although three of her children died at an early age. Most of her children settled in the Brookford area. Mark was one of the primary forces at the mill. Rufus managed the Company Store and post office for many years. Mae, Ruth, Stella, and Paul all worked in the mill at one time or another.

Mother Bolick ran the Boarding House for a number of years. The boarders were treated to Mother Bolick's good cooking. She had the reputation of being one of the best cooks around. In her last years she lived in the house now occupied by Lillian Holsclaw. Mother

**Mother Bolick**

Bolick passed away on May 5, 1972 at the age of ninety-four.

I was very fortunate in finding pictures of Mother Bolick's family. Lillian Holsclaw had them in her private collection. Naomi Bolick Taylor provided me with the single picture of her. If anyone reached the stature of being an institution on Mill Hill, Mother Bolick certainly attained it. Everyone in Brookford loved this kind, humble and generous woman. And she truly was Mother Bolick to us all.

## Fishing in the Beautiful Henry River

All of us at Brookford considered the river to be the best natural resource for the Mill Hill. Not only did it provide power to run the mill, but as mentioned previously it was a favorite swimming hole for many. In my opinion, fishing in the river was the best entertainment of all. I spent many days down on the river just fishing.

The first time I ever fished was there. My cousins, Charles and Jimmy Mitchell took me with them. I must have been around six or seven. It seems like someone else was with us, maybe Paul Pope. But about the fishing I can remember every detail. I can take you today to the exact spot we fished. Charles had me fish above them in shallower water. He fixed my pole and baited my hook. They went about 15 yards below me to fish in deeper water. They were experienced fisherman and they were going after the big ones.

Well, before you could turn around, I had hooked a fish. It wasn't a big one, maybe five inches long. But it was the first fish I had ever caught. Charles took one look at that scrawny fish and said to me, "He's too small to keep. We'll just have to cut him up for bait." My very first fish and they're using him for bait!

None of us caught any more fish that day. Served them right for using my fish as bait. But one thing was accomplished that day besides catching my first fish. I was hooked on fishing.

One day I saw my Uncle John coming down the road with a long string of fish. He was quite a fisherman. I asked him where he had caught those fish. He said, "In the creek behind the school house."

I thought to myself, Uncle John done found that magical creek just brimming with fish and it's behind the school house. I'll have to find that creek and fish it. I spent the best part of the afternoon looking for that creek. I knew the branch was a good ways down from the school, but I also knew it didn't have fish in it like the ones my Uncle John had caught. I looked and looked, but I couldn't find that creek.

Finally, it dawned on me. My Uncle John was just putting me on. The "creek" was the river and the "school house" was the mill. Duh! I suppose he knew how my mind worked and he was having fun with me. At least it kept me occupied for a whole afternoon.

Some days, if I couldn't get Buck Melton to go fishing with me, I'd take my dogs, Scottie and Pepper, instead. That was always a big mistake. Those dogs weren't nearly as interested in fishing as I was. They'd be playing around and usually one or both of them would end up in the river right where I was fishing. Ruined my fishing for that day. I would vow never to take them again, but I still did from time to time. I never claimed to be a fast learner.

My favorite place to fish was at the tail race. It presented one major problem, though. You had to wade across either the river or the tail race. But the fishing there was good and it was worth getting wet. Even if the fishing wasn't good that day, you could always find a stick and hit rocks up toward the dam. Any rock hit over the dam was a home run. If you couldn't find a stick, you could always skip rocks. I got to where I was pretty good at skipping rocks, a talent I passed on to my children.

Once I was fishing alone at the tail race when I hooked a big catfish. That fish gets bigger every time I tell about it, but it was a good size catfish. Buck Melton does catfish, I don't. I've always been scared to take them off the hook. Anyway I had the fish up on a rock and I was waiting for it to die so I could take it off the hook. (Where is Buck Melton when you need him?) That fish wiggled and wiggled until it got the hook out of its mouth and slipped back into the river. And I had a fish tale that nobody believed.

## The Saga of the Sawed Off Bat

How Jim Mitchell came into possession of the 36 inch bat I don't rightly remember. Knowing Jim, he probably remembers everything about the bat from the name of the player's signature on the bat to how he came to have it. One thing I do remember is that the bat was a Louisville Slugger and back then having a Louisville Slugger bat was like hitting the mother lode.

We all loved the bat, but at 36 inches it was too big for any of us to swing. It was almost like having a box of candy and not being able to get the lid off. We all put our minds together and came up with a brilliant idea. We could saw off the big end of bat so that it would only be 30 or 31 inches. I'm sure Jim had the greatest input into this idea. After all, it was his bat. We felt that we could all handle the bat at that length and that's exactly what we did. We were quite pleased with our efforts.

We couldn't wait to try out our new "invention", so up to the ball ground we went. We were not into the game very far when it became Jim Schronce's turn to bat. Jim was a pretty fair hitter, but he had one very bad habit. He was a notorious bat slinger. Jim Mitchell was on deck as the next hitter, when Jim Schronce hit the ball. And true to form, he slung the bat. The sawed-off end of that bat hit Jim Mitchell above the right eye and opened a gash. With blood all over Jim, we ran down to his house. Aunt Margaret sent one of us to fetch Jim's dad, who worked at the Company Store. They took Jim to Dr. Hunsucker to get patched up. It took five stitches to close the gash.

It was the only ball game I ever played in that was called on account of blood. And that sawed-off bat was never used in a game again. Do you think "Moonlight" Graham's name was on the bat?

> "Any rock hit over the dam was a home run."

# Rosa Collins Clinard

You had to attend Brookford School to understand the influence Mrs. Rosa Clinard had on all of her students. She had the respect of every one of us. It was almost as if we were in awe of her. Not one of us wanted to disappoint her or get in trouble with her. The worst thing that could happen to you at school was to be called into Mrs. Clinard's office.

When I started Brookford School in 1941, she had already been principal there for almost twenty years. She became the principal of the old school on Red Hill in 1919. From 1922 until 1925, Brookford School was consolidated with Grandview School located near Windy Hill. Mrs. Clinard took a teaching position at this school, but when the new school opened at Brookford in 1925, she became the principal. She remained in this position until her death in 1955.

The former Rosa Collins was born in 1898 in Cedartown, Georgia to George D. and Rosa Goodall Collins. Her father was a home furnishings merchant and her mother was a descendent of the Goodall family of Macon, Georgia. Miss Collins graduated from Cedartown High School and went to Georgia State College for Woman in Milledgeville, Georgia, where she earned a teaching degree.

After graduation, she returned to Cedartown to teach in the Polk County School System. She taught four months (one term) in a rural county three-teacher school. She became convinced that her financial future did not include being a classroom teacher. The principal at her school only made fifty dollars month and her assistant a mere thirty five dollars.

She was considering a course in Library Science, when the superintendent of the Polk County Schools recommended her to an official of A.D. Julliard Company, owners of Brookford Mills, for the principalship at the Brookford School. In an article written by Mabel Miller Rowe of the Hickory Daily Record on September 2, 1950 in the "Know Your Neighbor" column, Mrs. Clinard was quoted as saying, "It was too great a temptation to turn down".

The inducement from Brookford Mills was a guarantee of one hundred dollars a month salary with seventy five dollars a month for her assistant. Additions to the offer included an eight months school, railroad fares to and from Cedartown even for Christmas, a furnished home (the teacherage) to live in without cost, and a ten per cent discount on all groceries purchased at the Company Store. Needless to say, Mrs. Clinard quickly accepted this generous offer.

Miss Collins came to the Brookford School in 1919 and immediately set to task in improving the school. The school building was a small three room structure, but with the enrollment steadily increasing, two more rooms were added and five teachers were employed. Finally a cottage was taken over and a sixth teacher was added. Miss Collins brought two teachers with her from Cedartown, Miss Vera Reid and Miss Sara Purks. Later three more teachers from Cedartown came to Brookford to work with her. Among them was Miss Hallie Lloyd, who later married Dr. Henry Menzies.

On June 5, 1920, Miss Rosa Collins married J. Weston Clinard and the couple settled into an attractive home in northwest Hickory. Even though Mrs. Clinard no longer lived on the Mill Hill, her influence continued in the community. When the new Brookford School opened its doors in 1925, Mrs. Clinard became its first principal.

Brookford School was put on the accredited list in 1926. About 1932, the North Carolina State School Board set up the unit system in schools and Brookford was included in the Hickory Unit. The school continued to grow under Mrs. Clinard's leadership and at the time of her death in 1955, the school had an average of almost three hundred students per year. The school included not only students from the Mill Hill, but also students from Windy Hill, Pope Hill, and the Barger Church Road area.

In 1949 Brookford School won a coveted honor. It received an A-1 rating – the highest rating given in elementary schools. It was the only school in Catawba County given this citation.

**A Red Hill School class.**

In the Mabel Miller Rowe article, Mrs. Clinard says the success of the school was made possible by the splendid cooperation of Brookford Mills, the teachers and the community as a whole. This statement is certainly true because the mill always was very supportive of the school. From the time the mill was built in 1898, the mill had a facility for teaching the children of its employees. The old school was built over on Red Hill and the mill underwrote the cost of the school until Brookford School was accepted into the area school system. Even when the school system only paid teachers' salaries for six months, the mill supplemented the teachers' pay for an additional two months. Because of this supplement, Mrs. Clinard was able to assemble a staff of teachers that was second to none in this area. This staff included Mrs. Kathryn Brooks, who was Mrs. Clinard's able assistant, Mrs. Max Steelman, Miss Mary Kate Jerome, Mrs. Charles Hughes, and Mrs. Euphemia Fox.

The Brookford community gave Mrs. Clinard and her staff its complete support. Many of the parents had received very little education when they were growing up. A number of them had to go work in the mills at an early age(some as young as eight years old) to help support their families. They recognized that their children were receiving an excellent education and wholeheartedly supported Mrs. Clinard and the school.

However, the greatest amount of credit for the success of Brookford School has to go to the remarkable Mrs. Rosa Clinard. Without her leadership, the school would not have achieved this success. She sought excellence for herself, her school and her students. All of us who attended Brookford School are forever indebted to this dynamic woman.

In December 1955, Brookford and the entire Catawba County area were saddened by the untimely death of Mrs. Clinard. She received fatal injuries in an automobile accident in

One of the continuing results of Mrs. Clinard's work is the birdhouse project in the Brookford School—where boys in the shop classes make an annual affair of building a wide variety of houses and feeders. And they put them up.

Newton. The whole community mourned her death.

In a Living Memorial article written by Wake Bridges of the Hickory Daily Record, the community decided on a suitable memorial for this unselfish and distinguished woman, who had done so much for the Brookford community. The Rosa Collins Clinard Memorial Fund was established as a living memorial in the form of an educational fund for needy, deserving Brookford youths. The goal for the fund was quickly met and surpassed. Many of the Brookford people gave to the fund out of gratitude for all Mrs. Clinard had done in almost thirty five years for the Brookford School and community. They had witnessed first hand how their children had benefited from the excellent education they had received under Mrs. Clinard's guidance. Many of these students went on to become teachers themselves. And the credit goes to Mrs. Clinard and her staff at the school.

On May 20, 1955, a service for the unveiling of a memorial oil portrait and plaque honoring Mrs. Clinard was held in the school auditorium. Mr. James Gaither, chairman of the Brookford School Clinard Memorial Committee, reported that the Rosa Collins Clinard Memorial Fund had exceeded its original goal and that contributions were still being received. Mr. Gaither also announced that a workshop would be equipped with power and hand tools at the school to allow the pupils to continue the program of building bird houses and feeders that had been started by Mrs. Clinard. This program had earned state wide recognition for the school. The North Carolina Wildlife Commission had become aware of the efforts of Mrs. Clinard and Brookford School in the study of bird life as part of the curriculum at the school. She was the single most important individual responsible for Brookford becoming one of the first bird sanctuaries in this area.

The service at the school auditorium was a fitting tribute to a remarkable woman, who had become an important part of life in Brookford from her arrival in 1919 until her death in 1955. Her influence on all of the students who attended school in Brookford cannot be measured. As far as we were concerned Mrs. Clinard was Brookford School!

# The Forbidden Football Games

Football was never as popular as baseball on the mill hill, but there was one ritual that we observed every fall on a Sunday afternoon. Many of us met on the front lawn at the school for a game of two hand touch. The fact that the front lawn was forbidden territory made the game more appealing. We all knew Mrs. Clinard would never approve of our playing football there, but the front lawn was the perfect place for a game. And the chance of Mrs. Clinard coming by was remote.

There were plenty of other places to have the game. The field to the north of the school was just as good as the front lawn, maybe even better because it wasn't as close to the road. But Mrs. Clinard would not have minded if we played there. The outfield at the ball ground was another place, but it was mostly red dirt and for that reason it was quickly ruled out.

I don't remember ever getting caught playing on the front lawn. Whether Mrs. Clinard knew about the games or not, I'm not sure. We always felt she knew about everything but maybe we were giving her more credit than was due. It shows the influence she had over our lives even on a Sunday afternoon. The cardinal rule at school was you never wanted to get on Mrs. Clinard's bad side. It was not a pretty sight. Still the lure of that beautiful, lush front lawn was just too much temptation.

1930 Brookford School Grade 1A Class. Albert Wallace is on the second row, third from the left. Willie Foster is next to him. Tom Workman is on the same row, second from the right. Pearce Fox is on the top row, third from the left.

1930 Brookford School Grade 1B Class. Reba Foster Poovey is on first row, fourth from the right. Shyke Travis is on the second row, second from the left. Richard Sprouse is in the middle of the same row.

# Brookford School

Growing up in Brookford, it seems our lives revolved around school. During late summer it seemed the first day of school would never come. Although we all talked about how much we hated school, nobody would think of missing that first day of school. By the same token, it seemed the last day of school would never come either.

School always started in September back then and the most vivid memory I have of the first day of school is the smell of new overalls. In those days, denim had a distinct odor that is not present in the jeans today. All the boys had on their new overalls for the school year.

The Brookford School that I attended opened its doors in 1925. Stella Bolick Grubb tells me that her first day of school was the very first day the new school opened. The mill, from the time it opened, provided for the education of the workers' children. The first school in Brookford was a frame building located on Red Hill. Lillian Isenhour Holsclaw, Lil Pope Stepp, Katie Miller, and Neal Stepp all attended this school. The school building was used for storage after the new school was completed. It caught fire in 1927 and burned to the ground.

We are all very fortunate that Neal Stepp kept a picture of the school building and all the students attending the school. In the picture I think Neal was in the third grade. All of us are indebted to him for allowing a copy of that picture to be included in this book.

When the new school opened, one remarkable woman was made its first principal. She would remain the principal for thirty years until her untimely death in an automobile accident in December 1955. Mrs. Rosa Clinard was the main reason Brookford School became one of the best schools in the Hickory area. She would not settle for anything less than the best. Her teaching staff was the best in the system.

It was accomplished because of her effort and the crown jewel on the staff had to be Mrs. Kathryn Brooks. She taught the seventh grade and was almost like an assistant principal to Mrs. Clinard. There didn't seem to be anything that she could not do. She was the best teacher around. She was an accomplished pianist and if anyone was needed to take kids to ball games, Mrs. Brooks was right there. If Mrs. Clinard was indispensable at Brookford, Mrs. Brooks was just a half step behind. Between the two of them, they made sure the school was successful year after year.

When I attended Brookford School from 1941 to 1948, the teachers were: Mrs. Chuck Hughes, first grade; Miss Mary Kate Jerome, second grade; Miss Grace Mitchem, third grade; Miss Vera White, fourth grade; Mrs. Euphemia Fox, fifth grade; Mrs. Max Steelman, sixth grade; Mrs. Kathryn Brooks, seventh grade; and of course, Mrs. Rosa Clinard, Principal. Miss Jerome, Mrs. Steelman and Mrs. Brooks all taught many years at Brookford.

Mrs. Steelman's sixth grade class at a Hobo party in 1946 at the cow pasture where we played our famous cow pasture ball games. This is a wonderful picture of the class although Bart Milam (in the middle of the second row) seems to have lost his focus. The camera shy child is Joe Elders.

Just as Mrs. Clinard had the best teachers, she also had the best cooks for the lunchroom. The food was absolutely delicious. I don't think we appreciated how good the food was until we went to Green Park and Hickory High. What a culture shock it was for us. We all wanted to go back to Brookford for lunch. I've been told that whenever the Hickory School System had visitors from the state education department, they always arrived at Brookford School at lunch time. They also knew where the good food was.

The school had a janitor named Hazel, who worked there for many years. I understand that he took the job when his father, Walt, retired. Hazel was such a dependable person. He was kind and gentle to all of us kids. He kept the school spotless. And sometimes with great prodding he would dance for us. It was quite a treat for us because he was an accomplished dancer. I'm sure we got on his nerves sometimes, but you would never know it.

When you think about all the kids who attended Brookford School and went on to success in a variety of fields, it's difficult to comprehend. The profession that attracted the greatest number was the field of education. I believe the examples set before us by the teachers at Brookford had a great effect on all of us and that is the reason so many of the students became teachers. All of us should thank God that we were fortunate enough to

go to a school that had Rosa Clinard as principal and the teaching staff she assembled. They inspired us to be better at whatever we chose to be. We are all greatly indebted to them.

While writing this article on Brookford School, I started thinking about some of my favorite memories of the school. Here are some of mine; you are welcome to add some of yours!

The marble games before school and at recess. The rule of thumb was: don't get into a game with Ray Fisher if you didn't want to lose all your marbles. He was the champion marble shooter.

Bobby Holland: He had cerebral palsy and was adopted by the whole school. Everyone looked out for Bobby. You couldn't find a sweeter kid in the whole world or one with more courage. One year he was elected King of the school.

The assemblies during the war years had a patriotic theme. The all time most popular song was "Let's Remember Pearl Harbor".

Then there was the scrap metal drive. Everybody pitched in and we brought every bit of metal we could find on the Mill Hill and piled it high behind the school. That pile of metal looked higher than Baker's Mountain.

The baseball games at Oakwood School. We loved to go over there and beat the socks off those rich kids.

The basketball games with Oakwood at our gym, where they beat the socks off us. We Mill Hill kids could never understand a game where you had to bounce the ball.

One of our favorite school yells. "Strawberry Shortcake, Huckleberry Pie. V-I-C-T-O-R-Y, Are we in it, Well I guess, Brookford, Brookford, Yes! Yes! Yes!"

Do you remember our school song? Adelaide Bolick and Jackie Thompson supposedly wrote it, but I saw Mrs. Brooks' heavy hand involved. The song was sung to the tune of "On Wisconsin" and the words are: "Hail to Brookford. How we love thee. School we love so dear. Fondest memories we will cherish through each future year. Happy school days, Golden Rule days, we'll remember long. Then we will sing her praises loud and strong."

Safety patrol. Remember the white belt and safety patrol badge you got to wear if you were selected to be part of the patrol? Talk about feeling important! My favorite beat was the sidewalk just past the tennis court. You got to escort all the pretty girls across the street. Talk about fringe benefits.

Does anyone else remember this besides me? During assembly all of us sang "Little Sir Echo, how do you do?" We would then sing "Hello" and Robert Sigmon, who hid behind the piano and would sing "Hello". He was little Sir Echo, I suppose. He was selected to be the echo because he had the best singing voice.

Seems like everybody had a tonette band back then, and so did we. Later, Mrs. Brooks made this band the best in the area. I think this happened after they got rid of me. I had no musical ability and this is from a guy that secretly wanted to be Little Sir Echo.

Buck Melton remembered the sound of Mrs. Clinard's high heels clicking down the hallway. You always knew where she was by the sound.

And Deann Elders Hare remembers the fresh clean smell of the teachers. You might know a girl would remember this. It could be she remembers because most of Mill Hill kids only took a bath on Saturday night whether we needed it or not.

The sound of Janitor Walt's broom coming down the hallway was mentioned by Tom Workman.

I remember the year I was in the seventh grade, they needed more room for the cafeteria, so they converted the unused room at the left rear corner of the school into a separate dining area for the seventh grade. Talk about feeling privileged!

# The Company Store

The Company Store was built soon after the mill building was completed in 1899. It continued to be an important part of Mill Hill life until the closing of the mill. The building consisted of the Company Store and post office, a café, a barber shop and a pool room. Upstairs was a large meeting area with a stage and a basketball court. This area served many purposes for the community. Silent movies were shown here. Most of the adult education classes were held here also. It provided recreational activities. Town meetings were held and it even served as place for church meetings for awhile.

The store was managed by Rufus Bolick for many years. He served as the Postmaster of Brookford at the same time. A number of people worked in the Company Store. Joe Reinhardt worked as a clerk for many years. He had worked in the mill as a doffer until he came to work in the store. This is where he learned the grocery business and in 1943 opened his own grocery store, Reinhardt and Son Groceries. Bad Eye Starnes, Edwin Warren, Neal Mitchell and Dan Henderson also worked in the store. Mrs. Rena Kendell, who became the first woman mayor of Brookford, also worked in the store in the dry goods department.

The store sold all kinds of dry goods, as well as groceries. Most of the people on the Mill Hill traded at the Company Store. For one thing, it was the only place that would take dugaloo, although it was a known fact that your friendly bootlegger would also trade in dugaloo.

The Brookford Café was operated by a number of people through the years. Ken Hovis worked there for a number of years. Neal Mitchell also ran the café for a while. His son, Charles, eventually operated the café. Brookford has always been a little prejudiced about things Brookford, but it was a known fact that the Brookford Café made the best hot dogs and hamburgers in the world. If you don't believe me, just ask anybody who was raised on the Mill Hill.

The barber shop was the sole domain of the Cloer family. I can't remember anyone but Cloers cutting hair there. Tom Cloer ran the barber shop as I was growing up, but his father, Pink Cloer, had operated it before him. I don't think Tom ever cut my hair that he didn't complain about how kinky my hair was. Tom's uncle Roby Cloer also worked in the barber shop and I usually waited until Roby was free to get my hair cut. He was just a kinder, gentler barber. No offense, Tom.

The barber shop also had a shower stall and many of the Mill Hill people took advantage of it. When the mill added bathrooms to the employees' houses, the bathroom only consisted of a commode and lavatory. Eventually the mill would add full inside bathrooms to the houses, complete with a bath tub. I was a teenager before that happened.

Top Simpson was manager of the pool room for as long as I can remember. He also managed the swimming pool in the summer. The pool room was always a busy place, but on Friday nights it was a mad house. The mill paid off every Friday and a number of people sought to supplement their income by a friendly game of pool or buckboard. I'm sure there were a number of wives that wished Brookford didn't have a pool room, but on Friday nights in Brookford, it was the place to be.

## The Company Store

The mill hill had several other grocery stores. Probably the best known and busiest store was Will Pitt's Store. It was located on Hwy #127 about halfway between the mill and the river bridge. Will had a well-stocked store, but the one thing I remember about his store was that he had a dog inside a fenced area. And that dog could climb a tree! We went out a number of times just to see the dog. I don't remember if we ever bought anything or not. But the dog was worth seeing.

Abe Pitts had a store on down towards the bridge from Will Pitts' store. His store also had gas pumps (Esso). My uncle Neal Mitchell bought this store and operated it for a number of years. The store later burned down. I believe that Forest Smith was operating it at that time. Fletch Holland ran a grocery store for a long time. It was located just below where Hillside Baptist Church is now. Across the river near the Swinging Bridge, the Teague family had a small store in the basement of their home. The only other store I can think of in Brookford was a small store down in what we call Shanty Town. It was across the street from the Union Hall Building and was run by a woman who looked to be at least 140 years old. But this store held one big fascination for me. They had a punch board with gumballs of all colors inside. For a nickel you got five punches. If you were lucky enough to get a white gumball then you won a bar of candy. This was the ultimate win/win situation as far as I was concerned. I liked the gumballs, but the chance to win a bar of candy was just too much

**Jerm Foster on his Indian motorcycle. Taken 1918.**

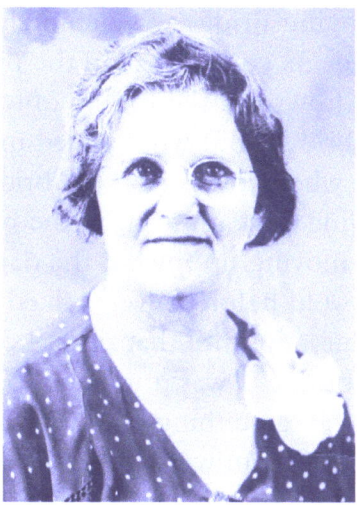

Rena Kendell, first female Mayor of Brookford. Right: Ivey Lowman in front of the Brookford Café.

temptation for me. Occasionally I did get a white gumball. What joy!

The Brookford Service Station was operated by Stewart Elrod as long as I was growing up in Brookford. It was located across the road from the mill office. The swimming pool was just behind the service station and Stewart did a lively business in the summer from the kids in the swimming pool, although I'm sure we were a headache for him from time to time. Still he did have a good selection of candy and drinks. On Fridays a lot of the mill workers would toss coins over the fence into the pool for us to dive in and get. Most of that money ended back in the service station I'm sure.

The service station is where the Hickory Daily Record dropped the Brookford papers off. Ray Fisher was in charge of delivering the paper to the customers. This was probably around 1946-1947. I helped Ray for some time by delivering the papers on the hill I lived on as well as Mexico and Possom Hollar. It is still a vivid memory of being down at the service station, folding the papers for delivery and listening to Fred Kirby singing "Atomic Power" on the jukebox.

## Motocross Track

An interesting bit of information I obtained in talking with many of the Brookford people is the fact that at one time Brookford had its own motocross track. I was told about this by more than one person and most of the older residents remembered it. The track started out about where Neal and Lil Stepp's house is now and went down toward the creek near the river and circled back. A number of Brookford residents raced their motorcycles on this track. I have been unable to find any pictures of the track or the races, but from what I can gather the track existed in the late 20's and early 30's. and was a very popular place to be back then. I have been able to find a picture of Jerm Foster on his Indian motorcycle, but whether he ever participated in any of the races I'm not sure. It was a real surprise for me to find the race track existed at all.

## The Scout Pond

By the time I came along, the scout pond down at the Union Hall Building had fallen into disuse. The dam, which was built by the Brookford Scout troop around 1921, had sprung a leak and the water there was no deeper than the rest of the branch. But in talking with people older than me, the scout pond was the place to be when the weather got warm. Every year the scout troop dredged out the pond and everybody was ready for swimming. Forest Gaines says that some days there would be as many as 25 to 30 kids there. For awhile the pond even had a diving board. In the middle of the pond the water was close to ten feet deep. It sounds like it provided a lot of good times for the kids.

Everybody I talked to had a favorite story about the pond. My brother, Jerry learned to swim there. And my mom told me that during lunch at the school, Jerry had to take a quick dip before heading back to school. Lil Stepp says she was there one day and somehow got in water over her head. She couldn't swim and had to be dragged out by my aunt, Margaret.

All in all it sounds like the scout pond was a lot of fun for the kids on the hill. The one question about the scout pond that no one has been able to answer is why was the scout pond also called the Rathcobb? Maybe somebody reading this book will have the answer to that question.

## Swinging Bridge

The Swinging Bridge was located about five hundred yards below the dam and served the community a useful purpose. A number of people who worked in the mill lived across the river and used the bridge to get to work. If you didn't use the Swinging Bridge or walk across the dam (risky business) you had to walk all the way around to the bridge across Highway #127, which was a long way around. Not many people owned cars and walking was the only way to get around in Brookford. The Swinging Bridge was definitely the only way to go. As you can see in the picture of Myrtle Fox Lowman, there were only two planks for the bridge. But what scared me the most was that when you got on the bridge, the water flowing beneath it made the bridge look like it was moving up toward the dam. I was twelve years old before I ever walked across the bridge. Up until that time, I crawled across the bridge. I was not alone. A number of kids did the same thing, although I have to confess most of them were girls.

Whenever high water came, many people came down to the river to watch the Swinging Bridge get washed away. It was almost like a sporting event. "Let's go down to the river and watch the Swinging Bridge get washed away". In the flood of 1940, it was one of the first things washed away, long before a portion of the dam broke off.

On a Sunday afternoon you could always go over to the Teague house located just across the river and buy something they had in the store in their basement. A number of prominent families lived across the river. Besides the Teagues, there were the Wilsons, Winsteads, Isenhours, and Copases. You could sit on our hill and watched Mr. Wilson plowing out in his field. While I was still young, the Winstead house burned. You had almost a front row seat over on our hill to watch the fire.

## Union Hall Building

The Union Hall Building was just recently torn down when the state rerouted Highway #127. You would think I would have had enough foresight to have taken a picture of it. I knew that the new road would take it along with the dam for the scout pond. I was given

## Possum Holler

ample warning that the road was going to take them, but did I get pictures of them? No. Babe Thompson's daughter, Carolyn, furnished the picture of the Union Hall Building to me. I am thankful she had taken a picture of it.

Down through the years the building was used for a variety of purposes. I have been told that originally the building was used as a grocery store. Fletch Holland ran a store there at one time. It also served as a movie house and as a dwelling. In 1948 the Union at Brookford Mill occupied it and it has ever since been known as the Union Hall Building. It has served as a church building on several occasions. Hillside Baptist Church used it for a time until they built their present building. Other churches also used it for meetings. But like so many buildings and dwellings in Brookford it became a casualty of time and circumstance.

# Windy Hill

If you really have to want to find Windy Hill, the best way to get there is turning on 14th Avenue SW off the old Sub-Station Road (now Second Street SW). You won't find much of the Windy Hill I remember. The old Grandview School, which was used from 1913 until 1925, was torn down in the '60s. The ball field has been taken over by a housing development. A few of the houses are still standing, but for the most part Windy Hill is no more.

When the decision to tear down the school was made, Mrs. Irene Hayes Barger got together a reunion of all the people who attended the school. An article on Grandview School is included in this book. The article is in Mrs. Barger's handwriting and the pictures were from her daughter's, Betty Barger Lafone, collection.

In 1922, a decision to close the old school on Red Hill was made. The kids from Brookford attended the Grandview School until the new school in Brookford opened in 1925. You will recognize many of the Brookford people in the reunion pictures. The Grandview school was then closed and the Windy Hill kids came to the new Brookford School.

The old ball field on Windy Hill was used for a number of years after the school closed. Kids from Brookford had some spirited baseball games with the Windy Hill bunch on this field. It seems that we could never beat them on their field. It wasn't much of a ball field and bad luck always happened to us there. The Windy Hill kids got all of the lucky breaks. Could this have been the start of the home field advantage? It has been good to remember about the good times and games over on Windy Hill. Are you one of the fortu-

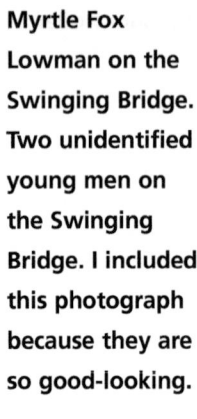

Myrtle Fox Lowman on the Swinging Bridge. Two unidentified young men on the Swinging Bridge. I included this photograph because they are so good-looking.

nate, who can say you were born and raised on Windy Hill?

## The Churches

Mill towns have always had the reputation of being one of the worst places to live. Some people would argue this reputation was well earned. The cotton mills often attracted the worst sorts of people. Many of the workers came from farms or other mill villages, often with a bunch of kids in tow. Most of them were uneducated, with almost no chance to improve their lot in life. A low paying job in the mill was their only hope of surviving.

Many took their frustrations out by drinking, gambling, and fighting. Reading any history book on cotton mills will bear this out. Mill hills were places to avoid.

From the very beginning of Brookford, the two churches, the Faith Reformed Church and the Brookford Baptist Church, had a tremendous influence on the lives of the people. The church is supposed to be a beacon in the community and both churches were the light that the people needed. Everyone needs a refuge and the churches certainly provided that for Brookford. I give the churches the most credit for taking the hard edge off the mill hill life. Obviously the mill was very important for providing work for the people.

**Clockwise from top left: Union Hall Building; Union Hall at 1951 strike, l to r, Carrie Travis, Bess Johnson, Tom Workman, Gene Weaver; New Highway 127 that took the Weaver home, Fisher home, Company Store, Union Hall Building, most of the first row on Red Hill and the Gaines home; part of the line at Union Hall Building during the strike of 1951.**

The school was equally important for it provided the education for the children so that they could have choices of other work - choices their parents did not have. But in my mind, the churches were the most important part of our lives.

Faith Reformed Church was the first church to be formed. In 1901 Corinth Reformed Church started mission work under the direction of Dr. J. L. Murphy. A lot was donated for the mission work by Mr. E. L. Shuford and the members of Corinth agreed to underwrite the expense of building the first church. The building was completed and the first service was conducted by Dr. Murphy on May 12, 1901. A history of the church tells us that a large and happy assembly gathered in the new church in the new town of Brookford.

Four days later, on May sixteenth, the church building was struck by lightning and burned to the ground. Immediately, the people of Brookford and Hickory set about to rebuild. And on November 3, 1901, the first service in the second church was again conducted by

Dr. Murphy, with the sermon given by Dr. J. C. Clapp. Practically the entire cost of the two buildings was borne by the members of the Corinth congregation.

The actual organization of the congregation into Faith Reformed Church, Brookford, North Carolina, was enacted by Dr. Murphy on March 5, 1905, with 22 charter members.

Faith Reformed Church, now Faith United Church of Christ, has been blessed with many outstanding pastors in its history. Two of its most outstanding ministers served this church while I was growing up in Brookford: Dr. H. D. Althouse and Dr. A. Wilson Cheek. Dr. Althouse served the Brookford Church twice, while also serving full time at Corinth. He served as supply pastor in 1938-39 and again in 1947-1948. Imagine a 12 year old boy growing up in the Baptist Church who would go over to the Reformed Church on Sunday night to hear a sermon. But that is exactly what I did, after going to the Baptist Church on Sunday morning. I cannot think of a higher recommendation for a pastor than that – to get a twelve year old boy to come for the second time on a Sunday just to hear him preach.

But Dr. Althouse was that kind of preacher. You were enthralled by every word of every sermon. He made God's word come alive. Dr. Althouse served the Corinth Church for many years. All of us are indebted to this servant of God. He was a great pastor and a great man.

Dr. A. Wilson Cheek was probably the most beloved of all of the pastors who served Faith Reformed Church. He was there from 1939-47. He served the church during one of the most trying times of this country- World War II. Under his leadership, the church grew to a total of 226 members by 1945. The church had 52 of its members serve their country in the armed forces. The second great tragedy of the church occurred while he served as its pastor. On December 22, 1944 the church caught fire and burned to the ground. I can still remember, as a nine year old, standing on the sidewalk across from the Company Store and watching this terrible event.

Under the leadership of Dr. Cheek, the church began the plans to rebuild once again. The war would definitely slow the process of rebuilding. For the next two years the church received permission from the Hickory School Board to use Brookford School as its Sunday meeting place. The present church building was completed and occupied in early 1947. Dr. Cheek was to continue as pastor until November 30, 1947, when he became Director of Youth Work for the denomination. It was with sad hearts that the congregation said goodbye to this wonderful pastor and friend.

In 1907, the First Baptist Church of Hickory decided to sponsor a mission church in Brookford. Just as in the case of Faith Reformed Church, the mill donated land for the church. On April 27, 1907 the founding document of Brookford Baptist Church was signed and Rev. C.M. Robinson was called to be the first pastor. The church sanctuary was completed in late 1907. In 1927 the church completed an addition, which was used for Sunday school classes. In 1944 they completed another addition, which included a kitchen and dining area as well as more classrooms. The church occupied this building until April 2001, when it moved to a new facility near the Brookford Community Building.

Rev. W.C. Laney was called to be pastor of Brookford Baptist Church in 1928. He would remain pastor there until his death in 1976, a total of 48 years. During his ministry the

**Top:** After the Faith Reform Church burned in December of 1944, both Vacation Bible School classes met at Brookford Baptist Church in the Summer of 1945.
**Left:** Preacher Laney

church became widely known in two important areas - missions and race relations.

Preacher Laney, as he came to be known, believed strongly in giving to missions and because of his endeavors Brookford Baptist Church became known as one of the most mission-minded churches in North Carolina. In 1972 the Biblical Recorder published an article in which it stated that Brookford Baptist Church gave more per member to missions than any other church in North Carolina. This is an astounding accomplishment and the credit goes to Preacher Laney and the faithful members of the church. The church was not wealthy by any stretch of the imagination and it shows how dedicated the whole church was to missions. I can still remember my aunt, saving money for the whole year to give to the Baptist Orphanage at Thanksgiving and she was not an exception. Everyone in the church

Faith Reform Church VBS: Lillian Holsclaw is third from the right on the back row. Dean Elrod is to her right.
Deann Elders, Joe Elders, David Isenhour, Mary Sue Copas, Pauline Bolick, Bruce Bishop at Ridgecrest.

felt just as strongly about missions.

In the area of race relations, Preacher Laney was way ahead of his time. He believed that all men are created equal. Not only did he believe this, but he put into practice his belief. Starting in the '30s, he began his ministry in race relations. He organized numerous meetings with all races. Brookford Baptist Church, through the efforts of Preacher Laney and the congregation, became widely known for these efforts. In the early '50s, a young reporter, Julian Scheer, from the Charlotte News visited the church and wrote a long article about the church's work in race relations. This was long before the Civil Rights Movement and segregation existed all through the South. It took great courage for Preacher Laney to lead his church in this explosive area. Time has proven him right, even though today there is still a ways to go to have complete acceptance of all races. Perhaps it will never come. It is sad that the most segregated places in America are the church sanctuaries on Sunday morning.

I still consider Brookford Baptist Church to be my home church, even though I was never on the church roll. I grew up in the church. I attended Sunday school regularly, but managed to skip out fairly often from the preaching services. It was just too hard for a youngster to sit still that long! I suppose the reason I went to Brookford Baptist was because my aunt and uncle, Christine and John Elders, attended there along with their children, Joe and Deann. My mom and my granny were never church goers; however, this didn't prevent the church from getting my mom to cook for their Monday night suppers. They knew she was the best cook on the Mill Hill.

Growing up in Brookford Baptist, I was exposed to some of the best Sunday school teachers anywhere and I am eternally indebted to all of them. The first teacher I can remember was Mrs. Etta Bolick. She was the kindest person I have ever met and she knew just how to teach a class of squirming kids. She died not too many years after I had her as a teacher and Brookford Baptist lost one of its best members.

When I was about 10 years old, I was fortunate to have Preacher Laney's son, J.W., as my teacher. He was still in high school at the time. His lessons were always interesting and helpful. The only time he ever lost our attention was the Sunday morning Top and Hettie Simpson's house burned down. We couldn't wait to get out of Sunday school so that we could go see the fire. I guess J.W. understood it was just too hard to compete with a fire. J.W. was later called into the ministry, following in his dad's footsteps. He is now retired and living in Maryland. As a Sunday school teacher, he was the best. Coming from a ten year old, there is not a higher compliment.

During my teen years, Seth Miller was my Sunday School teacher. How he could relate to us teenagers, I'll never know. Seth and Katie had no children of their own, but his lessons were just what we needed. Maybe he could still remember what it was like to be a teenager. All of us guys respected Seth and we listened to what he said, which was no small feat for Seth since we were at the age where we thought we knew everything. His lessons were always to the point and helped each of us. Besides, how could you not love a guy who could always pick out the best watermelons in the world. I used to hang around his house for days on the pretense of playing with Danny and David Thompson in hopes that Seth would cut open a watermelon. Some of life's best lessons are not in the classroom or in church. Seth lived his beliefs and his witness was evident to us all, even teenagers. I still miss Seth Miller- he could always put things in the right perspective.

George Flowers taught us as young adults. Just as the other teachers in the church, George was a very good Sunday School teacher. At the time he taught me he was still a young man and the lessons were right to point for us. We all loved to hear him talk. He definitely did not have a Catawba County accent.

I feel myself very fortunate to have gone to Brookford Baptist Church. All the teachers had a great influence on my life and to attend a church where history was unfolding was a moving experience. Sometimes when I hear a hymn or read a passage of scripture, I'm back at Brookford Baptist Church in my memory.

## Mary's Beauty Shop

Brookford had its own beauty shop. Mary Hilton Wallace became a licensed beautician around 1934 and shortly thereafter opened a beauty shop in the basement of the house now occupied by Paul Bolick. At the time Mary rented the space from the mill, the house was occupied by Red Austin, who was the maintenance supervisor for the Mill Hill.

Mary opened the shop before she was married and operated it there in the basement for over ten years. After she married Bud Wallace, she would bring her children with her to the shop. She trained a number of women, them Sytha Harter, Jackie Stewart, Lois Wallace, and Ceserine Hudson.

Finally Mary had to move her beauty shop into her home as her family grew and she needed to be there. It was sad to see Brookford lose its own beauty shop. Mary kept many of her Brookford customers, but it was awfully convenient to have a beauty shop on the Mill Hill. Mary has to be the prettiest beautician there ever was.

# Boarding House

The mill built the boarding house across from the Company Store not long after it had completed the store building. The boarding house served a real purpose for the Brookford community. The structure had two floors with an attic, that had two bedrooms. It had a total of 15 rooms with two baths. The house also had a kitchen and dining area. It provided rooms for single employees. Many times the mill would get young men to come into work for the summer and play baseball for the mill. Usually they would stay at the boarding house. Babe Thompson tells me that when the mill hired her dad, J.J. Stepp, he lived in the boarding house until he could move his family from Georgia.

The boarding house was managed by someone employed by the mill. I remember when I was growing up, Mother Bolick managed it. Mary Cranford also managed it at one time. The need for the boarding house declined after World War II and it eventually was torn down sometime in the late forties. The house across the street in the flat was moved to the site of the boarding house. Pearlie Sherrill has occupied this residence for a number of years.

During the twenties and the thirties, the boarding house was a meeting place for young people. Many of the eligible bachelors lived there. The front porch was just made for courting and after all the boarding house was located in downtown Brookford.

In compiling this book, I started looking for a picture of the boarding house and had struck out until Babe Thompson's daughter, Carolyn, found the picture of Red and Dolly Austin standing behind the Boarding House. It is a good picture of the Austins, although not a good photo of the Boarding House.

**Far right: beautyshop Mary's Beauty Shop Right: Red and Dolly Austin. The Boarding House is in the background.**

## The Swimming Pool

During the Depression, the mill built the swimming pool and the ball field with federal money. This was part of the recovery plan of President Roosevelt and it provided jobs for many of the men on the hill. No one is more grateful to President Roosevelt and to the mill than I. I spent half my childhood either at the ball field or at the swimming pool.

On a hot summer afternoon, the swimming pool was definitely the place to be. Most of the kids on the hill were down at the pool. Not only could you swim and dive to your heart's content, but you could also look at all the pretty girls. Seeing Yvonne Melton in a bathing suit was worth the price of admission. Nobody could fill out a bathing suit quite like Yvonne.

Top Simpson ran the pool for a number of years. He also ran the pool room at the same time. I guess for job description, pool was the key word. He ran a tight ship at the pool. No one wanted to break any of Top's rules and be banned from the pool. All of us more or less behaved.

It seemed like every year the mill had nurses come from the county health department and set up shop at the entrance to the pool. Anyone who needed a tetanus shot had to get one before they could swim in the pool.

Talk about being between a rock and a hard place. They knew that they had us. They also had the records of who needed the shots. No shots, no swimming. Our love for swimming exceeded our hatred of needles. The pool won out every time.

Some of my happiest times were spent at the Brookford Swimming Pool. I believe most of the kids on the hill felt the same way.

## Rubber Gun Fights

Rubber gun fights were popular on the mill hill for a good long while. The fights had some loose unwritten rules that needed to be followed. You had to make your weapon yourself. It had to be from a block of wood made into the shape of a hand gun. You taped a clothes pin at the back of the handle. Strips from an old inner tube served as the ammo. You stretched the rubber strip from the front of the barrel and secured it with the clothes pin. The choice of rubber strips was very important. Buck Melton preferred strips from red inner tubes (the inner tubes were made of real rubber-none of this synthetic stuff would do). I always went along with Buck. My pockets were stuffed with red rubber strips. Some of the guys had very sophisticated weapons-a few had double barrel guns. I had hands-down the sorriest weapon in the fight. Maybe this was why I was one of the last taken when we chose up sides for the fight.

> "I guess you could call it street fighting. We had a lot of fun with these fights. If you are ever in a rubber gun fight, the cardinal rule is: Choose Ray Fisher."

The best fighter in the game was Ray Fisher. He was good at any game that required hand and eye coordination. At school, he was the best marble player and later, at Mountain View, he had a stellar career in basketball. In choosing sides, you definitely wanted Ray on your side.

The rules of the fight were pretty simple. The side that had the last man standing won the fight. Get hit by a rubber strip and you were out of the game. The fights were usually held in downtown Brookford around the Company Store. I guess you could call it street fighting. We had a lot of fun with these fights. If you

"*On a hot summer afternoon, the swimming pool was definitely the place to be. Most of the kids on the hill were down at the pool. Not only could you swim and dive to your heart's content, but you could also look at all the pretty girls.*"

**On the diving board from the left: Buck Melton, Bo Hill, Barbara Jean Melton, Becky Austin. Holding onto the board: Ray Fisher with Mickey Sronce behind him.**

are ever in a rubber gun fight, the cardinal rule is: Choose Ray Fisher.

In preparing this piece on rubber gun fights, I got to thinking this would be the perfect way to fight all wars. Do away with all the weapons of mass destruction that kill and maim, and settle all disputes with rubber guns. If you're hit with a rubber strip (preferably red), you're out of the battle. You now belong to the other side and must perform humanitarian acts until the war is over. Seems to be a sensible way to settle disputes, and nobody gets hurt.

## Brookford's Calaboose

Did you know that at one time Brookford had a calaboose? I didn't either. I was talking with Lil Stepp and she casually mentioned the calaboose to me. According to Lil, it was located behind the Company Store just beyond the row of garages. I remember the row of garages well for that was the site of some of our best bottle cap baseball games. And I seem to remember a separate building from the garages, but I assumed it was just another garage.

It seems that if you became drunk and disorderly you could earn yourself a stay in the calaboose. A fine had to be paid in order to get you out. The mill provided police protection for the mill hill and the calaboose was part of that protection. Some of the men who worked as policemen were John Warren, Tom Adams, George Gilbert and Dewey Austin. The police work was part time, as these men held full time jobs in the mill. You had to be on your best behavior or you could end up in the calaboose.

**Copy of arrest made on June 13, 1926.**
**Note the fines paid.**

Brookford Mills

# Brookford Mills

In 1898, two men, Henry L. Holbrook and E.L. Shuford, organized a cotton mill on Henry River to be operated as The E.L. Shuford Manufacturing Company. The town was named by combining the last parts of the names HolBROOK and ShuFORD. The site they chose for their mill could not have been better. The river would provide the power to run their mill and the Mill Hill area was one of the prettiest tracts of land in Catawba County. They built the dam that is in existence today to harness the power of the river.

The following year, 1899, Mr. Holbrook brought machinery from a mill in Springdale, Maine and supervised its installation. The machinery came from a mill owned by Mr. Holbrook's uncle, Edwin Holbrook. Over the years, the mill would eventually have three more additions to bring its area to 120,000 square feet by 1940.

Mr. Holbrook moved his family to Brookford in the summer of 1899 into a large white house located on the top of the hill overlooking the mill. The Holbrooks would occupy this house until 1917, when the mill was sold. In 1919 the house was occupied by Mr. David Howard, the overseer of the mill, until his retirement around 1945. It was then occupied by Mr. A.O. Hefner and family, who became superintendent of Brookford Mills. The house is now owned by the Sam Hill family.

In 1917, under bankruptcy proceedings, the mill and all of its properties was sold at public auction. The properties were purchased by A.D. Julliard and Company of New York City. Legend has it the public auction was held on the steps of the Company Store and the top bid was $276,000. A.D. Julliard and Company would operate the mill under the name of Brookford Mills. They would continuously operate the mill under this name until 1953, when the mill was sold to United Merchants and Manufacturers. United Merchants was another company owned by A.D. Julliard and Company. They

*Brookford Mill Heads*

DAVID L. HOWARD
General Manager

MARK A. BOLICK
Mayor of Brookford and Mill Agent

Exterior View Of Main Building At Brookford Mills Plant

would operate the mill until the mill closed in early 1957.

From the time the mill was built and the Mill Hill was formed the mill owners sought to provide facilities for educational and religious purposes. The mill built a frame school building over on Red Hill. It originally had three rooms, and as enrollment increased two more rooms were added. The mill hired all the teachers and paid their salaries. There are people still living who attended this school. When the new school was completed in 1925, the old school building was used for storage. It burned down around 1927. The mill also provided a teacherage in the house just below the house Mark Bolick and family occupied for many years. When Mrs. Clinard came to Brookford in 1919 the mill provided the teacherage rent-free to her and the other teachers she brought with her from Georgia.

Even after Brookford School was taken into the county school system in 1930, the mill continued to be involved in the school. The county only paid the teachers' salaries for six months of the year. The mill supplemented their salaries for two more months so that the school could be state-accredited.

The mill also provided Adult Education classes. The classes started in 1934-35 and most of the classes were held upstairs over the Company Store. The classes were free to the employees of the mill and their families. Students' ages ranged from 25 years old to 70 years old. It was estimated that 85% of the people who could only make an X for their names learned to write. These adult classes met a real need for the community. Many of the mill employees started working in the mill at an early age, some as young as 8 years old. They had to go to work out of necessity to help their families survive and their education was very limited.

Truck unloading cotton at the Mill.

The mill also donated two lots to be used for church purposes. The Faith Reformed Church was organized in 1901 and Brookford Baptist Church was organized in 1907. Both churches continue having worship services in the community today. The mill also allowed a Lutheran church to use the area over the Company Store until its church building could be completed. This church was led by a Reverend Wise.

By 1940, the mill had expanded to its present size. It had 120,000 square feet for manufacturing purposes. It also had a large mill office, a warehouse in Brookford and another warehouse in Hickory. It manufactured all kinds of fancy cotton and rayon goods. In a September 1940 article by Mabel Miller Rowe in the Hickory Daily Record, she states that the mill had 712 looms and 13,368 spindles. Its output was 90,000 to 100,000 pounds weekly, which translates to about 5 million pounds annually. The mill had added new equipment to bring the hydro-electric plant to peak efficiency. A new water wheel replaced the old direct drive wheel. The same dam built in

1898 continued to operate the waterwheels although they had to add five feet to it.

The article also credited three men for the tremendous growth of Brookford Mills- David Howard, Mark Bolick and A.O. Hefner. Mr. Howard was born in Denver, North Carolina near the Lincoln-Catawba County line. In 1907 he took a job with A.D. Julliard and Company. Except for the two years he served in the army during World War I, he was employed by the same company until his retirement around 1945.

His first job was in Aragon, Georgia. When he returned from the service in 1919, he was sent to Brookford as overseer of the mill. In 1927 he was made manager of Brookford Mills as well as in charge of A.D. Julliard owned-mills in Aragon, Georgia and in Rome, Georgia.

Mark Bolick, a native of Caldwell County, joined Brookford Mills in 1921. He started out in a small job in the office and advanced steadily to the position of agent for the corporation. He was always supportive of all community affairs, especially Brookford School.

He would serve as mayor of Brookford from 1935 until 1948. Of the three men mentioned in the article, he was probably the main force behind the growth of Brookford Mills. Mr. Howard had to spread himself too thin in his job of managing three mills in two states. Mark Bolick was a dynamic man, who didn't mind making the tough decisions.

A.O. Hefner came to Brookford Mills soon after Mr. Bolick. He too took a minor job in the office and was promoted gradually until he was made superintendent of the mill. All three men provided excellent leadership for the mill, but the mill also had many capable men who headed up the various departments in the mill. Most of them were long time employees of Brookford Mills and each played an important part in the growth of the company. The names of these people are familiar to anyone who grew up on the Mill Hill. Some of these department heads were, J.J. Stepp, J.W. Lipscomb, L.E. Beamon, J.D. Greene, Tom Cloninger, James Holsclaw, Will Lowman, B.B. Bishop, George Flowers, Red Austin, Tom Gadd, Charlie Nance, June Gaines, Frank McCune, Tom Clark, Jack Thompson and Loy Deitz.

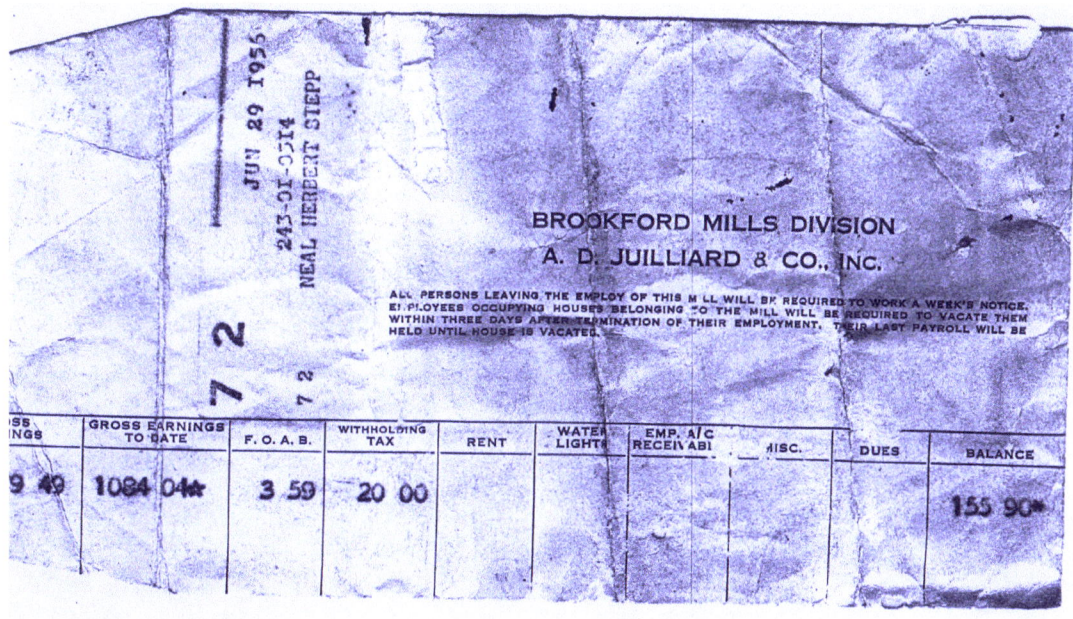

**Neal Stepp's last paycheck from Brookford Mills.**

Clockwise from top left: Doc Warren at Union Hall Building during the strike. Charlie Jolly is on the left. Unidentified man on the right.
Supervisor Row after snowstorm.
Striking workers line up.

These men are credited with making Brookford Mills one of the premier cotton mills in this area and they should be. But equally important was the work force. Without these people there would have been no success. These people were very loyal to Brookford Mills and always gave their best effort. The mill was very fortunate to have such a devoted work force.

Until 1953, the mill owned the whole village, which included not only the mill facilities, but also the Company Store, the service station, the school building and ball field, the boarding house, the swimming pool and about 120 mill houses. The workers rented their houses. They paid so much per room per week. The rent was taken out of their pay.

The mill was responsible for all upkeep on the houses. The house I was born in only had a cold water spigot. An outdoor johnny was provided for bathroom purposes. The house was not underpinned and insulation was unheard of in those days, so the house was freezing in the winter and hot as blazes in the summer. Our house and the house just below us were the two oldest houses on the Mill Hill and had clapboard siding. All the other houses had plank siding. The houses on Boss Man's row all had hot and cold water and inside bathrooms. Only supervisors occupied these houses, although for a time the mill used one of the houses for a teacherage.

The mill eventually paved all the streets on the Mill Hill and gradually upgraded all the employees' homes. Inside bathrooms were added as well as hot and cold running water. Our house and the house below us were remodeled. The old kitchen and the back bedroom were torn down and a new kitchen and back bedroom were added along with a new bathroom.

The mill continued to operate at peak capacity all through World War II and with the return of the men in service there was no shortage of labor. In 1948 a union was voted in at Brookford Mills. It was not known at the time, but this action initiated the demise of Brookford Mills. In 1951 a general strike was called and from that time on conditions changed. I believe the decision to close the mill was made after the strike.

In 1953 the mill sold all the Mill Hill houses. The mill offered the houses to the employees at a fair price and most of them purchased the houses they were living in. A.D. Julliard and Company sold the mill facilities to United Merchants and Manufacturers in 1956 and it was just a matter of time before the mill closed its doors. The decision came at the end of 1956.

You hear different reasons the mill closed. The official reason United Merchants and Manufacturers gave was that production had fallen off and that they could not operate the mill profitably. Another version was that United Merchants and Manufacturers said that Brookford Mills had too many seconds. All the machinery in Brookford Mills was moved to a mill United Merchants owned in Georgia. Supposedly this mill had 46% seconds. Brookford Mills never had more than 2% seconds, but the mill in Georgia was non-union. Makes a person wonder.

It was sad to see the closing of the mill. To remember how much a part of our lives the mill was and then to see it gone was almost like a death in the family. My mom, like many of the workers, spent her entire working life at Brookford Mills. Mom never worked in a cotton mill again. She was 50 years old when the mill closed.

The team. Front row, from left to right: Bill Gaines, Darrell Dietz, Tony Smith, Tony Gaines, Bobby Fox. Back row: Bob Taylor, Chad Mitchell, Donald Bowman, Richard Laney, Jerry Copas.

# The Mill's Basketball Team

From 1952 to 1956 Brookford Mills sponsored a semi-pro basketball team. Bob Taylor coached the team and they won their league title every year they played. Their league consisted of teams from Morganton, Blowing Rock, Granite Falls, Newton, Valdese, and Denver. The team also played in a number of tournaments in Gastonia, Cramerton, and Blowing Rock. There is a very good reason the mill team was successful. If you look at the team pictures, you will recognize some very good basketball players. The players on the team were Jerry Copas, Richard Laney, Chad Mitchell, Bill and Tony Gaines, Darrell Deitz, Tony Smith, Robert Sigmon and Bobby Fox. The only player on the team with no Brookford connection was Donald Bowman, who grew up in the Oxford section. They only let him be on the team because he was one heck of a basketball player.

Naomi Bolick Taylor provided the pictures of the team and talked about how much fun the team had. Jerry Copas filled me in on some of the particulars for the article. He was a fountain of information about the team. One year they were playing in a tournament in Gastonia in which the winner of the tournament got to go to the national tournament in Kansas City. Brookford advanced to the finals and was to play a team from Gastonia (not a good sign). What made it even worse, when they took the floor to start the game, there on the Gastonia team were two All-Americans from North Carolina, York Larese and Len Schaffer. Brookford didn't make it to Kansas City.

Another year the team played in a tournament at Cramerton and got into the finals again only to run into a team from Camp Lejeune. You can't beat the Marines no matter how hard you try. All the players on the mill team were good at basketball. Jerry tells me he made some lasting friendships with some of the players they played against. It certainly sounds like they all had a lot of fun playing.

# The Mill's Christmas Party

Growing up in Brookford, there were certain events you looked forward to with great anticipation. I've already written about two events – hog killing time and the letting off of the dam. The mill's annual Christmas party was another such event. It was always held in the auditorium at school and as a kid, you wouldn't miss it for the world.

Usually one of the grades at school presented a Christmas program. Carols were sung and there was a visit from Santa Claus. Mark Bolick had a few words to say. He was mayor of Brookford as well as a top supervisor at the mill. He thanked the school for the good job they had done all year and the employees of the mill for their hard work.

Then it was time for the real reason we came to the party. The mill always handed out a bag of Christmas treats for all the kids. The treats were in a brown paper bag and included fruit, nuts and candy. To us kids, it was a very special gift because it came from the mill. It made us feel good that the mill thought enough of us kids to bag the treats just for us.

I couldn't wait to get home and show my mom and my granny my very own bag of treats from the mill. I can still remember the joy I felt as a kid. I guess it's much too late to thank the mill, but here goes anyway. Thank you, all those who planned so carefully to make Christmas so special for us kids.

# The Flood of 1940

In August 1940, the whole Catawba Valley area was hit with heavy rains that caused severe flooding. Brookford Mills was hard hit by the rising waters. I have been able to come up with four pictures that show the flooding in various stages. The first picture is taken from the top floor of the mill showing how high the water had risen. The second picture is taken about the same time from ground level with a number of people in the foreground. The third picture is taken after the flood had burst the dam. Brookford Mills was built in three different stages. As the mill became bigger, it needed more hydro-electric power and the mill added an additional five feet to the dam. In the third picture, the dam broke off at

## MILL FETE HELD AT BROOKFORD

The auditorium of the Brookford school was packed to overflowing when the Brookford Mills held its first annual Christmas party for employees and their families Saturday evening.

A. O. Hefner, superintendent of the mills, declared in his address of welcome: "This is one of the greatest pleasures I have ever had." He then gave a special welcome to mothers, saying that those who do not work at the mill also play an important role.

Mr. Hefner, who has been with the company for twenty-six years, gave the employees and their families credit for making the Christmas party possible, adding that one and all had cooperated to the fullest extent.

M. A. Bolick, agent of the mills, brought greetings to the employees and their families after which the children sang carols.

**Music and Movie**

The program opened with music by Miss Naomi Bolick and an invocation by Rev. B. J. Wessinger, pastor of Zion Lutheran church. The children sang Christmas carols.

A motion picture, 'Twas the Night Before Christmas," was shown, also pictures of the Brookford school in technicolor. The audience sang "White Christmas," and a play "Christmas in Happy Valley," was staged by the children. Miss Marie Warren gave a recitation.

Then Santa Claus entered to start the presentation of gifts.

The mills employ 650 persons and 700 children under sixteen years of age received treats at the party. The treats consisted of apples, tangerines, oranges, four different kinds of candies, and mixed nuts. In addition to treats, 580 children under twelve years of age received a gift.

Long before the party got underway, the 650-place auditorium was filled and benches were brought in from other parts of the school building.

C. E. Taylor, overseer of the weave shop, and others were kept busy trying to find seats for the men, women and children. Bright eyed children, many of them puzzled by the proceedings, had the time of their lives and ate apples, oranges and candies until their tummies bulged out like Santa Claus, played by Ab Pitts.

In the afternoon, a Christmas party was held for the fifty colored employees of the mills and their families, with Mr. Hefner playing the role of Santa Claus.

Delighted over the large attendance, Mr. Hefner and Mr. Bolick said the mills plan to make the party an annual event.

Mrs. J. Weston Clinard, principal of the school, and other teachers were on hand to help with the party held Saturday night.

An article from The Hickory Daily Record describes the event we most looked forward to all year.

this five foot level. The fourth picture shows the dam after the water had receded. You will note in the bottom right of the picture what looks like a bolts of cloth.

The mill was flooded in the basement level. There was a weave room down there. Naomi Bolick Taylor tells me that her dad, along with a group of people, were moving some of the machinery out of the flooded weave room. Her dad said that all of a sudden the water stopped coming into the mill. He reasoned that the sudden drop in the water happened when the dam burst.

# Brookford People

# Joe and Hat Reinhardt

Joe Reinhardt was born May 19, 1902 in the Fallston area, one of 13 brothers and sisters. By 1911, the Reinhardt family had moved to Brookford and at nine years of age Joe was working in the mill as a doffer, standing on a box in order to do his job. He worked in the mill until management moved him to the Company Store to work as a clerk. The store was managed by Rufus Bolick and some of Joe's co workers were Wes Bollinger, Dan Henderson, Edwin Warren, Neil Mitchell, and Bad Eye Starnes. It was in this job that Joe learned the grocery business. Another of Joe's co-workers was a woman named Rena Kendall, who became not only the first woman mayor of Brookford, but also the first woman to be mayor of any town in Catawba County.

Hat Hilton was born April 17, 1901 in Granite Falls. Hattie was her given name but everyone called her Hat. She was also one of 13 brothers and sisters. Her family also moved to Brookford and it was there that she met Joe while working in the Spinning Department. They were married in 1922 and in 1924 their only child, Ralph, was born.

Joe continued to work in the Company Store until the early '40's, when he went to work for Newton Upholstery. While working there he was approached by Will Lowman about opening a grocery store on property that Will owned just across the road from the ball field. They opened their grocery store in 1943. Each one owned 50% of the building, and 50% of the stock. Early on, Joe realized that Will was not cut out for the grocery business and he went to Will with a proposition. He told Will he would trade either his share of the building for the stock or vice versa. Will decided to trade his share of the stock for

**Joe and Hat Reinhardt with Lil Stepp.**

**Hat Reinhardt with Ada Scronce**

ownership of the building. This is the arrangement they had until the grocery store closed in 1984. Joe owned all the stock and paid Will rent for the building. Evidently this worked out for the best for both of them. I know it did for the people of Brookford for I can't imagine life there without the Reinhardt Grocery store. Joe's son, Ralph, came into the business in 1948.

It was in the grocery business that Joe excelled and became indispensable as far as Brookford was concerned. Joe or Ralph would come down on the mill hill and take grocery orders. These orders were filled and delivered, with most of them on credit. Joe always worked with his customers. I don't know if he ever refused an order. Ralph said that many times Joe sold groceries on credit even though he knew that he probably would never be paid. But that was the kind of person Joe was, generous to a fault. It was this generosity that made Brookford so indebted to him. He broke almost all the rules of business and yet he had a successful business.

People trusted Joe. You knew he would do exactly what he said he would do and that the groceries he sold to you were the best he had. Of all the people I knew in Brookford, Joe was the kindest and friendliest man and one that had the interest of the whole community mostat heart. His biggest supporter had to be his wife, Hat. She was just like Joe – kind and friendly. My mom counted Hat as one of her best friends. Joe and Hat had a marriage that lasted until Hat's death in 1992, almost 70 years.

If Joe's greatest loves were Hat and the people of Brookford, his love for baseball wasn't close behind. Joe started going with Earl Hollar and others to see the Washington Senators play in the early '20's. The Senators had a pitcher by the name of Walter Johnson, who was called the Big Train. He was basically all the Senators had in those days. He was eventually elected to the Hall of Fame. He recorded over 400 wins, but to me, his greatest record is the 100 shutout wins he had. No one else has ever come close to this record. Joe became a good friend of Walter. In an interview before his death in 1994, he told me that he had some letters that Walter had written to him. I have wished a thousand times that I had gotten copies of these letters to include in this book, but I didn't. I told Ralph about the letters, but he has not been able to find them. They would be a valuable part of history. Let's keep our fingers crossed that Ralph will one day find the letters.

Joe also had a Western Carolina League baseball that was signed by Babe Ruth, Ty Cobb, Ted Williams, and Casey Stengel. But also on the ball there is a signature by Bill Bass as well as a signature by some one named "Cline". This tells you something about Joe, that he would consider the signature of Bill Bass as important as he would that of Ruth or Cobb or any of the others.

In 1955, Joe was in Cleveland, Ohio with Top and Jim Simpson to see a game between the Indians and the New York Yankees. On the mound that night for Cleveland was a young lefthander by the name of Herb Score, who was fast becoming one of the premier pitchers in baseball. He was hit in the face by a ball off the bat of Gil McDougald of the Yankees. The blow almost killed Score. He finally recovered from the injury, but he never became the same pitcher again. And for that matter, Gil McDouglad was never the same ballplayer again. Joe, along with Ralph and others, were in New York in 1956 to see a World Series game between the Yankees and the Dodgers. The game they saw was the day before Don

Larsen pitched the perfect game for the Yankees. Talk about rotten luck!

Joe was almost ninety years old when I interviewed him in 1991, but his love for baseball was still as strong as ever. All he wanted to talk about was his beloved Braves. He never missed one of their televised games. Hat was right there beside him.

Joe lost his life mate on January 22, 1992. He was to live two more years until he too passed away on February 20, 1994. Brookford had lost two of its best people. No one did more for the mill village of Brookford than Joe and Hat.

## Mark and Gertrude Bolick

In my mind, the person most responsible for the success of Brookford Mills has to be Mark Bolick. He came to Brookford in 1921 after graduating from Lenoir College (now Lenoir Rhyne College). His first job in the mill was payroll clerk. From there he steadily progressed in management until he became agent of the mill. He remained in this capacity until the mill closed in 1957.

Mark was born November 19, 1898 in Caldwell County to Jacob L. and Mary O. Woods Bolick, who became known eventually on the mill hill as Mother Bolick. Mark was educated in the Caldwell County School. Upon graduation, he entered Lenoir College. I'm told by his daughter, Naomi, that part of his tuition was furnishing the use of his cow. He literally took his cow to school with him. It stayed on campus with him and provided milk for the student body and faculty. He has to be one of the few people who can claim his cow helped them through college.

World War I interrupted his stay in college. Mark served his country in the U.S. Army. Mark was stationed in Kentucky, but the war was over before Mark was sent overseas. When the war ended, he returned to Lenoir College and graduated in 1920 with a degree in business.

> "Joe was almost ninety years old when I interviewed him in 1991, but his love for baseball was still as strong as ever. All he wanted to talk about was his beloved Braves."

After Mark had begun work at Brookford Mills, he went on a date with a woman whose last name was Barger. It was at this event that he met the woman, who would become his life mate, Gertrude Barger. From that time on Gertrude became the only woman in Mark's life. They were married on May 21, 1922 and would become life long companions until Mark's death in 1995, a total of seventy three years of marriage. Ironic as it may seem, the Barger lady that Mark escorted to that social event also married a man whose last name was Bolick.

Gertrude was born on January 27, 1902 to Abel and Sarah Workman Barger. Her family lived in the Houck's Chapel area at the time of her birth. They later moved just off Highway 127 north of Brookford. They say behind every successful man is a strong woman. She was the perfect mate for Mark and in her own way was every bit as gifted as Mark. While Mark's energies were directed to helping Brookford Mills become the force it was in business, Gertrude gave all of her attention to being a wife and mother. Both of them succeeded greatly.

Both Mark and Gertrude were active members of Bethlehem Lutheran Church, where Gertrude was a life long member. Mark joined Bethlehem after his marriage to Gertrude and over the years became one of its most active members. He served on the Church Council, was a member of the Lutheran Brotherhood and served the church as Sunday School Superintendent. He also sang in the choir for many years and taught a Sunday school class for over fifty years. His pastor, Rev. Peeler, often referred to him as his "Assistant Pastor". At one time he held the distinction of being the oldest member of the congregation.

Mark was a lifetime member of Hickory Masonic Lodge 343 and was an honorary life member of American Legion Post #48. Mark actively supported sports in the Catawba valley area, particularly the Hickory Rebels.

Mark and Gertrude were blessed with seven children: five daughters – Marie, Thelma, Naomi, Adelaide, Elaine, and two sons – Ray and Carroll. All are still living. Thelma lives in Virginia, Marie in Lenoir, Naomi in Hickory, Adelaide in Florida, and Elaine in Marion. Ray and Carroll both reside in Georgia.

**Mark and Gertrude Bolick before they were married.**

While Gertrude became a stay-at-home mom, Mark continued to have outstanding success at the mill. Dave Howard, who was manager of the mill for A.D. Julliard and Company, had two other Julliard mills to manage in Georgia. These duties left him precious little time to manage Brookford Mills. It didn't present a problem because he had two very capable men under him – Mark and A.O. Hefner, who eventually became superintendent of the mill. In a 1940 Hickory Daily Record article by Mabel Miller Rowe on Brookford Mills, it states that the mill was producing between 90,000 and 100,000 pounds of cloth a week. This computes to almost five million pounds of cloth for the year! Brookford Mills had come a long way since its beginning in 1899 and Mark Bolick deserves a large share of the credit.

Brookford's management team was selected by Dave Howard, Mark Bolick and A.O. Hefner, and was as strong as any mill's in this area. Many of the names of these supervisors, foremen, and section hands are readily recognized by anyone who grew up on the hill. They include June Gaines, Tom Cloninger, James Holsclaw, J.J. Stepp, Robert Lipscomb, Will Lowman, George Flowers, Bernice Bishop, Loy Deitz , Ed Taylor, J.D. Greene, James Hinson, Lewis Beaman, Frank McCune and Fred Crider. I'm sure you can add to the list.

But the one man, who personified what Brookford Mills was all about had to be Mark Bolick. He was never afraid to make the tough decision and his keen business sense enabled Brookford Mills to become a great success. As devoted as Mark was to his family, he was equally devoted to Brookford Mills and to the Brookford community. No one stressed education more than Mark. Brookford Mills always had the education of the people at heart. From the time the mill started, its management became involved in the education of the people, not only for the children, but also for the adults. The mill had many workers who could not read or write. The mill provided adult education classes for them upstairs over the Company Store. The school house on Red Hill was built by the mill for the children. Even after the new school was built, the mill continued to supplement the teachers' salaries so that Brookford School could hire the best teachers. Mark Bolick enhanced the mill's efforts. I suppose he had seen what education had done for him and he wanted to see success for the Brookford people. His efforts were not in vain as Brookford had many of its people to go onto higher education and become successful in teaching, the ministry, nursing, and yes, in business.

All of us who grew up on the mill hill are indebted to many people, none more so than Mark and Gertrude Bolick. Without the Bolick family, Brookford would not have been the place it was. Mark was mayor of Brookford from the time I was born in 1935 until I had finished the seventh grade at Brookford School in 1948. His community spirit was unsurpassed. He was proud of Brookford Mills and Brookford School, but his greatest pride was in the Brookford community and its people. He truly helped Brookford be the special place it was.

Mark continued to work for A.D. Julliard and Company after the decision to close the Brookford mill in 1956. This would have to be the unhappiest time in his career to see his beloved Brookford Mills being dismantled. His work with Julliard continued for several years. He eventually worked for Carolina Mills before his retirement from the textile industry. I interviewed Mark and Gertrude in 1991. Mark was then 93 years old. He was just as sharp mentally as ever and his face lit up when he talked about his days in Brookford and Brookford Mills.

Mark passed away at age 97 on December 31, 1995. His beloved wife Gertrude joined him in death on August 13, 1996.

## Lee and Ruth Melton

To have lived on the mill hill in Brookford was one of the great privileges in my life. To have lived next door to the Melton family practically my entire childhood was almost like a blessing from above. Ruth and Lee were two people that I loved and admired. Everyone on the mill hill felt the same about Ruth and Lee.

Lee was born in Cleveland County on June 5, 1905. He lost both his mom and his dad at an early age and ended up in foster homes. By the time he was eight years old he was working in a cotton mill near Shelby. In an interview before his death, he told me that he worked six days a week and brought home his pay. The man who provided the foster home took every penny that Lee had made. He was working just for a place to sleep and eat.

Before Lee went to work in the mills, he lived in a foster home where the man made his living in selling produce. Lee couldn't have been more than six or seven years old. This man would take Lee along with him on his trips from Shelby to Asheville to buy produce. They would travel in a horse and wagon and the trip would take about a week to go up to Asheville and back. Lee's son, Buck, told me that they would take a huge sack of flour with them along with fatback. They would stop for the night at farm houses along the way. The produce man would give flour to the woman of the house to make biscuits for her family and for them. This is how they survived on that long trip. I'm sure that Lee's foster dad had made the trip many times and he knew where he could stop for the night and where he couldn't. Nowadays we complain about having to go to the grocery store. In interviewing people for this book, I have been amazed at the hardships many of the parents of my generation had to endure. During the first half of the Twentieth Century, life in Brookford and for the rest of the country was extremely hard. This generation of the Lee Meltons and the Joe Reinhardts and the Perry Wallaces had to endure the ordeal of child labor, the Depression, and many of them had to fight for their country in the World Wars. The rest of us have no idea how very tough these times were. But I believe that the toughness of the times was also what made their generation so strong. They endured these tough times and it made them stronger. There is a saying that life is like a grinding stone. Whether it polishes you up or grinds you down is according to the stuff you're made of. These people were tough and they endured.

**Lee and Ruth Melton**

About 1925, Lee took a job on the farm of John Camp near Shelby. It was there that he met Ruth, John and Sally's daughter. Ruth was younger than Lee. She was born on June 7, 1911. Lee had not worked at the farm long before he fell in love with Ruth. He remembers the day he finally asked John Camp for permission to marry Ruth. He says that he and Mr. Camp were working out in the field hoeing and Lee was trying to work up enough courage to ask for Ruth's hand. They had worked all day in the field and he still had not found the courage to ask Mr. Camp. He could see that they were on their last row and if he didn't ask him he might never have the opportunity again. Finally Lee asked Mr. Camp for his permission to marry Ruth. Mr. Camp replied, " I wondered if you were ever gonna ask me. I know you will be good to Ruth and you have my blessing." Ruth and Lee were married in 1926 and shortly thereafter moved to Red Springs, North Carolina where Lee had taken a job as loom fixer. Their first three children, John William, Ellen, and Yvonne, were all born in Red Springs.

In 1933 the Meltons moved to Brookford, where Lee took a position as a loom fixer. Lee and Ruth eventually had five more children in Brookford: Leoma, Othneal, Alberta, Barbara Jean, and Charles. Ellen died a tragic death at age two. The death of a child can do one of two things to a couple. It can become a wedge that drives them apart or it can bring them closer together. Lee and Ruth became stronger and inseparable.

Their house was always open to any kid on the mill hill. My mom had heard about the Meltons over on the Red Hill, but had not met them. One day she met Ruth and introduced herself. Ruth said, "Oh, I know who you are. I've been cutting your son Jerry's hair for some time." We found out Mom had been giving Jerry a quarter to get his hair cut at the barber shop. Instead Jerry pocketed the quarter, went over to Ruth's to get his hair cut for free, and spent the money all on him. Mom quickly put a stop to that practice, but this shows the kind of neighbor Ruth was. Any way she could help out she was willing to do it.

It has been said that the more love you give the more love is returned to you. You could not go into the Melton home without feeling the love they had not only for their family, but for everyone. Ruth Melton was like a second mom to me and Lee was the dad I never had. I always like to think I was semi-adopted by the Meltons. At least I considered myself one of their children. That could have been self-delusion, but Ruth and Lee always treated me like one of their own.

A true story about me perfectly illustrates what I'm saying. A number of times when I was heading up toward the ball ground, I would go through the Meltons' back door, get myself a biscuit from off the stove (Ruth always had a pan of biscuits there), walk out the front door and never say a word to anybody. It was like I considered their house as my house.

Another story about the Meltons: Ray Berry, who lived over on Barger Church Road, came home with Buck one day and never left, at least not until he went into service. Lee and Ruth considered him as one of their own children. Ray was included in Ruth and Lee's will. Talk about an abundance of love – Ruth and Lee had it.

I'm sure the Meltons had it tough. With as many kids as they had, life had to be hard on them to make ends meet, but there was always enough to share with others. What is best though is they shared themselves with everyone around them and we are all richer for their generosity. If the world was full of Ruth and Lee Meltons, it would not be in the terrible shape it is in today.

In writing about the generation of Ruth and Lee, I'm finding that many of them had to start working in the mills at a very early age, some as young as eight years old. Their education was minimal at best and yet so many of them were very successful in life. You can find no better examples of being good parents, good neighbors and good friends than down at the mill hill in Brookford. Just look at the lives of Ruth and Lee Melton, Perry and Rose Wallace, Mark and Gertrude Bolick, Lillian and James Holsclaw, Ruth and Hubie Pope, Lil and Neal Stepp, Aileen and Clyde Wilson. All of these people had successful marriages and all were the kind of people you wanted for your next door neighbors.

Ruth had the ability to do what they called on the mill hill "talking the fire out". I found out about this gift one cold morning. I was standing too close to the coal heater we used to heat the house in the winter. I wasn't paying a lot of attention to what I was doing. I only had my underwear on and when I bent down to pet my dog, Pepper, I backed into the stove pipe. The image of the ribbed pipe (elbow) was branded on my behind. Mom sent me right up to Ruth's for her to talk the fire out. There I was bending over and bearing my backside to Ruth, but talk the fire out she did. I still had the branded butt, but the pain was gone.

Later in life, Ruth tried to pass the gift of talking the fire out to me. It could only be passed from female to male or vice versa. Evidently the gift didn't take in my case because I have no ability to talk the fire out, but thank goodness Ruth had the gift.

Both Ruth and Lee were active members of Faith United Church of Christ or Faith Reformed Church as it was called when we were growing up. They put their faith in action. Neither of them ever saw a need that they didn't meet. Even Lee's big truck was part of their ministry at the church. Lee was always taking kids to or from John's River Camp. The vacation bible school would not have been complete without Lee's truck. Their children followed the lead of their parents and all were very active in the church. Their daughter, Alberta, was called into full time Christian ministry. She got her degree from Catawba College and after graduation married a minister. They together have served their Lord and the church in Pennsylvania. They have just recently retired.

While Lee worked at the mill, Ruth stayed at home with the children. When the kids got older, Ruth worked for a time in the Brookford Café with Charles Mitchell and also handled the post office when it was in the café.

All of their children went on to lead productive lives. Their three sons, John William, Buck, and Charles were all career Navy men and are now retired. John William lives in South Carolina, Buck lives in the mountains above Wilkesboro in a house he built himself (do you detect a little bit of envy here?), and Charles lives in Hickory. Leoma spent her entire working career in nursing and is now retired. Yvonne was a supervisor in Carolina Mills before her death in 1995. She is the only one of their children to work in textiles. Barbara Jean is still working with Hickory Home and Gardens.

Lee's truck was a help to all of us kids on the mill hill. The summer after seventh grade, Mrs. Brooks, our teacher, planned a swimming party for the class at Kool Park Pool. She probably did this out of gratitude that we were finally leaving Brookford School. Lee's truck transported all of us down to the pool. It was the best party I ever attended. He also used his truck to get our summer baseball team to away games. I can still remember being on the back of that truck all excited about a game with Highland or Sweetwater. I don't know what his church or the mill hill would have done without his truck.

It seemed that Lee could do about anything that needed to be done (see Hog Killing Time). In the mill, he worked as a loom fixer, which was the best paying job for the regular workers. If it involved machines, Lee could fix it. Lamar Hunt reminded me of the time his dad and Lee took the motor out of Perry Wallace's car and repaired and replaced it.

Lee passed this mechanical ability on to Buck. I was always envious of Buck for that very reason. I am mechanically retarded. I have to get out a manual to use a screwdriver. Buck is like his dad. He can fix anything. When we were growing up, I'm sure Buck got awfully tired of fixing my bicycle.

About the greatest compliment that can be paid to people is that they made a difference in the lives of the people around them. This is never more true than for Ruth and Lee. All of us in Brookford are indebted to them for making our lives better, which is exactly what God had in mind for each of us.

Lee died June 26, 1993. After he died the light in Ruth's life had gone out. In her last days, I visited her at Catawba Memorial Hospital. I was telling her that she had to get better because we couldn't imagine life without her being in it. She looked straight at me and told me that life without Lee was just too hard and she was ready to go and be with him. I had no argument for what she was telling me because I could see how much she missed Lee. That is the last time I saw Ruth alive. She died October 12, 1993. I can still see that sweet face talking about being with Lee again. The Lord blessed her by taking her to be with Lee and we were all blessed by having them in our lives

## Lillian and James Hosclaw

On February 27, 1932 James and Lillian Isenhour Holsclaw were married in Gaffney, South Carolina. By the time they were married, James had been working at Brookford Mills about fourteen years. Lillian had been taken out of school at age fourteen by her father, and put to work in the mill because as he put it, the family needed the money. Lillian loved school and wanted to continue her education, but her father would not hear of it. Lillian had met James earlier in the Brookford community. Neither could have selected a better partner. Their marriage lasted until 1989, when James passed away. They were blessed with two daughters, Maxine and Martha.

James was born in Caldwell County on May 24, 1909. Not much is known about his immediate family. James was raised by his grandmother, Martha, on the mill hill in a house behind Faith Reformed Church. He went to work in the mill at age nine. Lillian tells me that James was so small when he went to work in Brookford Mills that on breaks Fannie Hollar, mother of Earl, used to hold James on her lap. I guess she missed being a stay at home mother. James progressed in the mill to become a weave room supervisor. He remained in that capacity until the close of the

James and Lillian in Greenville, SC.

mill in 1957. Lillian spent her entire working career as a weaver, a job she loved.

Lillian was born in Brookford on December 6, 1912 to Reid and Dora Belle Whitener Isenhour. Lillian had two sisters, Louise and May, nine brothers, William Lee, Elby, Fred, Edwin (Buddy), Reid, Jr., Franklin, Boyd, David, O.B. and one half-brother, Walter Bollinger. The Isenhour family was not without tragedy. William Lee, at eleven months, fell into a fire and died. Lillian's brother Elby was deep sea fishing with a group on the coast in 1963. A sudden storm came up and the boat Elby was on capsized. He was lost at sea. They never recovered his body. Lillian to this day still grieves over Elby.

While she was growing up Lillian wanted to be a teacher, but with her daddy taking her out of school at 14, this dream was unfulfilled. Later, as an adult, she considered going back to school and becoming a nurse. With the cares of raising her family while working in the mill, this dream never came to be. It is ironic that her oldest daughter, Maxine, spent her entire working career as a nurse. Her younger daughter, Martha, is starting her thirty first year as a teacher. She is planning to retire at the end of this school year. In a way, Lillian attained both her dreams through her daughters. She is very proud of their accomplishments.

Brookford Baptist Church would not have been the same without Lillian and James. Both lived for their Lord and His Church. Lillian has been a life long member there and is still very active in the church. James was just as active. James and Lillian both served as Sunday School teachers and Training Union Directors. Both sang in the choir. James served as Choir Director for a number of years. Lillian is still a member of the choir.

Around 1945, the church built an addition that included a fellowship hall downstairs and more Sunday school classrooms upstairs. I remember as a young lad going down to watch them work on this addition. I guess I had taken it on myself to supervise. The one person I remember working the hardest was James Holsclaw. He and Lillian were like that. If there was work to be done, they were there. What witnesses for the Lord that even a young boy recognized how hard they worked.

I have often thought how very fortunate I was to grow up in a place that had James Holsclaw, Lee Melton, and Perry Wallace living right at my door. I didn't have to look very far to see role models on how to be a husband, a father, and a neighbor. These three men were there to be observed every day and you could look the world over and not find better role models. James always took time for me when I was growing up. He was interested in me as a person and this made a great impression on me as a young lad. I can still hear that deep, soothing voice of his. I certainly never wanted to disappoint my mother.

I also never wanted to disappoint James Holsclaw. I miss him to this day.

Lillian will be ninety this year (I hope she won't be upset that I am advertising that fact). Her flowers are still the prettiest on the mill hill. Sometimes she works in the yard a little too much for her own good, but that's the way she is and I don't think she's going to change. She is never still because there is so much for her to do, with taking care of her flowers, feeding her birds, and doing all kinds of crafts. She has made her back yard a refuge. It is so peaceful sitting there and looking at all the pretty flowers and birds. She truly is a wonder at all she gets done.

Lillian has been an inspiration for me in putting this book together. Many of the pictures are from her extensive collection. Without her help and encouragement, I don't think this book would have ever been completed. The first copy of this book is reserved for Lillian. Many thanks for being the friend you are to me.

## Perry and Rose Wallace

Perry Wallace was born August 3, 1900 to Jay and Sarah Wallace in Conover. Rose Hefner Wallace was born in Catawba County to Lawson and Cora Hefner on October 1, 1903. They met while working in a cotton mill in Conover and were married on April 2, 1921. This marriage would last until Rose's death in 1988. They had three children, Albert, who passed away in 2000, Viola, and Fred.

Shortly after they married, Perry and Rose moved to Brookford where they both took jobs in the mill, Perry in the card room and Rose in the spinning department.

Perry worked continuously in the card room until the close of the mill in 1957. Rose was not working in the mill when it closed. After the mill closed, Perry took a job with Burlington Mills in Rhodhiss. He eventually took a job at the Shuford Mills plant in Longview known as Hickory Spinners. The mill had to change its computer programs because of Perry. Seems the programmers did not anticipate anyone eighty three years old would still be working! In all Perry spent almost eighty years working in cotton mills. He started working in the mills at age nine. The family finally coaxed him into retirement in 1983.

Perry and Rose lived across the road from us almost the whole time I was growing up. Rose

**Perry and Rose Wallace**

was my Granny's best friend. I can't count the number of times Granny and I went to keep Rose company until Perry got off from the second shift. It was always fun for me to be there with Rose and Granny. Rose was just fun to be around. She often reminded me of the night I looked at her and said in all seriousness "Rose it looks like our good times are over. Perry is on the first shift now and the kids come in early". I couldn't have been more than six years old. But it struck Rose as being funny and she laughed and laughed. It was true, however. We did have lots of fun. I have often wondered what in the world did I add to the conversations. Maybe I was just a good listener. I wonder how many six year olds can claim that one of their best friends was a married woman with three children. Rose was as much my friend as she was Granny's. And I think she felt the same way about me.

Almost every time Rose and Perry went to visit they invited Granny and of course, I had to tag along. We always had a good time on our trips with them. I can remember going to one of the Wallaces' reunions. All the food was on a long table out under some trees. The food was out of this world and we all had a grand time.

One trip I remember with them, we were going to Valdese for what purpose I don't remember. What I do remember is that about halfway up the hill to Valdese, we had a flat tire. Perry got out to fix the flat and I got out to "help" him. I was maybe seven or eight years old and really all I was good for was asking questions. Do you have a spare tire? Just so happens he did. Do you know how to change the tire? He did. Will we get home before dark? Perry assured me that we would get home before dark. A lesser man would have strangled me, but Perry took it all in stride. We had a wonderful time in spite of that flat tire. And we did get home way before dark.

Another trip we made with Rose and Perry was a picnic lunch to a big lake. It must have been Lake James. I know it wasn't Lake Hickory because we drove for a pretty long piece. I even think my mom was along on this trip. What really sticks in my mind besides the wonderful picnic lunch and feeding pieces of bread to these huge fish was that to get to where we had the picnic we had to drive across this earthen dam. Now most kids would not give that earthen dam a second thought. Unfortunately I am not like most kids. Even at that young age I was already developing into a world class worry wart. I worried for years that fool dam was gonna burst and everybody in Brookford would be drowned, myself included. I can't remember when I stopped worrying about that dam. I think it was in 1995.

Rose and Perry were suited for each other. Rose was so outgoing and so much fun to be around. Perry was quieter than Rose, but there was never a kinder, gentler man on this earth than Perry Wallace. For a kid growing up without a father, I certainly didn't have any problem finding role models on how to be a husband and a father. I had to look no further than across the street at Perry Wallace or next door at Lee Melton. I have so many wonderful memories I spent with my granny in the company of Rose and Perry.

From the time they moved to Brookford until their deaths, Rose and Perry were faithful members of Faith United Church of Christ. Rose died on February 10, 1988 and Perry passed away on October 2, 1998. In his last few years Perry lived with his son, Albert and his daughter-in-law, Clare. When Perry died at the age of 98, the world lost one of its most gentle souls.

## Jerm and Bertha Foster

William Jeremiah (Jerm) Foster moved with his family to Brookford from Wilkes County in 1906. Jerm was born on June 18, 1890 to George and Elvira Foster. His family moved from Wilkes County because they had heard that you could find work in Brookford Mills and there was no work in Wilkes County unless you wanted to make liquor, and that field was already overcrowded. The Foster family came with a bunch of kids in tow. Jerm was sixteen years old at this time and he found work in the mill as a doffer. But it was not long before wanderlust got to him. There is a picture of a young Jerm on an Indian Motorcycle in Bo Peep Grill. How he came to have the motorcycle is probably another story, but leave Brookford he did. His travels took him to Virginia and West Virginia, where he worked for a time as a coal miner. He eventually came back to his family in Brookford and told them from then on he wanted to work on the ground, not under it. It was at about this time he met Bertha Chapman who was a spooler in the mill.

Bertha Chapman Foster was born in the South Mountains of Burke County to John Schublo Chapman and Elizabeth Butler Chapman on September 22, 1900. The Chapmans had nine children, with Bertha being the youngest. The Chapmans lost three of their children in the Flu epidemic of 1901. Her mother became incapacitated after this tragedy and the care of Bertha was left with her sister, Mary, who was fifteen at the time. Bertha was eventually taken in by her uncle, Grover Wilkie, who owned a lot of property over near Hwy #18 where it joins Hwy #10. He leased most of his land to sharecroppers but he gave an acre of this land to Bertha. She was to work this land and the money she made from selling her produce would be what she lived on. (Reba called it God's Little Acre). Her uncle Grover worked in the mill at Brookford and was instrumental in getting her a job as a spooler.

In 1916, Jerm and Bertha were married. It was not long before the marriage suffered a tragedy. Bertha gave birth to triplets, two girls and one boy in 1918. Two of the babies were stillborn and the third baby died the next day. Jerm and Bertha overcame this horrific tragedy and would have eight more children,

**Jerm and Bertha Foster's wedding picture.**

Dot, William, Howard "Chink" who died in 1960, Frances, who died in 2001, David, Peggy Sue and Thomas, who died in 1937 at eighteen months. After the death of Thomas, Bertha went into a deep depression that lasted a year. Perhaps she was grieving not only for the loss of Thomas, but also for her mother and for the loss of the triplets.

In 1938, the Fosters would suffer another calamity. Their home burned to the ground. Jerm had the foresight to have the house insured and he wanted to take the insurance money and build a nice garage. He had found a partially finished stone house way out in the country that he wanted to buy, but this is when Bertha put her foot down and insisted that they rebuild on the same lot in Brookford. She wasn't about to be stuck way out in the country. Jerm did get his stone house but he had to make do without his garage.

I don't think there was a child growing up on the mill hill that did not go down to the Foster home at one time or another and admire this pretty home. All of us were just a little bit envious of a family that had a stone house with hot and cold running water and a bathroom inside. It would be years before most of us mill hill kids would have an inside bathroom with an actual bathtub.

Many people my age, who grew up in Brookford, are unaware that back in the 1920's, Brookford Mills had a brass band that played in numerous events on the mill hill. A picture of that band is included in this book. It had many well known people of Brookford, such as Dick Reinhardt, Will Lowman, Tom Cloninger, and Jerm Foster. He is on the back row fourth from the right. He played the trumpet and the trombone. I've been told that there was a gazebo-type structure near the service station in the flat where they held dances and, of course, the band played for these occasions. It also played in the town meeting room above the Company Store when silent movies were shown.

Both Jerm and Bertha continued to work in the mill, Bertha between babies. Jerm had always worked on cars and machines. He continued his mechanic work part time after his marriage to Bertha. When he was passed over for the position of head loom fixer, Jerm quit his job in the mill and started operating his garage full time. His oldest son, Willie, became his helper in the garage.

It was not long before Jerm's garage flourished. Jerm did excellent mechanical work and

**Bertha and Jerm Foster with their stone home in the background.**

at a fair price. It was great to see this hard-working unassuming man enjoy the success he did. It was richly deserved. Jerm and his garage became an institution in Brookford. Practically everybody who owned a car had it worked on by Jerm Foster. Brookford would not have been the same place without Jerm's garage. My uncle Neal owned the store just two doors up from the garage. I would go out to the store with my mom and sometimes I would sneak out of the store and go down to the garage just to watch Jerm work. He was a mechanical genius. Brookford's cars certainly ran better because of Jerm. After Willie got out of the service, he became Jerm's partner and was almost as gifted mechanically as his dad.

Bertha also had a thriving barber business. She would cut hair on Saturday for ten cents. The barber shop charged a quarter. Their house that burned in 1938 had a shower in the basement and Bertha rented the shower out to anyone who wanted to use it. Remember the only other shower for public use was in the barber shop. Bertha was in direct competition with the barber shop. But she was a good business woman as capable in her own right as Jerm. I guess working "God's Little Acre" on her Uncle Grover's land was good training for her.

Jerm and his family were long time members of Brookford Baptist Church. Jerm was a man without any prejudices long before it was fashionable. If Jerm was working on a black man's car and it came time to eat, that black man sat down at the table with the Foster family and this was when there was very little association on the mill hill with people of other races. Jerm and Bertha believed in tithing and set aside one tenth of their money for the Lord. They showed their faith by their actions, which is exactly as the Lord intended. And they were blessed abundantly by the Lord. Times were not always easy for Jerm and Bertha, but their faith never wavered.

With Jerm being eight years older than Bertha you would think that he would be the first to die, but it didn't happen that way. Bertha died in 1961 at the age of sixty-three. Jerm would live almost ten more years without his beloved Bertha. He passed away in 1971 at the age of eighty-three.

## Baxter and Annie Crump

In 1953 the Hillside Baptist Church was built just down the road from Reinhardt's Grocery Store. The two people most responsible for the building of this church were Baxter and Annie Crump. The first meeting place for Hillside Baptist Church was in their home on the mill hill. It was through their efforts and their prayers that the church became a reality.

From the prayer meetings in their home, the church moved to the basement of Bramon Martin, who lived close to where the church now stands. The church eventually moved to the old Union Hall Building, where the church was organized on March 4, 1951. It met in the Union Hall Building until its present building was completed.

Both Annie and Baxter worked in the mill, Annie in the spinning room and Baxter as a doffer. Baxter was born in Hildebran on January 20, 1906. Annie was born just across the river from Brookford on December 8, 1909. Annie and Baxter were married on December 15, 1924. They would remain married until Baxter's death on November 22, 1978. They had nine children, Edna, Helen, Bill, Jim, Claude, Max, Joe (who died at eleven months), Tony and David. Both Max and David became ordained ministers.

Annie and Baxter were working in the mill when it closed in 1957. Both found work at Henry River Mill. Baxter later went to Ivey Weavers and Annie went to Hickory Spinners before they retired.

In writing this book, I was told time and again that I had to put Annie and Baxter Crump in it. Ruby Travis especially recalled how the Crumps helped them get through some hard times. The Travises' mom and dad both died and the whole gang of children was left to be cared for by the older sister, Ruth, who was not much more than a child herself. Ruby tells me that if it had not been for the Crumps and Mrs. Rudisill, who lived next door to them, they would not have made it as a family. Through the kindness and the efforts of Annie and Baxter and Mrs. Rudisill, the Travis family was able to survive and not be sent foster homes.

Talking with Max about his mom and dad, he related how their family was members of Winkler's Grove Baptist Church at one time. The Crump family did not own a car, so they took the bus to the Pepsi Cola plant in Longview and the whole family walked to the church which must have been more than three miles. That's a round trip of about six miles just to go to church. But that is how Annie and Baxter were. They believed in the church and they practiced what the church preached.

That meant seeing the needs around and meeting those needs. It is amazing what can be accomplished if you have enough faith. Annie and Baxter had great faith and it culminated in the founding of Hillside Baptist Church. When they finally decided to build the church, the grading for the land was done by Pop Griffey's team of mules and a scoop.

The first pastor of Hillside Baptist Church was Rev. Oscar Walker, who came from (you guessed it) Winkler's Grove Baptist Church. Baxter later pastored the church from 1960-1965. David, the present pastor, has served Hillside for over thirty years. The church is still the beacon in the community that Annie and Baxter envisioned those many years ago, when they met for prayer meetings in their home. And the church owes a great debt to

**Hillside Baptist Church**

Annie and Baxter for having the vision and allowing God to work through them.

This is not to imply that they didn't encounter many hardships in their lives. Just being born around the turn of the century guaranteed you of a hard life unless you were lucky enough to be born into a rich family. There were no child labor laws and the only work you could find was on a farm or in the mill. Many people started to work in the mills while they were still children. Baxter started to work in the mill at age eleven, Annie when she was fourteen. They had a child, Joe, who died when he was eleven months old. In February 1964, their son, Bill, died in High Shoals, North Carolina at age 34. Bill was a kind and gentle man and his death was an extremely difficult experience for the whole Crump family. It had to test the faith of Annie and Baxter, but they never wavered in their trust in the Lord and it was that strong faith that helped them to get through this tragic event.

Annie is still living down on the mill hill in the house that was once occupied by Mrs. Rudisill. She is ninety-three years old and is in reasonably good health. Only three of Annie's children are still living: Claude, Max and David.

The community of Brookford owes a great debt to Annie and Baxter Crump for their faith and their foresight. Annie is still a living witness to her faith.

## Chop and Babe Thompson

I don't think I ever called Chop and Babe by their given names - Carroll and Edna. To me and everybody down in Brookford they were simply Chop or Choppy and Babe.

Chop was born May 10, 1915 in South Carolina to Charles Richard Thompson and Alma Thompson. Chop's family moved to Brookford when he was about seven or eight. His dad took a job with Brookford Mills as supervisor of the weave room. A picture of his young mother shows this beautiful lady, along with a wonderful view of the Company Store when it still had the balcony.

Babe was born in Georgia on May 27, 1918 to J.J. and Edna Stepp. She was six months old when her family moved to Brookford. Both she and Chop started school together at Brookford School about the time the new school opened. They were taught in the

**Chop and Babe**

fourth grade by Babe's older sister, Kate, which had to be an unusual experience for Kate and Babe. Usually kids from Brookford went to Mountain View for high school. Chop graduated from there in 1936 and was the valedictorian of his class. Babe's dad insisted that she go to Hickory High and she also graduated in 1936. Even though she and Chop attended different high schools, they started going together. After high school, Chop took a job in the weave room and fell in love with Babe. He asked Babe to marry him and on May 23, 1936 they were wed and moved into a house on the mill hill.

While growing up, Babe developed into quite a tomboy. It may have been the influence of being in a family with four brothers and only one sister, but Babe had a bit of a daredevil in her. She loved to swim and the lure of the river was too much a temptation for her. She regularly jumped off the Swinging Bridge. One day she decided that maybe diving off the dam to the water below would be more fun. After all, the water at the Swinging Bridge was not very deep and very rocky. So she started the questionable practice of diving off the dam. Word got back to her dad bout her exploits and he quickly put a stop to them. Babe was about fourteen at the time.

Not too long after they were married Chop and Babe bought some land next to her sister Kate and Kate's husband, Seth, where they built a house. She and Chop had five children, Danny, David, Jeanie, Carolyn and Cathy. Babe was fortunate enough to be a stay at home mom, while the kids were small.

Babe was definitely a hands-on mom. To us kids she was just a little bigger playmate of ours. The first time I ever played in the branch Babe took us. We dammed up the branch so that it was at least knee deep and we all had a wonderful time playing. I believe Babe had the most fun of all. She was always a pleasure to be around. She still is at age 84.

When gathering the information about Chop and Babe, I remembered a dog the Thompsons had. The dog's name was Cub. He was big and black and looked like he had some Lab in him. Cub was almost like another kid to us. We would give him a belt and then chase him trying to get the belt back. Cub had as much fun at this game as we did.

Once while we were walking through the woods above their house we all spotted a black snake. I believe Cub saw it first and he took out after the snake. The snake went down into its hole, but this didn't stop Cub. He took to digging up the ground and got that snake out and killed it right in front of us.

We took that snake to show Babe for we were all proud of Cub. She told us to get that snake away from her and take it down to the woods and bury it. We went across the road to the woods and started digging a hole. One of us accidentally stepped on the snake and something green popped out of its mouth. We got some paper and pulled at this green "thing". It was a completely whole green snake that the black snake had swallowed. We ended up having two snake funerals that day. None of us could talk about anything else for days after all this happened. Cub was our hero.

In writing about Cub, I could not remember what happened to him. Babe told me that one day he wandered off and they never saw him again. They looked and looked for him, but never found him. Knowing Cub, he probably wanted to save them the grief of burying him and just wandered off to die.

It seems I have gotten far afield here. I'm supposed to be writing about Chop and Babe, but Cub was a big part of all our lives. Chop and Babe were a little younger than the parents of most of the kids I played with. I think that is one of the reasons we felt comfortable around them. They just seemed to understand us kids better. Their home was always open to all of us kids on the mill hill. This doesn't mean the Thompsons didn't run a tight ship. Babe was quick to let us know when we did something to displease her. Once I took it on myself to teach Danny and David how to play cards. We were all engrossed in the card session, when Babe saw us. She quickly pointed out that she didn't want her kids to know about card playing and never to bring those cards to her house again. She didn't have to tell me a second time.

As a kid I always enjoyed being over at the Thompsons'. They just made you feel good about yourself which is exactly how you're supposed to feel as a kid.

Chop only worked at Brookford mills a couple of years after he and Babe were married. He took a job in the weave room at Burlington Mills at Newton. He spent the rest of his working career there. After all of the kids' were in school, Babe took a position with Zerden's in Hickory. She worked for them over twenty-five years and did not retire until just before the Zerdens closed their store.

Chop died on November 9, 1998. Babe is still living in the house she and Chop built. Her daughter, Carolyn, now lives with her. Babe has always had a zest for life. She has always been interested in others and what was happening in their lives. She is one of those people who make you feel good just being around her.

She and Carolyn have been a big help to me with this book. One of my main goals in starting it was to find a picture of the boarding house. I had struck out on finding that picture until September 15, 2002 at 12:05 PM, when Carolyn called to tell us she had found that picture. It is a picture of Red and Dolly Austin and in the background is the back of the boarding house. I knew there would be a picture of it somewhere. Many thanks to Carolyn and Babe. Maybe I should turn this book over to their capable hands. They seem to be able to get the job done.

## Seth and Katie Miller

Seth has already been mentioned in this book in the article on Brookford Baptist Church. He taught a class of teenage boys. He is my all time favorite Sunday school teacher and also one of my favorite people. Seth was born in the Statesville area on August 7, 1907. After completing his education, he took a job with Duke Power. After working there for about a year, he decided to come to Brookford and live with his sister and her hus-

**Seth and Katie Miller**

band. He had heard that there were job openings at the mill. He found a job in the machine shop there.

He met Katie not long after coming to Brookford. Katie was teaching the fourth grade at Brookford School. Katie and Seth fell in love and were married in December 1928. Katie had to give up her teaching position because at that time, you could not be a teacher if you were married. Katie loved teaching, but her love for Seth was greater.

Katie, a sister to Babe Thompson, was born on September 18, 1908 in Texas to J.J. and Edna Stepp. She attended school at the old school over on Red Hill. A picture of her with her brother Neil, along with other students, is included in this book. She finished her education at Lenoir Rhyne. Babe was telling me that Katie got to Lenoir Rhyne by riding the mill truck everyday to school.

After their marriage, Seth and Katie bought some land across the woods from the mill hill and had a house built. Because she had to give up her teaching position, Katie also found work in the mill drawing ends.

When the time the war started in 1941, Seth was drafted into the Army. He would be in service until the end of the war. The Army used his expertise as a machinist and mechanic to keep its equipment and guns operating. He served overseas, but never was in combat. Upon his discharge he resumed his position in the mill.

Katie and Seth loved children. I'm sure one of their great disappointments in life was being unable to have any children of their own. But they had their nephews and nieces next door and both of them dearly loved Chop and Babe's children and could not do enough for them. It was almost like having children of their own.

On June 12, 1954, Seth had a major heart attack and died. He was only forty seven, but his life made a great impact on many young lives at Brookford. All of us guys who were in his Sunday School class received wonderful instruction, but we also observed how Seth lived his life. He was a living witness to his faith.

Katie is now ninety four years old. She is still living next door to her sister, Babe. Going over to talk with Babe about the articles on her and Katie brought back so many memories. It was like I wanted to hang around in hopes that Seth would cut open one of his wonderful watermelons.

J.J. and Edna Stepp

## J.J. and Edna Stepp

J.J. Stepp was born in Georgia in 1882. As a young man he struck out to seek his fortune in Texas. Not long after he arrived in Texas, he chanced to see a pretty, young Texan riding by on a horse. He inquired around and found out that her name was Edna Freeman, and being a true Texan, she could ride a horse, shoot a gun and loved to hunt jackrabbits and snakes, especially rattlesnakes. J.J. was smitten by this Texas belle and it was not long before they were courting. J.J. had fallen in love with Edna and finally convinced her that she needed to be married to him and not some Texan. On May 10, 1905, they were married. Three of their children were born in Texas- Terrell, Kate and Clodell, who died of whooping cough at age six months.

J.J. became proficient as a mechanic and as the textile industry grew in the southeast, he took a job with A.D. Julliard and Company in Georgia. Edna's love for J.J. and her growing family was put to the test in moving from her beloved Texas. While in Georgia, their sons, Neal and Charles and their daughter, Edna (Babe) were born. Edna missed her native Texas and almost every summer she would pack up the kids and head back. An independent woman, she drove her Ford with the kids in tow from Georgia and from North Carolina to her home in Texas. Often, they had to camp out along the way and once had a bear eat their food. At times, they had to ford the Red River. Edna kept this spirit of adventure all her life and it was contagious. The kids had a ball on these trips.

A.D. Julliard and Company bought Brookford Mills in 1917 at a bankruptcy sale. One of their first moves was to bring the Stepp family to Brookford. J.J. had become a master mechanic and the Julliards needed his mechanical knowledge to set up their new operation in Brookford. He would remain head of the machine shop until his retirement. Brookford Mills would not have been the success it became without the capable leadership of J.J.

Edna was very active in the Brookford community. She taught over at the school on Red Hill for several years. In looking through some of the documents of the old school, Edna's signature as secretary is on many of them. After the birth of their son, Jack, Edna retired from teaching.

When J.J. retired from Brookford Mills, the Stepps built a house up the road from Reinhardt's Grocery store. Many of their children had settled in Brookford and they wanted to be close to their grandchildren.

In the early '60s when Shuford Mills bought the Brookford mill from A.D. Julliard and Company, they had J.J. come out of retirement to oversee setting up their operation at Brookford. Mr. Stepp worked for a number of years for Shuford getting the mill to run efficiently. Believe it or not, he ended up qualifying for a pension, something he never got from all his years working for A.D. Julliard and Company.

J.J. passed away in 1964 at age 82. Mrs. Stepp lived until 1966. Babe tells me that she was a Texan until the day she died.

## Pete and Ruth Hollar

Raymond was his given name, but to everyone on the mill hill he was known as Pete. He was born on March 10, 1910 to John and Florence Simpson Hollar. He attended Brookford School and eventually found a job in the mill as a slasher. The woman he was to marry, Ruth Travis Hollar, was born May 27, 1913 to James and Carrie Travis. Ruth also worked in the mill drawing ends.

**Pete and Ruth Hollar with their family.**

On October 25, 1930 Pete and Ruth were married. Both were life long members of Faith United Church of Christ. Pete's mom and dad were charter members of the church. Ruth's mom, Carrie, was also a charter member. Ruth was baptized by the minister that helped form the church. She was about four or five years old at the time, but she still remembers the event. She and Pete were very active in their church. Pete served on the church board for a number of years. Ruth was always active in the church. Still is as she approaches ninety. Down through the years she has taught Sunday school and helped with the girl scouts. Both Pete and Ruth sang in the church choir. Ruth was at the church for the dress rehearsal of the Christmas play on December 22, 1944 when the church caught fire and burned to the ground. Undaunted, she and the other actors performed the play at Brookford School on Christmas night.

Pete and Ruth were also very active in the Brookford community. Pete served the community as a policeman for 17 years. Ruth had a great interest in Brookford School. She served as a grade mother and also as the president of the PTA. A picture is included in the book, showing her and Mark Bolick presenting Mrs. Clinard with a washing machine.

On December 21, 1964 Pete passed away, a sad Christmas for everyone. Later their son, Charles, passed away in South Carolina. Their daughter, Jane, still lives in the area. It has been almost forty years since Ruth lost Pete. She has never remarried. She still maintains a keen interest in her beloved church and the Brookford community and remains one of Brookford's most gracious ladies.

## Hubie and Ruth Pope

Hubie was born down on the Brookford Mill Hill in Possum Holler on April 4, 1914. He was the son of Wilburn and Ray Reinhardt Pope. Ruth came to Brookford with her family from Caldwell County. She was the daughter of John and Mary Ollie Bolick and was born on May 25, 1919. She was christened Minnie Ruth Bolick. Her father was killed in an automobile accident when her brother,

Paul, was just a baby. This made it necessary for the family to move to Brookford. Ruth's oldest brother, Mark had taken a position with Brookford Mills and he persuaded his mom to move to Brookford so that he could help look after them. Ruth's mom managed the boarding house for many years and became one of Brookford's most beloved people (see Mother Bolick section).

Both Hubie and Ruth attended the new Brookford School. Hubie was older than Ruth, but she had noticed this handsome man. And as she grew older, she knew that Hubie was definitely the man for her. Hubie had certainly taken note of this lovely young lady and in due time, he asked Ruth to marry him. They were married on March 28, 1936 and began their journey through life together. They would be inseparable for almost sixty-two years of marriage. They were blessed with two sons, H.E. and Joe. In the summer of 1944, H.E. came down with polio in the epidemic. H. E. survived this scare.

They moved several times to New Jersey to work in the mills there, but the love for Brookford and their families always brought them back. They eventually moved back to Brookford permanently. They bought the house that Hubie's mom lived in and would remain there until their deaths in 1998.

Both Hubie and Ruth were very active in Brookford Baptist Church. Hubie served as a deacon, Sunday school teacher and sang in the choir. He was blessed with a beautiful singing voice and used it for the glory of the Lord. Ruth helped out wherever she was needed. Both were faithful in attendance. When Brookford Baptist sponsored a sign language class, Ruth attended even though it was painful to use her arthritic hands in signing. She was the best in the class at understanding the signs.

Ruth had rheumatic fever as a child and later in life developed serious heart problems. It became necessary for her to have extensive heart surgery at the Baptist Hospital.

**Ruth and Hubie Pope**

Fortunately Ruth survived the surgery to the relief of all her family. She never allowed her health problems to slow her down. When Hubie's health deteriorated, Ruth devoted her life to his care.

Eventually Ruth's heart problems became so severe that she had to be hospitalized. She would not survive this stay in the hospital. On March 5, 1998, Ruth's damaged heart gave out. No one at the Pope's home wanted to tell Hubie, because he was so frail, but Hubie had sensed the change and said, "My wife, Ruth, has died, hasn't she?" He was told that she had. When they later went back to check on Hubie after he had taken a nap, He, too, had passed away. It was almost as if he had willed himself to die. Life without Ruth would be no life at all.

H.E. and Joe had already made the funeral arrangements and the announcement of their mother's death. Both of them knew that their dad and mom would want to be buried together. The funeral home said that a double funeral could be performed. Many people went to the funeral home for the receiving of Ruth and there lay Hubie by her side. They were together practically all of their lives and they were together in death…a beautiful story of love and devotion.

## Brookford Mills Baseball

Most of the cotton mills in the Piedmont area sponsored a baseball team. Brookford Mills was no exception. The mill fielded a baseball team almost from the time the mill was built. Baseball games were almost all the entertainment on the mill hill. One of my favorite pastimes was sitting around and listening to the old timers talk about this team or that team. Arguing about who was the best player or which team was the best took up much of the conversations.

About everyone agreed that "Dice" Reinhardt was as good a ball player as there was on the mill hill. His brothers, Paul and Pete played with "Dice". His baseball play earned him a look from a number of major league scouts. He had all the skills to be an outstanding ballplayer. "Dice" ended up signing a minor league contract, but within two weeks, he was back in Brookford. He was too homesick. There were many good players on the mill team.

Dan Henderson played first base and was tall and could stretch out a mile. He also signed a minor league contract. He forever became known as "Dan, Dan, the rubber man". Other players of note from the earliest days of the mill until the early '50's were Murph Simpson, John Holler, Wilburn Pope, Will Pitts (yes, that Will Pitts), Dewey Austin, Charley and Kurt Nance, Burnice Bishop, Tom Gadd, Murphy Hefner, Archie Simpson, Charlie Bollinger, and the Stepp brothers, Terrell, Neal and Charles.

The first mill teams played at a field over on Red Hill. It was located near the School building. This field was long gone before I was ever born, but I heard talk from a number of people, who played for the mill there and from people who attended the games. One of my most vivid memories is listening to the old timers talk about a big (six feet, five and one half inches), rawboned left hand pitcher by the name of Cliff Melton, whom the mill enticed to come and pitch for the mill team one summer. He was all of seventeen years and came down from his home in Black Mountain to pitch for Brookford. He was so fast that you could hardly see the ball and as

Brookford Mills' Baseball Team. It seems they can't make up their mind to hunt or to play ball. Front row, from left to right: Reed Isenhour, John Hollar, Wilburn Pope, Cleave Hollar. Back row, from left to right, Jim Whitener, Billy Bolick, Teal Pope, unidentified, Henry Whitener, Will Pitts.

1912 Baseball team

wild as a buck, which made him even more effective. Little did the fans know that this tall, wild kid would one day be pitching in a World Series game. Later he became well known as "Man Mountain Melton". He made the majors with the New York Giants in 1937 and won twenty games and lost nine games in his rookie season. He pitched for the Giants in the 1937 World Series with the Yankees. The Yankees won the series, but Melton did an excellent job pitching against the powerful Yankees.

Later in his career, Melton developed bone chips in his arm and in 1942, he had surgery on his arm, but "Man Mountain Melton" never pitched in another major league game after the surgery. His lifetime major league record was 86-80 with an ERA of 3.42. Not bad for a mountain man from the Black Mountains of North Carolina.

The mill still sponsored teams into the 1950's. The teams for the most part were good teams, but they never achieved the success of the earlier teams. One year all of us on the mill hill suffered through a 0 and 19 start. Still it was our team and we showed up and cheered them on.

## Doc and Bruce Warren

No book on Brookford would be complete without including Doc and Bruce Warren. Doc began working as a policeman for Brookford in 1944. His son, Bruce, became his assistant in 1965. Doc retired in 1972 and Bruce became the police chief. He would serve Brookford faithfully until his retirement in 2001. The Warren family provided police protection for the Brookford community for fifth seven continuous years and if that is not a record, then it should be.

**Neal and Lil Stepp**

I think it is appropriate that the picture I'm using for this article shows Bruce using the radar gun. Brookford got quite a reputation during Bruce's many years of service as a place you did not want to speed. That is a good reputation to have and Bruce was persistent in pursuing speeders. He and the Warren family are to be commended for the years of excellent service to the Brookford community.

## Neal and Lil Stepp

Neal was born September 2, 1912 in Aragon, Georgia to J.J. and Edna Stepp. His family moved to Brookford in 1918, when A.D. Julliard and Company transferred Neal's dad from their mill in Georgia to oversee setting up the mill here that Julliard had just purchased. Lil was born in a house behind Faith Reformed Church on August 21, 1912 to Wilbur and Rae Reinhardt Pope. She would be the only girl in a family of eight brothers.

Lil and Neal started school together at the old school on Red Hill. They would be in the same class until Lil dropped out of school to help her mother make ends meet after her

**Bruce Warren and his radar gun.**

father was killed in an automobile accident. She started out as a sweeper and eventually moved to the spinning room. Neal continued his education through the tenth grade and became one of the best baseball players around. His baseball career is chronicled later in this book.

When World War II started Neal was almost thirty years old, unmarried and definitely fit for service. He entered the Army in 1942 and would spend the next five years in service. These years in service ended his career in baseball.

When Lil and Neal were growing up, they usually paired off together and there was a feeling between them that sometime in the future they would be married, but Lil did not know the future was about to arrive in September of 1942. Neal had come home on leave in late August. He had looked for Lil, but had not been able to get up with her.

Lil told me that about 9:00 Friday evening there came a knock on her door. She had just gotten home from a movie and was getting ready to go to bed, because she had to work at the mill on Saturday. It was Neal at the door and he asked her to go out for a sandwich. He finally talked her into going with him for a bite. They went to the Light House Restaurant in Hickory. Lil ordered a country ham sandwich and was eating it, when Neal asked her to marry him. Lil said to Neal, "Let's talk about this later". Neal answered her, "No, it is now or never". Lil says she could not take another bite of that sandwich, but she could see in his eyes that Neal meant what he said. At five minutes 'til twelve on the night of September 4, 1942, they were married in Gaffney, South Carolina by Judge Cobb. Runt Reinhardt and Ada Schronce were witnesses.

The wedding party made it home around two o'clock in the morning. The married couple spent the first night of their honeymoon in Hotel Hickory. Lil says she had to get up at five in the morning to be at the mill at six. It was her first day at work as a married lady.

Lil and Neal celebrated their sixtieth wedding anniversary in September. Not many couples have such a romantic story about their wedding night. Lil and Neal have been good for each other. Their children, Wally, Susan, and Joe are all attentive to their needs as the couple enters their ninetieth year. Neal's health is not so good these days. Lil is as spry as ever. Along with Lillian Holsclaw, she has been a great help to me on this book, especially in finding pictures to use and as a source of information. Many thanks to you, Lil.

## Neal Stepp's Baseball Career

As mentioned in the article, "Brookford Mills Baseball", Neal Stepp had to be considered one of the best baseball players, if not the best, to ever come off the mill hill. His family has allowed me to use clippings from the fam-

| J.A. HILLERICH PRESIDENT | DIRECTORS |
| L.W. GOESSLING VICE PRESIDENT | J.A. HILLERICH |
| F.W. BRADSBY SECY. & TREAS. | H.W. MORROW |
| JNO. H. POPE ASST. TREAS. | F.W. BRADSBY |
| | J.H. ACKERMAN |
| CABLE ADDRESS HILLBRAD | L.W. GOESSLING |
| | H.W. BICKEL |
| 434-436 FINZER ST.  LOUISVILLE, KY. | JNO. H. POPE |
| | CODE BENTLEYS |

Mar. 25, 1935

Mr. Neal Stepp,
c/o Birmingham Baseball Club,
Birmingham, Alabama.

Dear Mr. Stepp:

Your agreement duly signed and witnessed, giving us the exclusive right to use your name for advertising purposes on baseball bats, has been received, and enclosed find our check for $15.00.

Also, we have ordered the signature die, and as soon as it is received the two bats will be sent you, no charge, to show you how this signature will appear on Louisville Sluggers in the future.

We thank you for giving us this exclusive right, and wish you a successful future in baseball.

Yours very truly,
HILLERICH & BRADSBY CO.

Henry Morrow

HWM:MG

## Consistent Hitter

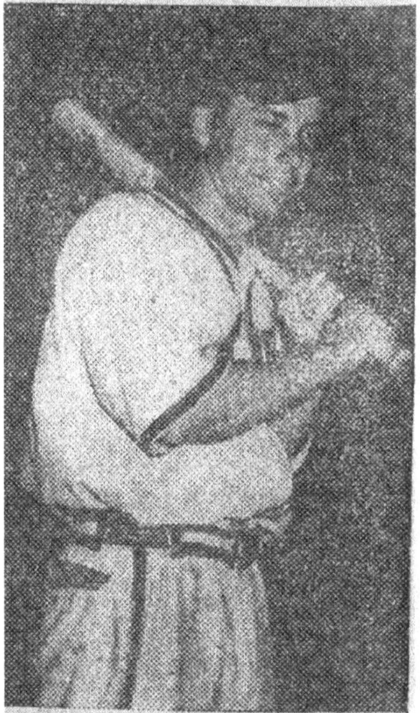

—Photo by Carter
eal Stepp, soft-spoken North Car-
inan, whose big bat is slamming
it many a hit for the Pensacola
Fliers this season.

MAR 10 1941
HICKORY, CATAWBA COUNTY
NORTH CAROLINA
(LOCAL BOARD)

3-10-41
(Date)

### NOTICE OF SELECTION

To Neal Herbert Stepp, Brookford, N.C., Order No. 447

You have been selected for training and service under the Selective Training and Service Act of 1940. You will receive an Order to Report for Induction—such induction to take place on or about March 22nd, 1941, 19......, when adequate facilities are expected to be available.

This notice is given you in advance for your convenience, and is not an order to report. Persons reporting to the induction station in some instances may be rejected for physical or other reasons. It is well to keep this in mind in arranging your affairs, to prevent any undue hardship if you are rejected at the induction station. If you are employed, you should advise your employer of this notice and of the possibility that you may not be accepted at the induction station. Your employer can then be prepared to replace you if you are accepted, or to continue your employment if you are rejected. The Order to Report for Induction will specify a definite time and place for you to report.

### Hickory H. S. Averages For B. B. Season

| Player | Games | AB | R | H | SH | SB | PO | A | E | 2B | 3B | HR | BB | SO | Bat. Ave. | Field Ave. |
|---|---|---|---|---|---|---|---|---|---|---|---|---|---|---|---|---|
| N. Stepp .... | 21 | 93 | 24 | 42 | 0 | 20 | 51 | 80 | 9 | 17 | 4 | 0 | 1 | 4 | .452 | .918 |
| Mullins ...... | 7 | 30 | 6 | 11 | 0 | 1 | 8 | 12 | 5 | 2 | 3 | 0 | 3 | 2 | .367 | [illegible] |
| Dale .......... | 23 | 74 | 14 | 27 | 0 | 3 | 22 | 9 | 5 | 4 | 0 | 0 | 3 | 5 | .365 | [illegible] |
| C. Stepp .... | 21 | [illegible] | 21 | 30 | 1 | 11 | 57 | 46 | 6 | 5 | 0 | 0 | 11 | 7 | .337 | .948 |
| Burns ........ | 22 | 94 | 25 | 29 | 1 | 13 | 186 | 12 | 6 | 0 | 0 | 2 | 4 | 17 | .309 | .971 |
| Payne ....... | 19 | 69 | 4 | 21 | 1 | 1 | 107 | 8 | 6 | 3 | 2 | 0 | 3 | 7 | .304 | .950 |
| Bivens ....... | 16 | 50 | 11 | 15 | 0 | 0 | 4 | 23 | 2 | 1 | 0 | 0 | 3 | 11 | .300 | .931 |
| Applegate .... | 16 | 30 | 7 | 9 | 2 | 4 | 22 | 5 | 2 | 2 | 0 | 0 | 2 | 12 | .300 | .925 |
| Rector ....... | 18 | 61 | 10 | 18 | 1 | 3 | 15 | 16 | 9 | 3 | 0 | 0 | 5 | 5 | .295 | .781 |
| Perry ........ | 16 | 55 | 9 | 16 | 0 | 4 | 18 | 1 | 1 | 1 | 0 | 2 | 6 | 4 | .291 | [illegible] |
| Norris ........ | 7 | 7 | 1 | 2 | 1 | 0 | 2 | 3 | 0 | 0 | 0 | 0 | 0 | 1 | .286 | 1000 |
| P. Harris .... | 20 | 47 | 7 | 11 | 2 | 4 | 14 | 8 | 11 | 1 | 0 | 0 | 1 | 5 | .234 | .667 |
| Hovis ........ | 20 | 85 | 18 | 19 | 0 | 2 | 30 | 6 | 4 | 4 | 0 | 1 | 10 | 14 | .224 | .910 |
| R. Harris .... | 7 | 22 | 6 | 4 | 1 | 0 | 4 | 7 | 5 | 0 | 0 | 0 | 1 | 6 | .182 | [illegible] |

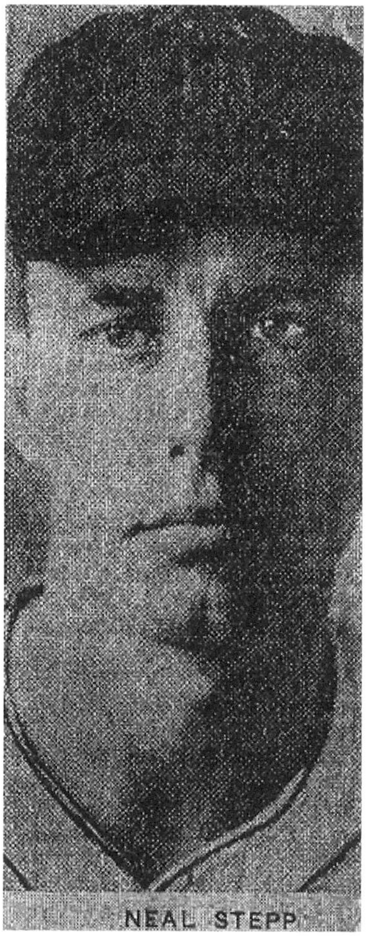

NEAL STEPP

### The National Association of Professional Baseball Leagues

PLAYER'S OFFICIAL RELEASE NOTICE

Cross Out Conditions Not Applicable

TO PLAYER Neal Stepp You are hereby officially notified of your release from this club on the following conditions:

1. ~~OUTRIGHT AND UNCONDITIONALLY.~~
2. ~~CONTRACT ASSIGNED TO~~ ........ CLUB OF ........ LEAGUE
3. OPTIONALLY ASSIGNED TO Tyler, Tex CLUB OF ........ LEAGUE
4. ~~PLAYER RETURNED TO~~ ........ CLUB OF ........ LEAGUE

W. H. Woodward President

Birmingham Baseball Club

Dated Feb 27 1936

ily scrapbook on his stellar baseball career. He played minor league ball in Atlanta, Birmingham, Pensacola and Tyler, Texas. There are many people in Brookford that felt Neal was ready to make the step into the majors, when World War II came along.

But after spending five years in service and becoming a husband and a father, he had lost his desire to continue his baseball career. Instead he came home and began working in the mill. Not long after he was home, some of the guys talked him into playing for the mill team. I had never gotten to see Neal play baseball, so I was very thankful that he consented to play. My uncle, Russ, was a bona fide baseball nut. He and my Uncle John went to Tyler, Texas to see Neal play. Russ was Neal's biggest fan. After getting to see Neal play for the mill team, I became his second biggest fan. Besides how can I not love a guy that still calls me by a long forgotten nickname "Slug".

You could tell from his smooth, powerful swing what a ballplayer Neal must have been in his prime. He was nearing forty years old, but he could still play a great game of baseball. One magical day, he came to bat and with that wonderful swing, he sent a ball out of the park. I can still see the arc of the ball as it left the ball park.

## Clyde and Aileen Wilson

Clyde and Aileen were ideally suited for each other. When they married on October 30, 1936, Clyde was twenty nine years old and Aileen was just sixteen years old.

The marriage lasted until Clyde's death in 1987. Aileen tells me that there was never an argument between them. I'm sure there has never been a nicer couple on the mill hill than Clyde and Aileen. They had three daughters, Nancy, Joan, and Jane and one son, Bill.

Clyde was born July 12, 1907 and Aileen was born on March 23, 1920 to Will and Ivey Lowman. Aileen had a twin sister, Pauline. She also had a brother, Winifred and another sister, Buna. In interviewing people for this book, I often come across tragic happenings in a number of people's lives. Aileen related one of the saddest happenings I have ever heard. When she and her sister, Pauline were about seven years old, they were out playing. Somehow Pauline was hit in the head with a rock. She seemed to be alright and no more was thought about the incident.

When their mother, Ive, was putting them to bed, Pauline looked at her mother and said "The Lord is coming for me". Her mother said, "What did you say Pauline?" She said again, "The Lord is coming for me". Her mother said, "Oh, Pauline, you are just imagining things". She kissed the children good night and closed the door.

When she went to get the children up, Pauline had passed away. Her premonition had come true for the Lord had come for her.

Clyde and Aileen both worked at Brookford mills. Clyde worked as a loom fixer and Aileen

**Clyde and Aileen Wilson**

as a weaver. Eventually, they built a house behind Aileen's mom and dad. Aileen still lives in this house along with her daughters, Joan and Jane. Her health is not the best these days. She has to be on oxygen all the time, but her difficulties have not kept her from being the same sweet woman I have known all my life. One of the great joys in life is getting an Aileen hug. It doesn't get any better. The house is lonelier without Clyde. It's hard to believe he has been dead for over fifteen years now. It was a real treat to be invited to their fiftieth wedding anniversary celebration. I did indeed get an Aileen hug.

Note: Aileen passed away November 14, 2002 before I had the opportunity to show her what I had written about her and Clyde. She is now in a far better place, where she is free of all her pain and suffering. Still those she has left behind are poorer for not having her in their lives. Perhaps it is a little bit selfish of us to want her back in our midst, but she was such a wonderful person that it brought all of us joy who knew her. She will be missed terribly, but she is with Clyde now and we are all blessed from having had her with us for eighty two years. I for one, Aileen, will miss those hugs.

## W.C. and Ethel P. Laney

Much has been written about Preacher Laney in Brookford Baptist Church and rightly so. He served as Pastor of the church from 1928 until his death in 1976. All of my memories of Brookford Baptist Church include Preacher Laney. That's how we referred to him "Preacher Laney", never Reverend Laney or Pastor Laney. He certainly was a force not only in the church at Brookford, but throughout the whole area and the state. Preacher Laney was born August 4, 1894 in Lincoln County. From an early age, he had felt the call to preach, but like so many people, he had received very little education. His labor was needed to help out his family and the call to preach was postponed for awhile. Eventually he surrendered to God's will and began to preach in area churches, but he knew his lack of education would be a great hindrance in his ministry and so at thirty years old, he went back for more schooling.

It was there in school, he met the woman, who would become his wife and helpmate. Ethel Mae Parker was born in Cherokee County, South Carolina on July 16, 1897. She went to area schools to receive her high school education and graduated from Gardner Webb College as valedictorian of her class. She had received a teaching degree and while teaching, she met Bill Laney. It can truthfully be said that Preacher Laney married his teacher. They were married on June 26, 1926 and thus began a partnership that would last until their deaths in 1976.

**left: Preacher Laney at campground.**
**right: Mrs. Laney**

**Mrs. Laney at a church conference.**

Mrs. Laney found that she did not like teaching and when Preacher Laney was called to Brookford Baptist Church, she devoted her full time to being a mother and a helper in the church. Through her efforts, she allowed her husband to devote his full energies to the work of the church. She was an accomplished pianist and played the piano for the church services and served the church in many other ways. But her main role was to look after her family and her husband. Preacher Laney would never have been the success he was as pastor of Brookford Baptist Church without the help and comfort of his wife. Mrs. Laney was a quiet, private person, but she was as much a force in the church and community as her husband. She just went about her call to full time Christian service a little differently than her husband.

The Laneys were blessed with four children, J.W., Mary Alice, Myrtle, and Richard. J.W. followed his dad into the ministry and Richard spent his entire career as a teacher and a coach. Mary Alice went to business school and was a secretary in business. Myrtle became a homemaker. All the Laney children are successful in their lives. J.W. and Richard are now both retired as is Mary Alice. Myrtle has served her community as an alderman for a number of years. She has lived in Brookford all her life and still lives in the house the Laneys occupied for many years.

Mrs. Laney passed away July 25, 1976. Preacher Laney lived just five months longer and he passed away on December 11, 1976. Both of these people left their mark on the Brookford community. Preacher Laney will forever be remembered as a visionary in race relations and Mrs. Laney for her quiet devotion to her church, her family and her husband.

Brookford Lives

# Brookford Memories of Joe Thomas Elders

In 1921 or 1922, as I recall being told, Christine Little married John Elders in Brookford, North Carolina. They were childless for many years until Mom had some kind of surgery. I was born September 1, 1934. On that date mills all over the south went out on strike. I never heard a lot about that, because no one would talk about it. I do remember being told that we ate a lot of spigot gravy (water and flour, I think).

I had a brother born on December 9, 1935. He was named Gary Robert Elders. He was fair haired and had blue eyes. As I was told, he was an angel, and I guess I wasn't. Then Mom was soon pregnant again. This time it was a girl! On May 16, 1937, Deann Bonzita was born with red hair and green eyes. But this was not a happy occasion, but it wasn't! Gary died with pneumonia about the same time as Deann's birth and Mom's tail bone was broken during childbirth. As I was later told, Mom was in the bed when Gary was buried.

I remember living in three different houses in Brookford. I don't remember living where I was born, it was a two room house, but I do remember the next place. I can recall several things that happened there. I remember once, while there, I had to have stitches in my tongue. I either cut it or bit it. I can remember standing under a lamp of some kind while Dr. Charles Hunsucker, who delivered me, sewed me up.

Growing up in Brookford was the most any kid could ever wish for. Brookford, where doors were never locked and windows were always open in the warm weather! Once I had gone quite a way from the house to where Granny and Aunt Mag and Dyke lived. I was spotted by the lady next door, Mrs. Melton, and she told me to get back home! You see-everyone knew everyone and knew where I lived. You can bet I went home in a hurry! I was only three.

Brookford had a big building in the middle of the village. It housed the Barber Shop, café, pool room and the Company Store. When I was very young, I think until 1946 or so, they would charge your groceries and then take it out of your pay at the mill. Once when my Mom was the only one working (more about why later) for two weeks' pay; after groceries, room rent (25 cents a room for your house) and I guess taxes and whatever else was taken out, she brought home fifteen cents. I'm pretty sure Deann has the pay envelope still!

I was teased into stealing some apples from there by some older kids and I got caught. I was about three or four years old! I got my butt busted that time.

Mom and Dad were married a long time before I was born - well it seems Daddy wore a flat top hat back then. He told all his old buddies, they always hung out around the store, that if he got a son he would hang that hat up and never wear one again. I understand the hat hung in the store for

John & Christine Elders

a long time. The store and the big porch was used for a lot of things. When I was young we used to roller skate on the store porch. My Daddy told me before they had radios some men used to listen to Morse code (I think it was) on the store porch and let all the men know how Babe Ruth and the Yankees were doing in the World Series.

I started school in 1940 almost on my birthday! School started on September first or the first Monday in the month then! One thing for sure-we had the best teachers in the world! Back then after your parents, the person with the most influence in your life was your teacher. You'd do what you were told to do! I very much remember first grade! Mrs. Hughes was my teacher! I fell in love with Carolyn Jackson that year! I still liked her in the second grad, but then she went to another school!

One family, who lived in the village, had relatives who lived on a farm outside of Brookford. I was in either the first or second grade and I used to go with them to pick cotton. We got a penny a pound for all we could pick. A good afternoon for me was six or seven cents. But one day my shoe came untied out in the field and this boy, who was younger than I, taught me to tie a bow. His name was Jerry.

I never stayed home. I was all the time out playing. We played in the woods an awful lot. We played in the branch (creek) a lot too. I learned to swim when I was seven years old in a pool in the creek. Later – we swam a lot in the river and also the company pool. It cost a dime to go swimming in the pool. When there was no money – we, the guys, went to the river. We had it all in Brookford.

Course in December 1941 the whole world changed. After Pearl Harbor we had a war to win! Everyone I feel had a part in winning that war. We kids would go anywhere to get scrap metal or old tubes or tires or whatever could be used. Razor blade were saved for scrap and grease from cooking and just about everything. I once walked from school all the way across Brookford to get a bag of scrap metal. Edith Warren had called the school to see if someone could come pick it up. I certainly didn't think that l would later marry her daughter. It rained on me before I could get back to school and I was soaked. It was almost a mile and a half round trip. We kept the scrap metal in the gym. We had so much it almost collapsed the floor.

When I was in the first grade, I was in a play that the fifth grade class had written. There were probably kids from every grade in the play. It was a story about a boy who shot a bird with his BB gun and killed it. It was supposed to be my daddy he killed. I play a baby bird and my line during the trial was "Momma, could I have a worm crouquette?" We did that play in every school in the Hickory School System, except one, I think. At the time our principal was trying to get a bird sanctuary in the whole area. That was to protect all birds. We must have done a good job with the play. I wore a bird costume made by the fifth grade. I was a baby robin.

In the second grade I got my first F on a report card. It was in writing- can you believe it now? As it turned out, it was the only F I had until the tenth grade. Miss Jerome was my second grade teacher. I don't think she liked me a whole lot. I remember once, after we had come in from recess to get water, she pinched the dickens out of my cheek because I drank too much to suit her. We left one guy behind in the second grade- the only one from my class who did not finish Brookford with me.

Our teacher at the beginning of the third grade was Miss Pitts, and at the end of the year, it was Mrs. Earnhardt. Mrs. Earnhardt got married and left our school after that year. I do very well remember crying the day school was out. She was tough but fair. Once she left the room and told us to read a certain chapter. When she returned, she was told I had been messing around, so she asked me what I had read. Needless to say, I didn't know and was embarrassed to death. When we got our report cards all during the seven years at Brookford, we would compare them. It seems we all wanted to do the best-thus we all learned, as we should have.

Remember these were the war years, so when we had singing each day, we sang patriotic songs. My daddy had been in the World War I and was wounded in France. He was in the army so I wanted to always sing the army song. My first cousin from South Carolina was in the Marines, so naturally I wanted to sing the Marine hymn. I had another cousin from S.C. who was a crew member of a B-25 bomber that was shot down over Europe. I've since talked to his sisters and they've been to France to see his grave. So you can see I wanted to sing the Army Air Force song too. Then there was Jerry, Dyke's brother, who quit school at sixteen to go into the Navy. Everything was related to the war. Almost all the movies were, and after we guys would come home from the show, we'd be whatever branch of the service we'd seen that day. We'd never play cowboys and Indians- always army. Mind you now, it cost nine cents to see the movie and a big bag of popcorn was a dime. Course my Mom and my Dad worked for less than a dollar an hour back then.

Once during the winter of the third grade we had a snowfall that was the Granddaddy of them all! We had to stay at home from school for a week. None of the teachers lived in the village and they couldn't get to school. Those were the days!

In the fourth grade we had Mrs. Steelman. She also taught me in the sixth grade. That was when someone discovered nicotine on her fingers and we discovered also she was human. I remember we were all shocked to know that our teacher smoked. I told you we held them in great regard. We were studying the delta of the Nile and I told the teacher I knew where there was delta not far from school, so we all walked down to the sewage plant. There was a creek right beside it and sure enough, where the creek ran into the river, there was a great buildup of sand and it was a mini-delta. Brownie points for me that time! Also in the fourth grade we were taught a little about art. There were paintings (copies of course) hung in our class and we had to learn the names of them and the painters. I still do remember lots of them.

In the fifth grade we were all taken to Hickory to hear the North Carolina Symphony Orchestra. They did "Peter and the Wolf" and I still remember the tune and that the oboe was the wolf! States and their capitals came that year. Most of them are still in my head somewhere. I told you – we had the greatest teachers in the world.

The summers were great then, too! Uncle Cape had a transfer truck and he took me with him one summer before the war was over. We went all the way to Pennsylvania. I got to see Washington, D.C., Baltimore and all in between. I was the only one from our crowd who'd ever been that far away.

I do very well remember when the end of the war came. First there was VE Day in May of 1945 and VJ Day in August. In 1945 President Roosevelt died in April just before the end of the war. I remember my Uncle Clarence talking about the atomic bomb. He said it would cause the whole world to explode and that was some heavy stuff for a ten year old. I would not have thought that one day I would pass thru the cities which we bombed. But-I did in 1955 when I was in Japan.

I mentioned my Dad not being home and Mom's pay check was fifteen cents. Well, he had a drinking problem. He would go months without a drink, but if he had one, he would usually stay on it for days or weeks. He used to leave Brookford and head for some of his family in South Carolina. Everyone in town worked at the mill or someway connected, so they all knew when Daddy was gone. They'd say "John's on another trip, huh". I heard that a lot back then. Not to get ahead of my story, but when Pat and I talked of marriage, her mother would often mention how my Daddy was and ask Pat if that was the kind of life she wanted?

**Pals Deann Elders and Patsy Helton**

Deann and I were spoiled as kids. We always seemed to get a lot for Christmas and I was the only kid I ever heard of who got a dollar on my birthday and was taken to the Dime Store to get what ever I wanted. A very big deal in the early '40's!

In the summer after the sixth grade, a year after the war, some man from the Hickory Recreation Commission came out and organized a ball team. I guess it was the first year of Little League. Anyway Dyke and I and eight or so other guys were on the team. I was the catcher and Dyke the pitcher and we did pretty darn good. We lost only one game and we won by scores of 44-4, 32-8, 32-2, and so on. What a great summer that was. We had to play games all over Hickory and we had no other way of getting to them except to walk. The games were all played in the mornings, and we's have to round up the guys and get going early. The walks home were always the best. We'd steal fruit, eat wild plums and just had a great time.

The seventh grade was great. Mrs. Brooks, our teacher, was the best. She was so patient yet very demanding. We all had to do a bird picture with pastel chalk that year, and mine won a blue ribbon. I remember my Dad and Mom went to the school that nite and came home and told me I'd won. They'd gone to a PTA Meeting.

Growing up in Brookford did have a few drawbacks! We had an outdoor toilet 'til 1946 or 1947. Ours was down the hill behind our house a good fifty feet or more. Course- we kept a chamber pot in the house for nite deposits. We didn't have hot water or bath tubs even after we got our first commodes. We always took our baths in the wash tub with water that was boiled on the stove. As best I can recall we sometimes had two baths a week. Otherwise, we'd wash off with cold water or we'd us a wash pan.

Those old mill houses were not insulated, so we froze in the winter and burned up in the summer. We heated our three rooms with a fireplace, a very small one which burned coal. The grate fell out once and our house nearly caught fire. We came home just in time to put it out. Speaking of house fires, the one next door to us burned when I was in maybe the third grade or so. The people who lived there were the Warrens, who later turned out to be my first wife's grandmother. She was one sweet lady, as I remember. She once, or maybe many times, baked sweet potato pie for us.

We moved from this house up to our last house in Brookford. Mom later bought it when the mill sold them all. I almost moved on with the story, but too many memories from this house are coming back.

I once chased the little girl next door when she had the mumps(we were playing) and her mom saw me and told my Mom. I had to get the hickory she used to switch my legs with, so I got a small one. It cut my leg and I bled and I think that was the last time Mom whipped me. She'd save it for Daddy!

I used to take these two brothers and their cousin to the kiddie show on Saturday mornings. Each of their mothers would give me a dollar. What a way to make money-seeing Roy Rogers, Gene Autry and the rest of the great cowboys, with loads of popcorn and candy.

There were other odd jobs back then, too. At one time I would cut wood and carry in coal for this lady for seventy five cents a week. I also cut grass. One man would pay me fifteen cents to cut his grass and I had to use a hand sickle and the guy next door paid me fifty cents and he had a push mower. Not one with a motor!

I also worked on a dairy farm one summer. We delivered raw milk, not pasteurized, six days a week. I'd meet the man, who owned the farm and operated the truck about six in the morning. We'd go all over Hickory and get back to the farm just after noon. His wife was a great cook and also a sister or half sister or some other relation to Mrs. Warren. After lunch I had to wash the bottles, put them in the sterilizer and then help with the milking. All I did there was to carry the room where the milk was bottled. Then I would, with a machine that was powered by me, fill the milk for next day's delivery. Two quarts at a time was all you could do. I made seven fifty a week back then. I'd have to walk home most of the time and that was a good mile and a half or two.

Once while waiting for a train to pass, I was hanging out the door of the truck and I got a cinder in my eye. It felt like a brick and I had to go to the eye doctor to have it removed. The trains were steam engines then and they burned coal and a cinder was a tiny piece of burned coal.

None of my family had good teeth or ever really took care of them back then! I remember one of my many toothaches especially. The tooth got infected and my jaw was all swollen and hurt like the dickens. Mom took me to this old dentist and he pulled it(it was a permanent jaw tooth) without numbing it at all. I was standing on the street afterwards and Ted Hefner came by on his bike. He saw me spitting blood in the gutter and asked me what had happened. I told him and he said he heard me yell when he was way, way down the street. I'm sure he did! It was a while before I forgave Mom for that one.

When the war came along, all things changed. They were building a new road thru Hickory and only gotten the thing graded. None of it was paved. We'd ride our bikes on it a lot. By the way-It was Highway 70- the one the malls are all on.

Too, we couldn't get candy much during the war. The man who delivered to the local service station came by on Friday evenings and we were always there. Sometimes he'd have a box of Hershey's or Milky Ways and we all have a nickel or a dime to get us one. That was in the early '40's. About five or six years ago I was going thru Cherryville and I saw a very familiar truck- the one the wholesale man used to drive. I stopped and talked with him and family and after all these years, he remembered coming to Brookford.

## Anne Pope Little's Memories of Pope Hill

The following article is written by Ann Pope Little. She wrote it after the death of her Aunt Booie. All the Popes were sitting around remembering growing up on Pope Hill after Aunt Booie's funeral. It was said that someone needs to write these down and the lot fell to Ann. You will see the Pope humor shine through on what Ann has written. One thing all the Popes had was a sense of humor. It has not been lost on Ann.

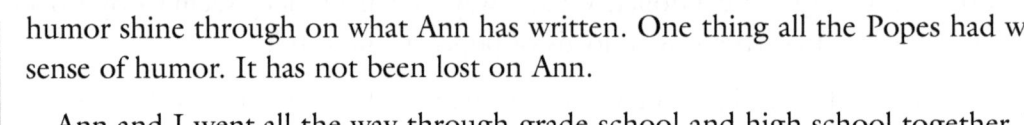

Ann and I went all the way through grade school and high school together. Her sense of humor has always been with her. I can remember that at one of our high school reunion we were all asked to stand up, introduce ourselves and our spouse. Ann got up introduced herself and then said "This is my current husband, Bill." brought the house down. Ann lost her "current husband" Bill, some years ago after a long and happy marriage.

At another reunion, she and Carolyn Nance came over to the table where I was sitting. Ann said, "Carolyn and I came over to get a closer look to see how you were holding up." I wasn't holding up very well, but Ann and Carolyn were doing just fine.

I know you will enjoy Ann's article on Pope Hill as much as I have. I was a little reluctant to put it in the book because she writes so well. Makes me wonder why I didn't get her to write the whole book.

## Pope Hill

We just buried my Aunt Booie, the last left of a generation of Pope's that will always be unique in my memory as well as the rest of my cousins especially the ones that we raised on Pope Hill. We were all brought up on tales of ghost, witches and magic letters that would protect you from silver bullets and if you tied it around a dog's neck and shot the dog it wouldn't die.

Grandma Daisy and Grandpa Ransom Pope had twelve children. Grandpa was about twenty years older than Grandma and I'm sure she worked much harder than he did. He had a country store and was a butcher. Grandma washed in a wash pot heated over a fire outside, made all their clothes and worked in the fields plus all the cooking so I'm sure she didn't have a whole lot of time to devote to each child and they were probably on their own a lot. I always thought Grandma Daisy was so stern and I guess she had to be with all the kids she raised plus twenty-five grandchildren and twenty of those lived on Pope Hill, so she never had a time that there weren't kids around. Now after raising my three children plus four grandchildren I can understand why she would say to me and Ginny, "Get on down that hill", when we would go up there. I don't know how she kept her sanity. Grandma used a hundred pounds of flour a week, that's a lot of biscuits. I think Grandpa would invite the whole church to come and eat on Sundays and he was always inviting somebody to live there.

I don't remember Grandpa Pope at all, he died long before I was born, but I remember Grandma saying he was so lazy he wouldn't strike a lick at a snake.

As my cousins and I sat reminiscing about old times after the funeral we each had our own interpretations of our memories Pope Hill so I decided to write this down while it was fresh in my mind, by next week I probably will have forgotten all that we talked about.

Clyde Jessinary was the oldest of twelve children. He was in WWI and worked for the railroad. He married Jessie, she had six children. He was either an exceptionally good man or incredibly stupid. I don't know which, but I don't think I would have taken on six of somebody else's children. His nickname was "Do". I think he got the name Do when he would come home from the war or work and all the children would run and say, "Do you have a nickel. I'm not sure about this but seems like I have heard this tale before of how he

**The Popes of Pope Hill. Left to right, front row: Bob, Dave, Jack, Arn and Ed. Second row: Sis, Clyde (Do), Lena, G-Pope, Maude (Booie), Hubert (Hub). Back: Edith (Tubby)**

got the nickname. Do never had children. He was a big man and probably the tallest of all the brothers.

Russell was the next oldest, and he married Myrtle Anery, a first cousin of my mother's. They had two children, Dot Noggle, who is the oldest grandchild and Brud. Russ was killed when he touched a 44,000 volt wire while working on a power line for Duke Power Company. Myrt was pregnant with Brud at the time. I think she was in her twenties, she was such a pretty woman, but she never remarried. She was one of my favorite aunts. I'll always think of her as being unique because she could DRIVE A CAR, I guess she was the only woman on the hill besides Mrs. Hunter that could drive and if you could drive a car that was something to be proud of because most women didn't drive.

Daddy and Ed were next I'm sure Grandma had her hands full with those two, I remember Grandma telling about when they were born they had a caul' over their faces and the mid-wife took it off and cut tools out and said they would be carpenters and she was right.

I don't remember too many stories about Do or Russ but Daddy and Ed must have been holy terrors. One Time they hooked a battery cable to the tail of a dog and it jumped through the window, Grandpa was sitting there reading the paper and he said, hellfluken boys what was that, another time they got new shoes one had a brown pair and the other had a black pair, they didn't like to be different so they put them in the oven and baked them so they would be the same color. I'm sure that's one time they got their butts whipped because I doubt they had much money to buy shoes. They hitched a baby carriage to a pony and put Sis inside and ran the pony round and round the house it's a wonder they didn't kill her. One time they put a cat in the oven and Grandma happened to come in from the fields and heard it meowing to get out. Grandma used to make dumplings for somebody on the Brookford Road and one time she had Daddy and Ed to take the dumplings over there, by the time they got there they had eaten all the chicken out of the dumplings and put the bones back in the pot. With that many people to cook for I doubt that they ever got much chicken so I guess they decided to get their fill for once.

Daddy and Ed both worked for Duke Power Co. Daddy retired from there but Ed quit and he and Daddy and David started a heating company and Ed ran it. While they worked at Duke Power they were working on telephones at opposite ends of town and somebody wrecked and hit the telephone poles they were working on and they both were knocked off the poles at the same time and they both arrived at the hospital at the same time I think Ed broke his leg but I don't think Daddy was hurt too badly.

Daddy married my Mother, Bernice Brown, nicknamed "Suz", in February of 1922. Mama was fifteen years old, and they lived with Grandma and Grandpa, after living there a while they moved in the house that is right beside our house now that Daddy and Ed built. There was six of us Bill, Midge, Mary, Joe, me and Bruce.

Ed married Bonnie Newton in August of the same year. She had just turned sixteen that May. Mama and Bon were best friends and since Myrt married Daddy's brother, he and Ed would ridge their motorcycles up to see Russ and Myrt and that's how they met Mama and Bon. Ed and Bon had three children Sam, Doris and Ginny.

Daddy and Ed built both their houses and lived across the street from each other all their lives, they would sit of the front porch and talk to each other all the time. It's almost like they knew what the other one was thinking.

Eubert, nicknamed Hube, was a loner I remember Grandma saying that he would get a biscuit and climb a tree and wouldn't come to eat with the rest of the family I guess he couldn't stand the chaos. He married Durland Stanley and they had two children, Sandy and Karen. Sandy gave me a letter over the week-end that someone had written his Dad in April 1938. Hube had stopped to help someone in a wreck and they had written a letter to thank him for his help. They lived in Statesville.

Ora"Sis" must have had a hard time with five older brothers I'm sure they probably tormented her to death. Sis married Morris Meadows and had two children Pete and Nancy Gail. She worked hard all her life, she mended socks at home and kept children I know she kept Jim Noggle and I think she kept Rick Noggle and I don't remember how many more, she also cleaned Grandma's and Lena's house in later years. She was an excellent cook. I can remember her washing her dishes and by the time she would finish she had to mop the floor. After Pete went into service she and Nancy Gail stayed up at Grandma's most of the time.

Dave was married to Pauline Bowman and they had three children Kay, David, and Lisa. He had a roofing business in Statesville and I don't remember hearing any tales about him growing up.

Maud, nicknamed Booie, where in the world that name came from I don't know. Booie was studying to be nurse in Gastonia, N.C. when she met Coit Litton. Coit was in WWII and after he got out I guess he went to work for Lennox Furnace Co. I don't know what his official title was but they traveled all over the world. They never had any children.

Jack was next he married Annie Wilfong and they had one child, Jean, she was close to my age and we would play at her house a lot because she had a playhouse it was like a real house, it had little window flower boxes and everything. Jack died when he was thirty five and Jean was in the first grade. I don't remember Jack that much but everybody on the hill was devastated. Jean and Annie finally moved in with her Grandmother Wilfong.

Lena, what can I say about her, she was special, Lena owned a beauty shop and it was on one end of Grandma's house. She worked hard all of her life but I never heard her complain, never heard her talk about people, she always had a smile and couldn't do enough for people. If you did something for Lena she always did something in return. I don't think she ever cooked while she worked, Sis and Grandma did most of the cooking and when Grandma got older Sis did the cooking and the cleaning. After Lena retired she started baking cakes and she would give them as Christmas presents and they were delicious. Before she retired she bought all the nieces and nephews presents for Christmas as long as I can remember. She was a special lady and everybody loved her and it just doesn't seem right to go down on Pope Hill and not stop to visit Lena. It's still hard t believe she's gone. Lena never married and it didn't seem to bother her at all she seemed very happy with her life.

Bob married Edna Ivey, she was from Charlotte, they had five children Glenda, Bobby, Judy, Janice, and Carolyn. They lived beside Grandma and Lena so they were closer to Grandma than the rest of us that lived on down the hill. Bob worked for the railroad and died four days after Lena.

Edith, nicknamed Tubbie, was the youngest she was always very smart. She married Clyde Triggs he was from Mississippi they had one son, Gary. Something was wrong with Tubbie's leg when she was younger but I don't know what it was I think she had to stay in bed for quite a while. Clyde died when Gary was in school I think I remember he was in his teens. Later in life she had a non-malignant brain tumor. When she was older she developed Alzheimers Disease and went to live with Lena and she lived there until she died.

I'll tell some funny stories that I remember hearing. I think the funnies one is about Daddy and Bob. One time they took Joe, Bruce, and Bobby to the mountains hunting. Joe was probably a teenager and Bruce and Bobby around ten. They let the boys out at a certain place and told them they would be back to get them but if they had any trouble to shoot their guns three times and they would come to get them. Well they waited and waited, it started raining and it was cold finally Joe said boys come on we're going back to the cabin. They got to the cabin and Joe started fixing them some soup about that time they hear three shots about fifty yards from the cabin so they ran to see what was wrong and they found Daddy and Bob sitting on a log with their heads down in their hand, Bob had this red stuff running down his face and Joe said oh my God Daddy shot Bob, he thought it was blood, they ran over and Bob had a black and red plaid hat on the kind that covers your ears and it was wet and the red dye from the hat was running down his face and it looked like blood, they were both drunk as skunks.

Daddy and Ed did everything together the would get mad at each other and you would think they hated each other one minute and the next they would be laughing. They could do just about anything and fix just about anything. I think Daddy and Ed both had dyslexia because they went to school but both only learned to sign their names they were both intelligent and could do anything. They worked in the Brookford cotton mill when they were about ten years old one would sleep while the other worked, they took turns working.

I think the twenty grandchildren that were raised on Pope Hill developed a special bond we were all in the same boat, we didn't have a whole lot but we had each other.

I don't know much about the older kids like Dot, Bill, Sam, Midge, Mary, Doris and Brud. All I remember is Midge and Mary telling about Bill and Sam giving them goat turds and telling them it was candy. I know they played in the creek and played Tarzen in the barn and did most of the things that the younger kids like me did. I'm sure we all went up to the store that was in front of Grandma's house everyday and walked up to the sub-station to get the mail that where it was delivered.

Every Christmas Eve we would go up to Grandma and Lena's and open Christmas presents, there were a lot of people there when all the kids and the families came, I don't know how they could stand all the noise and confusion but it didn't seem to bother them, they were always happiest with a crowd around. We had Grandma's birthday dinner I think she was born in February, from pictures I have seen we had coats on and we usually had the dinner outside if it was pretty. They would set up saw horses and put long boards on top of them and cover them with tablecloths, everybody would bring food and the table would be loaded. There were a lot of good cooks in the Pope family as most of us can contest too by looking at us, but we had fun putting it on.

Usually on Friday and Saturday night Ginny and I would go up to Grandma's and they would tell us ghost stories, when we went home it would be pitch dark, we would walk real slow until we got to Jack's house and then we would just fly, Jack saw a man that had died, in front of his house and the man owed Jack a nickel and he supposedly said "Here's the nickel I owe you We didn't waste any time getting by his house.

There was also a tale of the witch, her name was Minnie Fitt and she lived on the Brookford Road, Grandma said that when she needed milk she would go over to this towel and milk it. When she died Grandpa had a team of horses and he used to take people to the cemetery to be buried and he said that team of horses could barely pull the wagon and the woman only weighed about ninety pounds. He said all the witches from all around were on the wagon you just couldn't see them. Coming back from the cemetery, which was quite a way back then, it was in Conover, the horses ran all the way home.

Daddy built us a cabin down by the creek and we would spend nights down there and tell ghost stories and be scared to death. There was one tale about "Old Abe", who was a confederate soldier that was decapitated during the Civil War and he would walk up and down the creek looking for his head.

Another one was about the woman that drown in a well I guess she committed suicide. Every night you could hear her scream and hear water splash.

Daddy and Ed were working on a power line one night during a storm, they were at the Old St.Paul's Lutheran Church in Newton, they said they had mud up to their knees, they looked across the road at the cemetery and saw a woman in a white flowing dress floating above the tombstones and she didn't have a speck of mud on her. They said she was a witch but I think she was an angel to protect them.

Everybody on the hill at one time or another has heard the knocking, when Daddy and Ed built their houses they heard it and tried to find out what it was. It always sounded like it was coming from the Shell house but they couldn't hear it. Pearl Hayes and her family lived there at one time and he was a shoemaker and that's what it sounded like, somebody half soling shoes.

Midge told some of her friends in Northern Virginia and they just laughed and said she was crazy. They were going to Florida on vacation and stopped and spent the night with Mama and Daddy and they heard the knocking all night. I guess that made them a believer. Daddy always said that somebody would die when we heard the knocking it used to scare the bee-gees out of me. Once it started it would go on all night.

One day Daddy came home and said he had paid a witch off that had put a hex on Mama and Bruce. Mama said you're crazy and he said he had their pictures nailed under the door facing in their bedroom, Mama didn't believe him so the took the facing down and sure enough he did have their pictures nailed up there.

Daddy and Ed and I don't know how many in the family had copies of the magic letter that supposedly dropped from the sky I guess just for the Popes. It was suppose to protect us from silver bullets and all sorts of things if you tied it around a dog's neck and shoot the dog it wouldn't die, I hope they never tried that one. Witches couldn't put a hex on you and I don't remember what all else it could do. Booie was home visiting one time and she was telling about something that had happened to her at a club meeting she said the heel of her shoe, which was new, came off as she was going in and after she got in the handle to her purse came off and everything spilled on the floor. Daddy and Ed said, " Was somebody there that didn't like you?" and she said, "Yes" and they said, "Hell, she put a hex on you. You'd better get a copy of this letter". So one of them left their letter with her to copy. Ed started to leave and Daddy said, "Hold on , I have to go with you so I'll be protected by your letter". When all my bad luck started happening Daddy made me take a copy, but I can't see that it helped that much. I'm still having bad luck.

I'm sure there are many more ghost tales that I don't remember that some cousins do remember. I just remember all the good times we had together and try to forget the sad and unhappy things, which were many.

Sometimes especially when I lived in Danville I would get so homesick for Pope Hill it was almost like a magnet pulling me back down on the hill. After I would go back there I would be okay until the next time I got homesick. Last summer Lisa and four of my grandchildren and I went down to the creek and found where the creek used to be dammed up and where the old cabin had been. I could just visualize all the grandchildren that we raised on Pope Hill playing in the creek, catching crawdads, playing Tarzen, making play houses out of moss and acorns. We didn't have a lot of toys to play with, but we had each other and our imagination and a common bond of being family and caring about each other that has lasted throughout most of our lives as we remember where we came from and are proud of our heritage. We remember all the ones that have gone on before us and remember them fondly and lovingly as we think of Pope Hill, a special place in our memories.

**By: Ann Pope Little**

Brookford Photos

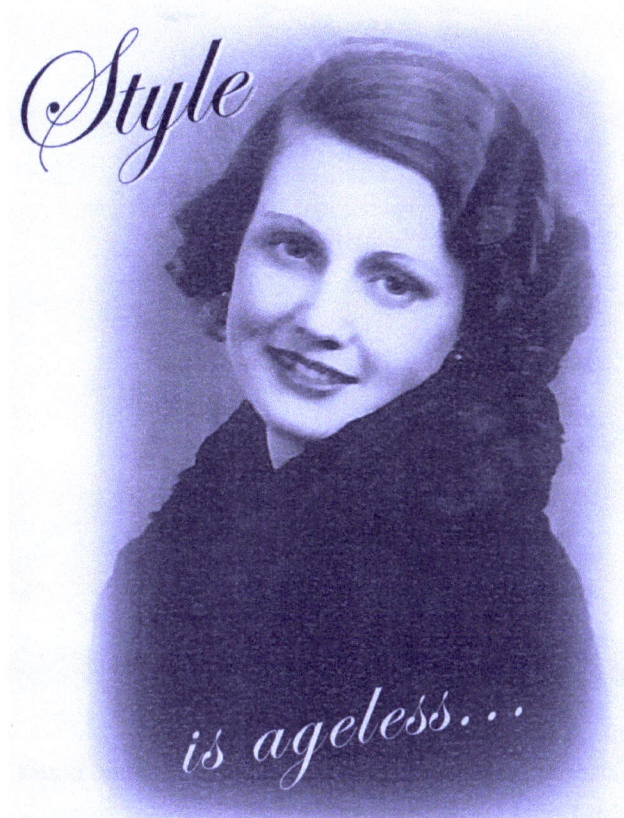

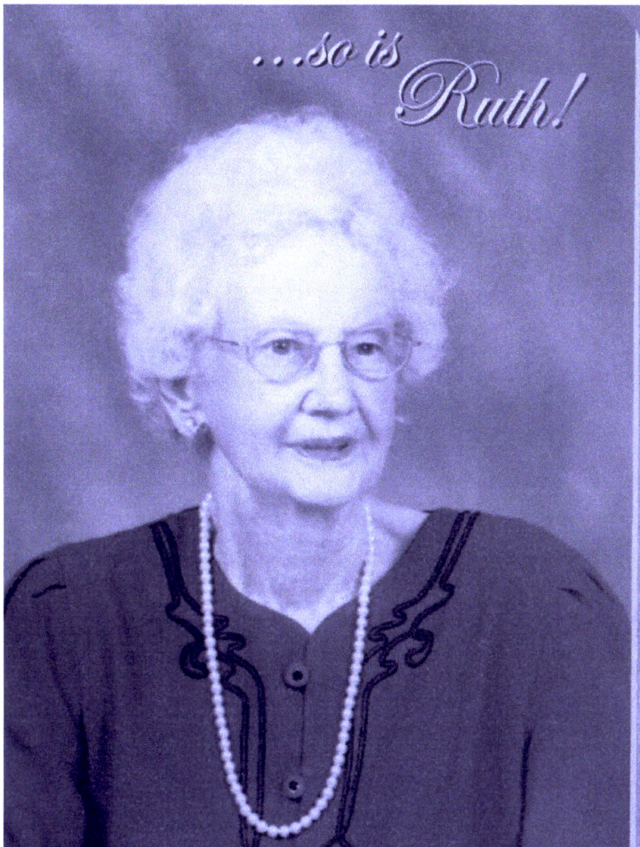


You are Invited to Celebrate
the 90th Birthday
of
Ruth Travis Hollar
at
Faith United Church of Christ
Fellowship Hall

Sunday, May 25, 2003
(2-4pm)

Please drop in to share any memories,
funny stories or photos you may have.

No gifts please.

For questions or directions, please call:

Ruth Hollar (828) 294-4825
Susie Drum (828) 327-2550

Myrtle Hunt's Sunday school class at Easter taken about 1932. Note Boarding house and Company Store to the right and Truck Garage and Corner of Faith Church on the left.

**Class at Brookford School**

Left: Marvin Keller taken in the early 40's.
Top: Good view of Mexico
Right: Katherine Keller taken in the early 40's
Bottom: Bleaka Reinhart and Bonnie Pruitt with swimming pool in the background

Left: Bub Pope on the swinging Bridge. Right: Bonnie Workman Mitchell.
Bottom left: Seth Miller with Dannny and David Thompson. Bottom right: Bill Fox "holding" Lanny Pope

**Left: Two of Brookford's finest Lee Melton and Perry Wallace. Right: Ruth Travis Holler and Ruth Bollinger Earl. Bottom left: Mike Schrone and daughter Lela. Bottom right: Back of Brookford Mills.**

Top: A young Lucy Reinhardt Simpson taken in her back yard. The mill is in the background on the right.
Bottom left: Forest Gaines. Bottom right: Alma Thompson, Chop Thompson's mother note balcony on Company Store.

Top left: Iron Steps. Left to right: Shilda Berry Burns, Ruth Berry Bumgarner, and Dewey (Bill) Berry, Jr. Top right: Mary and Bud Wallace. Bottom: Dewey Berry family with Brookford Townhouse in the background, l to r: Shilda, Bill, Gloria, Dewey in the back. Skees Crider walking past in her Easter finery.

Top left: Fletch Holland's store. Top right: Pete Hollar. Bottom left: Jim Mitchell, Billy Ray Hunt, Myrtle Smith and Lamar Hunt.

Top: Dewey Reinhardt with the service station in the background. Bottom: Joe Reinhardt at store

Top left: Buddy Lewis and pals at the pool. Top right: Ruth and Hubie Pope. Bottom: Vacation Bible School class at Brookford Baptist Church. Taken Summer of 1947.

**Top: Back of Brookford Mills during high water. Bottom: Mrs. Clinard at school.**

Top: Mother bolick's extended family. Bottom: Mother Bolick's family with spouses.

Top: Brookford Mill Band
Bottom: Brookford Mill Band in uniforms.

Top: Red Hill School and students. Bottom: Brookford Mills Basketball Team. First row l-r: Bobby Fox, Bill Gaines, Chad Mitchell, Tony Smith, Bob Taylor(coach). Second row l-r: Mark Bolick, Jerry Copas, Richard Laney, Robert Simon, Donald Bowman.

Left: Brookford Service Station.
Bottom: Brookofrd Mill Supervisors, photo taken about 1948.
Next page: Red Hill School class

Brookford Memories · Brookford Photos

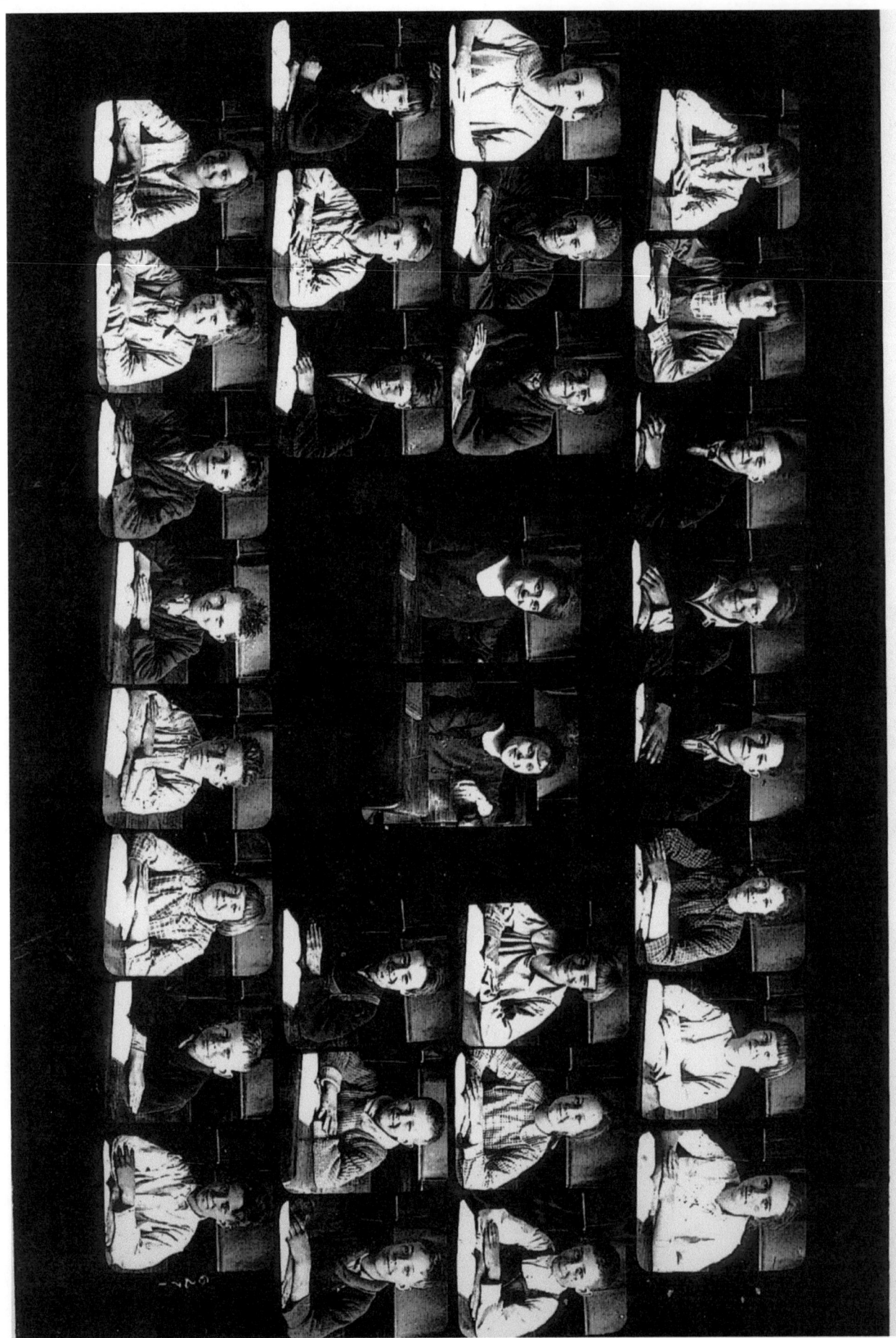

Brookford Memories · Brookford Photos

# Rosa Clinard's Album

The following album was kept by one of Miss Rosa Collin's friends to record her first year at the school on Red Hill in 1919 – 1920. As you can see the album becomes much more than that. It becomes a beautiful love story. Rosa meets J. Weston Clinard and falls in love with him. Her father tells her to hand in her resignation and get herself back to Georgia. Unfortunately for her dad the mill refuses to accept her resignation and as they say, the rest is history. She stays at Brookford School and marries J. Weston Clinard in June 1920.

*Sarah, Vera, Julia, Emmie Mae, Arney*

*Sarah's class*

Rosa and Julia take a little recreation and encounter a fierce beast

This is the school house where the three little (?) girls entered upon their famous career

Weston arrives on the scene and calls on the girls with Doug.

*Vera is thinking of the somebody who already came to meet her.*

*Emmie Mae, Julia, Vera, Sarah*

J. Weston Clinard was that somebody.

Rosa gets Weston "up a tree".

This is the Jay's home where the two glad hearts were joined together.

Rosa getting "up a tree" herself on account of Weston.

Both out of the tree and on firm ground

Rosa writes home that "Weston is a wonderful man because he can go like a mule". Her father replied for her to have nothing to do with any of those "Tar Heels".

Rosa appears to be rather amused over the situation but Sarah is sure enough mad. They are all ready to go back to Georgia after the "big fuss" stirred up by " an early acquaintance to be long remembered".

However, they did not go, and a close study of this picture may reveal why at least two people were very glad that they remained.

Sarah Parks - Rosa Collins - Vera Reed -

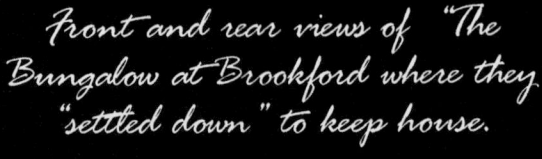

*Front and rear views of "The Bungalow at Brookford where they "settled down" to keep house.*

*Getting aquainted with the wood pile and beginning to feel at home.*

*These three little (?) girls left a perfectly peaceful home away down in Georgia to teach school in North Carolina.*

*How could Rosa do such a thing when she to tear herself away from this charming man?*

*This is where they landed.*

*The superintendent and his family, who were good, reliable friends to the teachers*

"Pals" Julia Mitchell and Emmie Mae.

Mr. and Mrs. Wilburn.

Sightseeing in the city of Brookford

Mrs. Goodwyn.
Oh, yes, they went to church–occasionally!

# BROOKFORD MILLS COMPANY

EGRAPH AND SHIPPING POINT
HICKORY, N. C.

**BROOKFORD, N. C.**

February 16th, 1920.

Miss. Rosa Collins,
Brookford, N. C.

Dear Miss. Collins:-

    We acknowledge receipt of yours of 14th, inst., tendering your resignation as teacher of the Brookford school, and after due consideration we ask that you reconsider tha matter. This committee has faithfully fulfilled its contract with you, and has rendered every possible assistance to the school. We desire to have the school continue without interruption, and to this end we feel it our duty to decline to accept your resignation.

    Respectfully,

    Brookford School Committee,

    *C. S. Glass*

        Chairman.

# Grandview School

When I started this book on Brookford I had never heard of a school on Windy Hill called Grandview School. The school opened in 1913. Students from Brookford attended this school in 1921 until 1925 when the new Brookford School was opened.

In the early 1960's the Grandview School building was condemned and Mr. Irene Hayes Barger organized a reunion for all students who attended Grandview. Her hand written notes are included along with a picture of the school and the students and teachers. Mrs. Barger is in the middle of the first row in the white dress and the page boy haircut. Pictures of the reunion are also included. You will recognize many of the people who attended.

# Grandview School

Grandview school opened in the fall of 1913 with 30 pupils attending. Bro. Billy Bolick gave the land and a generous donation. The building had one room. You went up to the teacher to recite your lesson. He was seated upon on a platform. We always made a ring around the platform. He gave us head marks if one of the pupils missed a word and you spelled the word you went up in the ring to where the word was first missed. Then you crossed over and started at the bottom again. You got a head mark.

The first school board consisted of Mr. J. Luths Bolick, Mr. R. T. Pope, Mr. F. L. Holland, B A Miller, C D Day and Mr Kale Reinheart

1913 - 1st Teacher The teacher was a Mr Mace 2nd teacher Mr M. L. Sherrill who taught 3 terms 1915-1916, 1917 3rd teacher Mr Gordon Whitener who taught 2 terms then Mr. Baxter Baker who taught 1 term Mrs. B Taylor who taught 2 yrs Mrs Clyde V Price who was Principal until the school closed.

1962
1936
---
36

in 1922. It consolidated with Brookford but the building was not ready until the fall of 1925.

Primary Dept

In the spring of 1918 They built another Room. It had folding doors that we opened each morning for the opening of Hymn, scripture and Prayer. Mrs Flow Frazier was the first Teacher she taught. She taught 3 terms. Mrs Roberts, she now taught primer, First and 2nd grade. Then Mrs Laura Brannock Yount She taught 2 terms, Mrs Kate M Combs, Mrs Ora Hahn, Mrs Kathleen Keener Pursnell She is now. Also the last teacher was Mrs Jessie McGill Hocking. She was the last teacher in first and 2nd grade. They added another Room in the spring which made 3 as it stands today. Organist for these programs were Irene Black and Sadie Hefner. Mrs McGill married Jason Gordman while teaching at Grandview.

Now would all the teachers please stand so we can make your pictures with the elementary Grades and Mr Whitener with the older classes

The next year another room was added. They hired another teacher Mrs. Kathleen Keener Presnell was is married and living in Norfo Virginia. She taught 2 and Third. Mrs. Frazier, Roberts 1st 2nd. After Miss Keener left Miss Ora Hahn who is now in Greensboro. N.C. After Her Mrs. Laura Brannock, Yount, She taught The Years Beginning 1917- 1918- 1919. The next and last Teacher was Mrs Jessie McGill Goode Marring Mr. Jason Goodman While she taught There. Will all The Teachers besides myself please stand that is present. We will have our pictures made with the group of Grades Elementary Grades 4th, 5th 6th 7th 8th. Primary Grades Primer 1st 2nd 3rd. Mrs. Yount will you please stand with the pupils that are here today that were in those Classes Imediately following the School Honor Roll and Memorial service.

Grandview School opened in the fall of the year 1913, with 30 pupils. Consolidated with Brookford when the new school building was built in the year 1925. Mr. Billy Bolick gave the land and gave a generous donation to the school. When it was built. It was a one room school.

The first teacher was a Mr. Moose. The first School Board member consisted of Mr. J. Lewis Bolick, Mr. R. F. Pope, F. L. Holland, B. K. Miller, C. P. Day, Kale Reinheart, Berry Starnes.

2nd year Teacher was Mr. M. F. Sherrill. He taught from the fall of 1914 until spring 1917, or 4 yrs.

3rd Teacher Mr. Gordon Whitner from 1917 4th 1918. 5th Mr. Baxter Baker 1 yr. 1919. Mrs D. B. Taylor 2 yrs 1920-21. Mrs. Clyde V. Price 3 yrs. 1923-24-25.

Primary Dept 1st Teacher Mrs Flow Frazier Robert at this time another room was added with folding doors between the 2 rooms. They were folded back each morning for our opening program of Scripture Hymns, Prayer, Organist Irene Bolick, Sadie Barger.

Mrs. Frazier taught Primer, First, Second

## Pupils who attended Reunion

Fred Goodman.
Margaret Campbell Goodman.
Milford Cloer
Pauline Reinheart Rozelle
Georgie Travis
Gwendola Pooley Kahill.
Earl Starnes
Irene Sprouse Hollar
Arnold Pope
Eward Pope
Ura Pope Meadows
Teacher Gordon Whitener
Paul Reinheart
Lona Bell Walker Reinheart.
Nell Reinheart Eckard.
Ethel Hollar Holt.
Vennie Starnes Settlemyre
Ethel Murphy Vervoat.
Kermit Hollard.
Vergil Cloer Holland.
Laura Cloer Kahill
Vivian Hayes Teague
Cecil Badger
Leslie Hollar
Mildred Sprouse Hollar.

A. P. (C. D. Day) Home Day $50.00.

Alice Herman Overcash
Colleen Holland Parker
Paul Hunt
Maude Warren Hunt
Pauline Pope Baker
Barbra Pope Glass
Lena Pope
Ida Mae Starnes Isenhour
Harly Hollar
Arlene Reinheart Hollar
Hobart Warren
Von Walker
Edna Mae Goodman Seitz
Nora Walker Carson
Sadie Starnes Eggers
George Starnes
Irene Hayes Barger
Laura Brannock Yount

The school building at Grandview School and the teachers and students. School opened in 1913 and this picture was taken soon after that date.

Brookford Memories · Grandview School

Mill Property

Copies of the original deeds when Mr. E.L. Shuford purchased the property for Brookford and the mill in 1898-1899. There is also a copy of the deed when the property changed in 1917 to A.D. Juillard and Company. Also when the property was sold to Shuford Mills in 1958. Plats of the town of Brookford are also included. These plats were done about the time the mill houses were sold. Lyrics to "Mill House Dream" written by my neighbor, Christopher Revis are included.

E. L. Shuford From Jason Yoder

State of North Carolina, Catawba County—

Know all men by these presents that we Mrs Jane Yoder and Jason Yoder, her husband, of Catawba County, North Carolina, for and in consideration of Two hundred Dollars ($200.00) to us paid by E. L. Shuford of Catawba County, State of North Carolina, receipt of which is hereby acknowledged, have given, granted, bargained and sold, and do by these presents give, grant, bargain, sell and convey unto the said E. L. Shuford & his heirs and assigns the right and privilege to dam and back the water in the Henry's Fork of the South Fork River against and upon our land and river bank, which land and bank begins at the bridge known as the "Iron Bridge" across the said River about two miles South of Hickory, North Carolina, and running as far up the said river as our land now runs, provided, however, that neither the said E. L. Shuford his heirs nor assigns shall dam and raise the water in the said river above the certain point at ordinary water mark, designated upon a rock at the head of the last shoal, and more particularly described as follows: Marked by a cross on said Rock on the west side of the river {Stamp} So that the said E. L. Shuford, his heirs and assigns, shall forever have the right and privilege to raise the water to and at the point as indicated and reaching and conveying any portion of our land which may be naturally reached and covered by said damming and backing without let or hindrance, or without any claim for further compensation or damages in any way arising through or because of the right and privilege above granted upon the part of ourselves our heirs or assigns for all time. And I the said Jason Yoder, join herein for the purpose of conveying such right and privilege as to my estate in the said lands, and in further token of my full and free assent to my said wife's execution of this Conveyance. In Testimony Whereof we have hereunto set our hands and seals this the 19th day of December A.D. 1899.—

Jane Yoder (Seal)
Jason E. Yoder (Seal)

Witness A. A. Yoder—

State of North Carolina, Catawba County—

I, A. A. Yoder, Justice of the Peace, do hereby certify, that Jason Yoder and Jane Yoder, his wife, personally appeared before me this day and acknowledged the due execution of the foregoing instrument and the said Jane Yoder, being by me privately examined separate and apart from her said husband, doth state that she signed the same freely and voluntarily without

18

or compulsion of her said husband, or any other person, and that she doth still voluntarily assent thereto. And the said Jason Yoder doth state that he freely assents to his said wife's execution of the said instrument. Witness my hand and private seal, this the 19th day of December 1899.

A. A. Yoder J.P. (seal)

State of North Carolina, Catawba County —

The foregoing certificate of A. A. Yoder, a Justice of the Peace of Catawba County, is adjudged to be correct. Let the instrument, with the certificates, be registered. Witness my hand, this the 27th day of December 1899.

L. H. Phillips
Clerk Superior Court.

Filed for registration at 11 am.
Dec 27th 1899 — P. M. Dellinger, Register of Deeds.

## E. L. Shuford from Abel Whitener & wife

State of North Carolina, Catawba County —

This Deed, Made this the 11th day of November A.D. 1899, by Abel Whitener and wife, Margaret P. Whitener, of Catawba County, State of North Carolina, parties of the first part, to E. L. Shuford of said county and State, party of the second part. Witnesseth: That the said parties in consideration of the sum of Sixty-seven and 40/100 Dollars ($67.40) to them paid this day by the said E. L. Shuford, receipt of which is hereby acknowl. have bargained and sold, and by these presents do bargain, sell and convey unto the said E. L. Shuford and his heirs that certain tract of land lying and being upon the South side of the Henry's Fork of the South Fork river, in Hickory Township, Catawba County, North Carolina, just South of what is known as the Iron Bridge, and which is fully bounded and described as follows, viz: Beginning at a Stone near the Iron Bridge on the South side of Henry's Fork River and about 2½ poles from the Bank of said River and in Abel Whitener's line, and running South 16¾ West 14 7/25 poles to a Gum; thence North 64 East 10 1/25 poles to a White Oak; thence North 75¾ East 4½ poles to a White Oak; thence South 65 East 6½ poles to a Spanish Oak; thence North 81 East 6½ poles to a Stake; thence North 63½ East 5¾ poles to a bunch of Maples; thence North 44¾ East 11½ poles to a dead Black oak; thence North 68 East 5 poles to a Hickory; thence North 39¾ East 14 3/5 poles to a Stake; thence North 38 East 8 poles to a dead Black-Oak; thence North 7½ poles to a pine; thence North 9½ East 4 7/25 poles to a White-oak; thence North 60 East 3½ poles to a white oak; thence North 16 East 10 4/5 poles to a pine; thence North 38¾ East 9 3/5 poles to a Laurel; thence North 30 East 4 3/5 poles to a White oak; thence North 36 East 4 poles

20

a post oak near the Iron Bridge, Abel Whitener & Jason Yoder's corner and runs North with the old Butts line 4 chains to the Fork, thence up the Fork as the river meanders and then crossing to the Beach which is the beginning corner of grant N. 588 to Peter Mull — In Testimony Whereof, the said Abel Whitener and Margaret P. Whitener have hereunto set their hands and Seals, this the 11th day of November, A.D. 1899 —

attest: E. B. Cline                    Abel X Whitener (seal)
                                              his mark
                                        Margaret X Whitener (seal)
                                              her mark

State of North Carolina, Catawba County —

I, E. B. Cline a Notary Public, do hereby certify that Abel Whitener and wife Margaret P. Whitener personally appeared before me this day, and acknowledged the due execution of the annexed deed of conveyance; and the said Margaret P. Whitener, wife of the said Abel Whitener, being by me privately examined, separate and apart from her said husband, touching her voluntary execution of the same, doth state that she signed the same freely and voluntarily, without fear or compulsion of her said husband, or any other person, and that she doth still voluntarily assent thereto. Witness my hand and official seal, this the 11th day of November A.D. 1899.

                                        E. B. Cline (seal)
                                        Notary Public

State of North Carolina, Catawba County —

The foregoing certificate of E. B. Cline a Notary Public of Catawba County, is adjudged to be correct. Let the instrument, with the certificate be registered. Witness my hand and official seal this the 27th day of Dec. 1899 —                      L. H. Phillips
                                        Clerk Superior Court

Filed for Registration at 11 a.m. Dec. 27th 1899. P. M. Dellinger Register of Deeds

## E. L. Shuford From A. E. Rowe

State of North Carolina, Catawba County —

This Indenture, made this the 17th day of November A.D. 1899 between A. E. Rowe and Mollie L. Rowe, his wife of the County of McDowell and State of North Carolina, of the one part, and E. L. Shuford of the County of Catawba, and State of North Carolina of the other part. Witnesseth: That Whereas, on the 12th day of January, 18— the said A. E. Rowe and wife did sell and convey their interest in the tract of land hereinafter described to P. J. Rowe of Catawba

22

deed is and was at the time of signing the same an acting justice of the Peace for said County, and full faith and credit are due to his official acts. Given under my hand and official seal this the 29th day of November 1899.

Thomas Morris Clerk
Superior Court McDowell County

State of North Carolina Catawba County –

The foregoing Certificate of Thomas Morris C.S.C. for McDowell County is adjudged to be correct. Let the same with this certificate be registered. Witness my hand, this 27th day of Dec. 1899.

L. H. Phillips
Clerk Superior Court

Filed for registration at 11 am Dec. 27" 1899. P. M. Dillinger, Register of Deeds

---

E. L. Shuford From E. B. Cline Commr

State of North Carolina, Catawba County –

This Deed, made this the 8th day of November A.D. 1899, by E. B. Cline Commissioner of the Superior Court of Catawba County, party of the first part, to E. L. Shuford of Catawba County, State of North Carolina party of the second part. Witnesseth: That Whereas, in Special proceeding for partition of certain lands known as the Linnie Rowe Dower Lands, brought by A. P. Ward and wife J. E. Ward, and J. W. Tate and wife Mattie Tate and others against M. A. Rowe in the Superior Court of Catawba County, there was a decree and order of the Court to sell the lands hereafter described, and the said E. B. Cline was appointed by the Court as commissioner to make said sale, and, Whereas under said order and decree and under order and decree of resale signed by the Court, on the — day of September A.D. 1899, the said E. B. Cline, Commissioner as aforesaid, advertised the lands hereafter described for thirty days in the Times Mercury, a weekly newspaper published in Hickory, Catawba County, North Carolina, and on Saturday, the 7th day of October 1899 at 2 o'clock P.M. before the First National Bank in Hickory, North Carolina, offer said lands at public outcry to the highest bidder, upon the terms stated in the decree and notice of sale, and at said sale H. L. Mace became the last and highest bidder for said lands at the price of Thirteen hundred and fifty dollars ($1350.00) and assigned his bid in writing to the said E. L. Shuford, and, Whereas, on the 6th day of November, 1899, said sale to said E. L. Shuford was duly confirmed by the Court, and title ordered to be made, upon payment of the purchase money, and said a post oak near the iron bridge, with thence _____ yards east, and runs North with the old Butts line 4 chains to the Fork, thence up the Fork as the river meanders, and then crossing to the Beach which is the beginning corner of grant N. 588 to Peter Mull — In Testimony Whereof the said Abel Whitener and Margaret P. Whitener have hereunto set their hands and Seals, this the 11th day of November. A.D. 1899 —

attest — E.B. Cline

Abel X Whitener (seal)
his mark

Margaret X Whitener (seal)
her mark

State of North Carolina, Catawba County —

I, E.B. Cline a Notary Public, do hereby certify that Abel Whitener and wife Margaret P. Whitener personally appeared before me this day, and acknowledged the due execution of the annexed deed of Conveyance; and the said Margaret P. Whitener, wife of the said Abel Whitener, being by me privately examined, separate and apart from her said husband, touching her voluntary execution of the same, doth state that she signed the same freely and voluntarily, without fear or compulsion of her said husband, or any other person, and that she doth still voluntarily assent thereto. Witness my hand and official seal, this the 11th day of November A.D. 1899 —

E.B. Cline (seal)
Notary Public

State of North Carolina, Catawba County —

The foregoing certificate of E.B. Cline a Notary Public of Catawba County, is adjudged to be correct. Let the instrument, with the certificate be registered. Witness my hand and official seal this the 27th day of Dec. 1899 —

L.H. Phillips
Clerk Superior Court

Filed For Registration at 11 am
Dec 27th 1899. P.M. Dellinger Register of Deeds

## E.L. Shuford From A.E. Rowe

State of North Carolina, Catawba County —

This Indenture, made this the 17th day of November A.D. 1899. between A.E. Rowe and Mollie L. Rowe, his wife of the County of McDowell and State of North Carolina, of the one part, and E.L. Shuford of the County of Catawba, and State of North Carolina, of the other part. Witnesseth: That Whereas, on the 12th day of January, 1880 the said A.E. Rowe and wife did sell and convey their interest in the tract of land hereinafter described to P.J. Rowe of Catawba County

412    **E. L. Shuford   From   J. Frank Bollinger and wife**

State of North Carolina. Catawba County —

This deed, made this the 9th day of September A.D. 1899 by Sarah C. Bollinger and J. Frank Bollinger, her husband, of Catawba County and State of North Carolina, parties of the first part, and E. L. Shuford of said County and State, party of the second part. Witnesseth: That the said Sarah C. Bollinger and J. Frank Bollinger, her husband, for and in consideration of the sum of Fifty-eight dollars and forty-five cents to them paid by the said E. L. Shuford, the receipt of which is hereby acknowledged, have bargained and sold and do by these presents bargain, sell and convey unto the said E. L. Shuford and his heirs, that boundry of land lying partially upon and partially near to the Henry's Fork of the South Fork River about two miles from Hickory and in Catawba County, North Carolina, bounded and described as follows, viz: — Beginning at a Hickory, Whitener's corner on the West bank of the river and running North 26½ West 4 poles to a Stake; thence North 65½ West 8 poles to a Stake, formerly a hickory near the ford; thence South 87 West 28 poles to a maple; thence S 68½ W 12½ poles to a pine stump; thence S 88 W 5 poles to a maple; thence South 76 West 8¼ poles to a gum; thence South 74 West 8 poles to a White Oak; thence 65½ West 10 poles to a gum; thence South 81½ West 11 7/5 poles to a large rock in Abel Whitener's line; thence with his line South 37 East 7 poles to a maple; thence North 70 East 32 poles to a maple; thence South 66 East 4½ poles to a Maple; thence South 80 East 7½ poles to a pine stump; thence 49½ East 11 poles to a White Oak; thence No. 87¼ East 20 7/5 poles to a Walnut; thence South 69½ East 12½ poles to a Stake in Whitener's line; thence North 66½ East 4 Poles to the beginning. Containing 3 acres and 30 poles more or less. And the said Sarah C. Bollinger and J. Frank Bollinger for the consideration aforesaid do further sell and convey to the said E. L. Shuford and his heirs, all their right, title and interest in and to the river bed unto the middle of the Stream where the said land at its Eastern end lies upon the bank of said River and further all right, title or interest which they have or ought to have in and to that land which lies at any point between the above bounded land and the middle of said Henry's Fork River and which is included in the deed from G. E. Bollinger and wife to Sarah C. Bollinger dated December 26" 1890 and registered in Book 45, Page 140, office of the Register of Deeds for Catawba County, the intention of the Grantors herein being to quit claim unto the said E. L. Shuford and his heirs any interest they may have in the strip of land conveyed on the 20th of May 1872 by Abel Cook and wife and Abel Whitener and wife to Linnie Rowe and others and also in the acre of land near the old Rowe dam which was reserved by Abel Whitener in his deed to Abel Cook & To Have and to hold the aforesaid lands and premises to the said E. L. Shuford his heirs and assigns to his and their only use and behoof forever. And the said Sarah C. and J. Frank Bollinger covenant with the said E. L. Shuford his heirs and assigns that they are seized

414  E. L. Shuford  From  Mrs M. A. Bumgarner Guar. & others

State of North Carolina. Catawba County.

This Deed, made this the 7th day of September A.D. 1899 by Mrs M. A. Bumgarner guardian of Walter W. Rowe, L. R. Whitener Guardian of Lizzie and Nora Rowe and Mrs Hattie Rowe Guardian of Peter, Anna and David Rowe, all of Catawba County and State of North Carolina, parties of the first part to E. L. Shuford of said County and State, party of the second part Witnesseth: That Whereas the said Walter W. Lizzie and Nora Rowe, children of P. J. Rowe, deceased, are the joint owners of a one-sixth interest in the land hereinafter bounded and described, and the said Peter, Anna and David Rowe children of Andy Rowe, deceased, are the joint owners of a one-sixth interest in said land; and Whereas all the said infants, by their Guardians as above named, on the 29th day of August 1899, joined in an Exparte proceeding in the Superior Court of Catawba County, to obtain an order of Court to sell and convey the aforesaid interest in the land hereinafter described at private sale to the party of the second part and Whereas on the 2nd day of September 1899 His Honor O. H. Allen judge holding the Courts of the 10th judicial district, made an order in said Proceeding confirming the order of L. H. Phillips, Clerk of the Superior Court of Catawba County, directing the aforesaid guardians to execute to said E. L. Shuford a deed in fee for the interests of their respective wards in said land, which said proceeding and all the orders and decrees therein are hereby referred to as fully authorizing the execution of this deed. Now Therefore, in consideration of the foregoing and for the purposes aforesaid and in further consideration of the sum of Fifty Dollars paid by E. L. Shuford to Mrs M. A. Bumgarner and L. R. Whitener Guardians and of Fifty Dollars paid to Mrs Hattie Rowe Guardian as aforesaid the receipt of which is hereby acknowledged, the said Mrs M. A. Bumgarner Guardian of Walter W. Rowe, L. R. Whitener of Lizzie and Nora Rowe and Mrs Hattie Rowe Guardian of Peter Anna and David Rowe have bargained and sold and do by these presents bargain, sell and convey to the said E. L. Shuford and his heirs all and entire the right, title and interest of their respective wards in and to that certain parcel of land lying and being in Hickory Township, Catawba County, State of North Carolina, about two miles from the town of Hickory, below what is known as the Iron Bridge lying partially in the bed and partially on the bank of the Henry's Fork of the South Fork River and bounded as follows: to wit: Beginning at a Stake in the middle of the River, Siria Rowe's line 12 poles below the mill dam, and runs South 30 East 4 poles to a maple thence South 68½ W 12⅞ poles to a pine stump and pointers;

408  E. L. Shuford from C. M. Rowe & wife

State of North Carolina, Catawba County.

This Deed made this 2 Day of September A.D. 1899 by Charles M. Rowe and Belle Rowe, his wife, of Catawba County, State of North Carolina, parties of the first part to E. L. Shuford of said County and State party of the second part. Witnesseth: That the said Charles M. Rowe and wife for and in consideration of the sum of Fifty Dollars ($50.00) to them paid by the said E. L. Shuford, the receipt of which is hereby acknowledged, have bargained and sold and do by these presents bargain, sell and convey unto the said E. L. Shuford and his heirs an undivided One-Sixth interest or any and all interest which the said Charles M. Rowe and wife may have and own in and to that parcel of land lying and being in Hickory Township, Catawba County, State of North Carolina, about two miles from the town of Hickory, below what is known as the Iron Bridge lying partially in the bed and partially on the bank of the Henry Fork of the South Fork River and bounded as follows to-wit: Beginning at a stake in the middle of the River, Lena Rowe line 12 poles below the mill dam, and runs South 30 East 4 poles to a Maple; thence South 68½ W. 12⅔ poles to a Pine Stump and pointers; thence South 88 W. 5 poles to a Maple; thence S. 8 W. 8¼ poles to a Small gum; thence S. 74 W. 8 poles to a white oak; thence S. 65½ W. 10 poles to a Black Gum; thence S. 80 W. 18 poles passing over the face of a large rock E to a gum; thence S. 66 W. 15 poles to a Pine; thence S. 41½ W. 14½ poles to a Red oak at the head of the first shoal; thence S. 26½ W. 20 poles to a large Black gum; thence S. 17 W. 16½ poles to a Birch; thence North to a stake in the middle of the River; thence down the middle of the River to the beginning containing two acres, more or less. Also another tract beginning at the aforesaid stake, the beginning corner of the first tract and runs South 30 E 4 poles to a Maple; thence N. 81½ E 28 poles to a Small Hickory on the Bank of the River below the Ford; thence the same course to a Stake in Linnie Rowe's line in the middle of the river; thence up the middle of the River to the beginning. This land was conveyed by Abel Cook and wife and Abel Whitener and wife to Charles M. Rowe and others by deed of May 20" 1872 which is registered in Book 8 page 353 and 354 in the office of the Register of Deeds for Catawba County, reference to which conveyance is hereby made. To Have and to hold an undivided One-Sixth interest or entire interest of the said Charles M. Rowe in the aforesaid land and premises to the said E. L. Shuford, his heirs and assigns, to his and their only use and behoof forever subject only to any reservation contained in said deed of May 20" 1872. And the said Charles M. Rowe does hereby covenant with the said E. L. Shuford, his heirs and assigns that he is seized in fee of said land

416 E. L. Shuford From M. A. Rowe

North Carolina, Catawba County —

Know all men by these presents that I M. A. Rowe of Catawba County North Carolina have agreed with E. L. Shuford of said county and State and do hereby agree and bind myself to the following proposition to wit: That upon the payment to me of the sum of Two hundred and Fifty Dollars ($250.00) at any time within six(6) months from the date hereof by the said E. L. Shuford, his heirs or assigns, I will execute to the said E. L. Shuford his heirs and assigns a deed in fee simple conveying unto him my entire interest in and to that parcel or lot of land on the Henry's Fork of the South Fork River in Catawba County, North Carolina, lying a short distance below the Iron Bridge about Two 2 miles from Hickory N.C. and bounded and described as follows. Beginning at a stake in the middle of the River Linnie Rowe's line 12 poles below the mill dam and runs S 30 E 4 poles to a maple; thence S 68½ W 12⅔ poles to a pine stump & pointers, thence S 88 W 5 poles to a maple; thence S 76° W 8¼ poles to a small gum; thence S 74 W 8 poles to a white oak; thence S 65½ W 10 poles to a black gum; thence S 80 W 16 poles passing over the face of a large rock to a gum; thence S 66 W 15 poles to a pine; thence S 41½ W 14½ poles to a Red oak at the head of the first shoal; thence S 26½ W 20 poles to a large black gum; thence S 17 W 16½ poles to a birch; thence North to a stake in the middle of the River; thence down the middle of the River to the beginning — Also another tract beginning at the aforesaid stake, the beginning corner of the first tract and runs S 30 E 4 Poles to a maple; thence N 81½ E 28 poles to a small Hickory on the bank of the river below the ford; thence the same course to a stake in Linnie Rowe's line in the middle of the River; thence up the middle of the river to the beginning — The said E. L. Shuford may accept the foregoing proposition at any time within the said six months from date and as soon as he shall tender said purchase money I or my heirs or legal representatives will immediately execute a deed for my interest in said land as aforesaid — This proposition is to be null and void if not accepted within said time — And I hereby acknowledge the receipt of one Dollar as binding myself my heirs executors & administrators to this contract. Witness my hand and seal this the 7th of September 1899.

Witness N. Martin {Stamp} M. A. Rowe

State of North Carolina Catawba County —

The Execution of the foregoing instrument was this day duly proven before me upon the oath and examination of N. Martin the subscribing witness thereto — Witness my hand and notary seal this the 8th day of September 1899.

{Seal} E. B. Cline
Notary Public

North Carolina, Catawba County —

The foregoing certificate of E. B. Cline a Notary Public of Catawba County is adjudged to be correct. Therefore let the instrument with this certificate be registered — Witness my hand this the 13th day of Sept 1899.

L. H. Phillips C.S.C.

Filed for registration at 8¼ a.m.
Sept 13th 1899

with his co-tenants, and has a right to convey his interest
in fee-simple that said interest is free and clear from all
encumbrances, and that he will warrant and defend the title
the same against the claims of all persons whomsoever.
In Testimony Whereof, the said Charles M Rowe and Belle
have hereunto set their hands and seals, the day and year a
written.
C. M. Rowe
Witness A A Yoder
Belle Rowe

State of North Carolina, Catawba County.
I, A. A. Yoder J.P. do hereby certify that Charles M Rowe
wife Belle Rowe personally appeared before me this da
acknowledged the due execution of the foregoing dee
conveyance. And the said Belle Rowe being by me
vately examined, separate and apart from her said
band, touching her voluntary execution of the same
state that she signed the same freely and voluntarily
out fear or compulsion of her said husband, or any
person and that she doth still voluntarily assent the
Witness my hand and seal, this 2nd day of Sept. 1899

A A Yoder
Justice of the Pea

State of North Carolina
Catawba County
The foregoing certificate of A. A. Yoder J.P. of ta
ba County is adjudged to be correct. Let the i
strument with the certificate be registered
Witness my hand and official seal, this 1t
4th day of Sept. 1899.

L H Phillips
Clerk Superior C

Filed for registration at 6 PM
Sept 4" 1899

396   4065

State of New York }  This is to certify that that
County of New York }  undersigned –

- Augustus D. Juilliard — 70 wall st. N.Y.
- Chester A. Braman         "   "   "   "
- Fredric A. Juilliard       "   "   "   "
- Duncan D. Sutphen         "   "   "   "
- Philip M. Smith           "   "   "   "
- Robert Westaway           "   "   "   "
- Frederick W. Johnson      "   "   "   "

will conduct as partners a manufacturing and mercantile business at Brookford, Catawba County, North Carolina, under the name of Brookford Mills Manufacturing Company, and that the names and post office addresses of the partners are as set forth above.

This January 4th, 1916

- Augustus D. Juilliard — 70 wall st. New York
- by Fredric A. Juilliard, His attorney in fact
- Chester A. Braman — 70 wall st. New York
- Fredrick A. Juilliard — 70 wall st. New York
- D. D. Sutphen — 70 "   "   "
- Philip M. Smith — "   "   "   "
- Robert Westaway — "   "   "   "
- Frederick W. Johnson — "   "   "   "

State of New York }  The due execution of the foregoing
County of New York }  Certificate was this day acknowledged before the undersigned Notary Public, by each of the subscribers thereto in person, except A. D. Juilliard, and as to him, the same was acknowledged by F. A. Juilliard, as his attorney in fact.

Witness my hand and notarial seal this the thirty-first day of January in the year of our Lord one thousand nine hundred and sixteen.

Chas. Von Riper
Notary Public

North Carolina }  The foregoing Certificate of Chas. Von
Catawba County }  Riper a N.P. of Kings County N.Y. is adjudged to be in due form and according to law, therefore let the instrument

North Carolina,
Catawba County.

This Deed, made the 28th. day of August, 1917, by and between Augustus D. Julliard, Chester A. Braman, Frederic A. Julliard, Duncan S. Sutphen, Phillip M. Smith, Robert Westaway and Fred W. Johnson, trading and doing business as A. D. Julliard & Co., a partnership of the City of New York, State of New York, hereinafter referred to as the parties of the first part, and Brookford Mills Company, a corporation organized under the laws of the State of North Carolina, hereinafter referred to as the party of the second part, WITNESSETH:

That in consideration of One Dollar ($1) and other good and valuable considerations, the receipt whereof is hereby acknowledged, the said parties of the first part do by these presents, bargain, sell, grant, alien and convey unto the party of the second part, in fee simple, the following described real property; namely

All those certain tracts, parcels or lots of land and water rights situate, lying and being in Catawba County, North Carolina, more fully described in the following deeds which have been duly recorded in the Office of the Register of Deeds of Catawba County North Carolina,; that is to say:

(1)

Deed from E. L. Shuford and wife to E. L. Shuford Manufacturing Company, recorded in book 63, page 130

(2)

Deed from E. L. Shuford and wife to E. L. Shuford Manufactueing Company, recorded in book 63, page 153.

(3)

Deed from J. W. Sublet and wife to E. L. Shuford Manufacturing Company, recorded in book 70, page 224.

(4)

Deed from J. P. Whitener and wife to E. L. Shuford Manufacturing Company, recorded in book 70, page 225.

(5)

Deed from E. L. Shuford and wife to E. L. Shuford Manufacturing Company, recorded in book 70, page 226.

(6)

Deed from E. L. Shuford and wife to E. L. Shuford Manufacturing Company, recorded in Book 70 page 227.

(7)

Deed from E. L. Shuford and wife to E. L. Shuford Manufacturing Company, recorded in Book 70 page 228.

(8)

Deed from E. L. Shuford and wife to E. L. Shuford Manufacturing Company, recorded in book 70 page 229.

(9)

Deed from E. L. Shuford and wife to E. L. Shuford Manufactueing Company, recorded in book 75 page 78.

(10)

Deed from E. L. Shuford and wife, to E. L. Shuford Manufacturing Company, recorded in book 75 page 91.

(10a)

Deed from E. L. Shuford and wife to E. L. Shuford Manufacturing Company, recorded in Book 75 page 162.

362

(11)

Deed from W. H. Shuford and others to E. L. Shuford Manufacturing Company, recorded in book 76 page 109.

(12)

Deed from C. M. Rowe and wife to Brookford Mills, recorded in Book 86 page 238.

(13)

Deed from J. A. Whitener and wife to Brookford Mills, Inc., recorded in book 86, page 240.

(14)

Deed from John L. Whisnant and wife to Brookford Mills, Inc., recorded in book 86, page 243.

(15)

Deed from L. P. Whisnant and wife to Brookford Mills, Inc., recorded in Book 95, page 190.

(16)

Deed from R. L. Martin and wife to Brookford Mills, Inc., recorded in Book 98, page 456.

(17)

Deed from E. L. Shuford and other trustees to Brookford Mills, Inc., recorded in Book 95 page 193.

(18)

Deed from T. J. Leonard and wife to Brookford Mills, Inc., recorded in book 86, page 75.

(19)

Deed from L. J. Leonard and wife to Brookford Mills, Inc., recorded in Book 75, page 399.

(20)

Deed Farabee Abernethy and husband, W. L. Abernethy to Brookford Mills, Inc., recorded in Book 99, page 477.

(21)

Deed from George McCorkle, Commissioner to Brookford Mills, Inc., recorded in Book 95 page 197.

(22)

Deed from A. A. Shuford and K. C. Menzies to Brookford Mills, Inc., recorded in Book 8C page 191.

(23)

Deed from Hickory Milling Company, to Brookford Mills, Inc., recorded in book 112 page 483.

(24)

Deed from Hickory Milling Company to Brookford Mills, Inc., recorded in Book 112, page 486.

And also all other lands, rights and easements in land and all water rights of every kind whatsoever which formerly belonged to Brookford Mills, Incorporated, and which were conveyed with the above described lands by Henry J. Holbrook, Trustee in Bankruptcy of the Estate of Brookford Mills, Incorporated, bankrupt, to the parties of the first part by deed dated the 4th. day of January 1916, and recorded in the office of the Register of Deeds of Catawba County in book 121, page 363.

The parties of the first part also sell, assign and convey to the party of the second part, its successors and assigns, all the factory buildings, warehouses, tenant houses all buildings, machinery, fixtures, tools and appliances, and all live stock, wagons, buggies and farming implements belonging to the parties of the first part at said mills at Brookford, Catawba County, North Carolina, or elsewhere in said Catawba including those purchased by the said parties of the first part from Henry J. Holbrook, Trustee in Bankruptcy aforesaid of Brookford Mills Company, Incorporated, except so much of said personal property as has been otherwise disposed of by said firm since such conveyance, and also all other machinery, appliances, instruments, tools, stock in process of manufacture at said mills, and cotton on hand at said mills fuel at said mills, supplies and material of all kinds at said mills at Brookford Catawba County, State of North Carolina now belonging to said parties of the first part and acquired since said conveyance, and all books and office fixtures at said mills, together with the good will of the manufacturing business and other business now carried on by the said firm of A. D. Julliard & Co. at Brookford, Catawba County State of North Carolina, also all stock of goods, wares and merchandise in the store building at Brookford aforesaid belonging to the parties of the first part.

To have and to hold the same together with all privileges and appurtenances there unto belonging, to it, the party of the second part, its successors and assigns, in fee simple, free and clear from all liens and encumbrances of any kind whatsoever.

In witness whereof, the said parties of the first part do hereunto set their hands and seals, the day and year first above written.

|  |  |
|---|---|
| WITNESS:::: | A. D. Julliard Co. (SEAL) |
|  | By |
| CHAS. VAN RIPER. | Augustus D. Julliard (SEAL) |
|  | A. D. Julliard (SEAL) |
|  | Chester A. Braman (SEAL) |
|  | Frederic A. Julliard (SEAL) |
|  | Philip M. Smith (SEAL) |
|  | Duncan S. Sutphen (SEAL) |
|  | Robert Westaway (SEAL) |
|  | Fred W. Johnson (SEAL) |

State of New York,
County of New York.

I, Charles Van Riper, a Notary Public in and for the County of Kings in the State of New York, with certificate filed in New York County, do hereby certify that Augustus A. Julliard, Chester A. Braman, Frederic A. Julliard, Duncan D. Sutphen, Phillip M. Smith, Robert Westaway and Fred W. Johnson personally appeared before me this day and acknowledged the due execution of the foregoing deed for the purposes therein expressed.

In witness whereof, I have hereunto set my hand and notorial seal,

State of New York,
County of New York.        No. 53027 Series B.

I, William F. Schneider, Clerk of the County of New York and also Clerk of the Supreme Court for the said County, the same being a Court of Record do hereby certify that Chas. Van Riper, whose name is subscribed to the deposition or certificate of the proof or acknowledgement of the annexed instrument, and thereon written, was, at the time of taking such deposition or proof and acknowledgment, a Notary Public, acting in and for the said County, duly commissioned and sworn and authorized by the laws of said State to take depositions and also acknowledgments and proofs of Deeds, or conveyances for land, tenements or hereditaments in said State of New York. That there is on file in the Clerk's office of the County of New York, a certified copy of his appointment and qualification as Notary Public of the County of Kings with his autograph signature. And further, that I am well acquainted with the handwriting

NORTH CAROLINA                      QUITCLAIM DEED
CATAWBA COUNTY

THIS DEED, Made and entered into this 14th day of January, 1958, by and between A.D. JUILLIARD & CO., INC. a corporation organized and existing under the laws of the State of Delaware, with its principal office in the City of New York, State of New York, and authorized and licensed to do business in the State of North Carolina, and having an office and place of business in Catawba County, North Carolina, hereinafter referred to as the party of the first part, and SHUFORD MILLS, INCORPORATED, a corporation organized and existing under and by virtue of the laws of the State of North Carolina, and having its principal office and place of business in Catawba County, North Carolina, hereinafter referred to as the party of the second part;

WITNESSETH:

That, whereas, on September 7th, 1957, the parties to this deed entered into an agreement under the terms of which A.D. Juilliard & Co., Inc. agreed to convey to Shuford Mills, Incorporated by quitclaim deed a small tract of land, approximately two (2) acres in size, located southwest of Brookford on the Mountain Grove Road, which tract is and has been used as a grave yard, and,

WHEREAS, under the same agreement above referred to, Juilliard & Co., Inc., agreed to convey all of its interest in certain water power rights of way and easements on Henry Fork River to Shuford Mills, Incorporated;

NOW, THEREFORE, party of the first part for and in consideration of the sum of ($10.00) TEN Dollars and other valuable considerations, to it in hand paid, the receipt of which is hereby acknowledged, has remised and released and by these presents does remise and release and forever quitclaim unto the party of the second part, and its successors and assigns, and does grant, bargain, sell and convey, and has by these presents granted, bargained, sold and conveyed, without any actual or implied warranty of title, unto the said second party, its successors and assigns, all right, title, claim and interest of the party of the first part in and to the following tracts of land, including any and all easements for water rights; said properties being described as follows:

BEGINNING at a Pine stump, an old corner on the South side of the Mountain Grove Road (which beginning point is the same as that set forth in the deed from A.D. Juilliard & Co. Inc. (Brookford Mills) to Blackwelder, as set forth in Book 336 at page 196 in the office of the Register of Deeds for Catawba County); and runs thence with an old line South 56° West 22 poles, more or less to an old corner; thence with another old line North 42½° West 15½ poles, more or less, to a point in the old County Road; thence along said road approximately South 75° East 25 poles, more or less, to the beginning.

The water right easements included in this conveyance are described as follows:

All rights set forth in the deeds described in the following records in the office of the Register of Deeds for Catawba County:

Conveyance L P Whisnant and wife, to Brookford Mills, Inc., dated September 19, 1908, and recorded in Book 95 at pages 190-192, inclusive;

Conveyance John L Whisnant and wife, to Brookford Mills, dated May 5, 1908, recorded in Book 86 pages 243-245, inclusive;

Conveyance J A Whitener and wife, to Brookford Mills, dated August 17, 1907, recorded in Book 86 Pages 240-242 inclusive;

Conveyance R L Martin and wife, to Brookford Mills, dated October 10, 1910, recorded in Book 98 at page 456;

Conveyance C M Rowe and wife, to Brookford Mills, dated March 12, 1908, and recorded in Book 86 at page 238;

Also Conveyance from Mrs. Jane Yoder and husband, to E L Shuford in 1899 as shown of record in Book 60 at page 17; together with any and all other water power right of ways which are owned by, or in which A.D. Juilliard & Co., Inc., or its successors in title, have any interest.

Rev. $.55

The intent and purpose of this conveyance, as far as the easements are concerned, is to transfer to Shuford Mills, Incorporated all such interest as A.D. Juilliard & Co., Inc., has in and to any water rights on the Henry Fork Branch of the South Fork River.

TO HAVE AND TO HOLD the aforesaid tracts or parcels of land and all privileges thereunto belonging to it, the said party of the second part and its successors and assigns, free and discharged from all right, claim, title or interest of the said party of the first part, or any one claiming by, through, or under them.

IN TESTIMONY WHEREOF, said party of the first part has caused its name to be signed hereto by its President and attested by its Assistant Secretary, and its corporate seal hereto attached, all by order of its Board of directors, on this the 14th day of January, 1958.

IN TESTIMONY WHEREOF, the said A D Juilliard & Co., Inc, has caused this instrument to be signed in its name by its President, and its corporate seal to be hereunto affixed, and attested by its Assistant Secretary, all by order of its board of directors duly given, this the day and year first above written.

A D JUILLIARD & CO., INC.

ATTEST: Martin J Schwab
Assistant Secretary        (CORPORATE SEAL)

BY: Harold Ackerman
President

CITY OF NEW YORK
STATE OF NEW YORK

On this 14th day of January, 1958, personally came before me Harold Ackerman, President, with whom I am personally acquainted, who, being by me duly sworn, says, that he is the President, and Martin J Schwab is the Assistant Secretary of A D Juilliard & Co., Inc., the corporation described in and which executed the foregoing instrument; that he knows the common seal of said corporation; that the seal affixed to the foregoing instrument is said common seal, and the name of the corporation was subscribed thereto by the said President, and the said President and Assistant Secretary subscribed their names thereto, and said common seal was affixed, all by order of the board of directors of said corporation, and that the said instrument is the act and deed of said corporation.

Witness my hand and notarial seal this 14th day of January, 1958.

Hildegarde E Brett
Notary Public

My commission expires: March 30, 1958 (LS)

NORTH CAROLINA
CATAWBA COUNTY

The foregoing certificate of Hildegarde E Brett, a Notary Public in and for said City and State, is adjudged to be correct. Let the instrument and the certificate be registered.
Witness my hand this 1 day of Feb., 1958.

Eunice W Mauney, Asst
Clerk Superior Court

Filed at 11:55 A M on February 1, 1958, and recorded February 3, 1958, in Book 558, Page 629-632.

Register of Deeds

Thomas P Pruitt

Brookford Memories · Mill Property

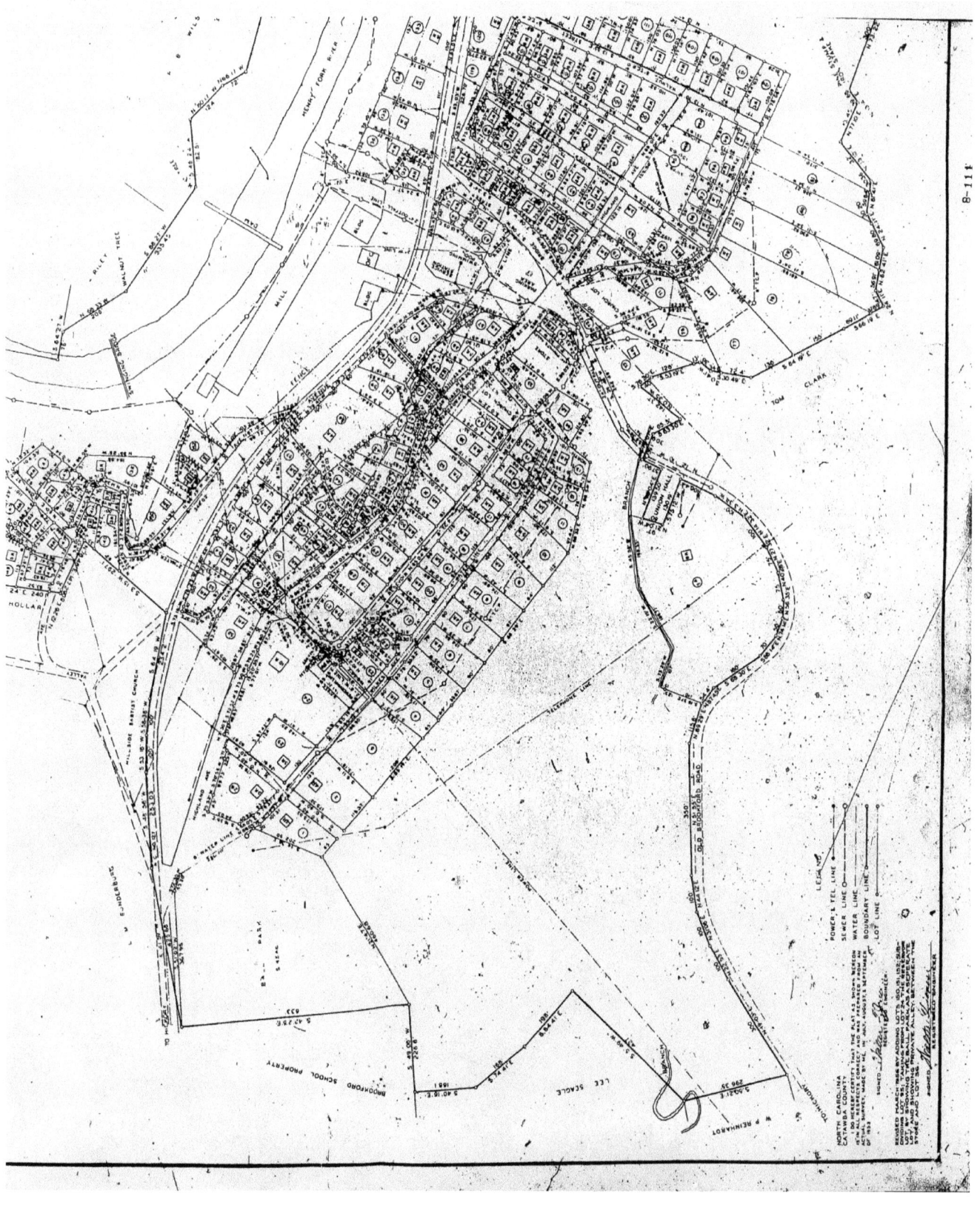

Brookford Memories · Mill Property

## Town of Brookford
### BROOKFORD, N. C.

A meeting of the Town Board of Brookford was held Tuesday, February 23, 1937, with the Mayor and all Aldermen present.

After the meeting was called to order by the Mayor, a motion was made by Mr. Tom Bloninger and seconded by Mr. L. R. Beaman that J. R. Hollar be retained to assist C. E. Gilbert in his police duties.

By a motion made by T. M. Cloninger and duly seconded by L. R. Beaman, a resolution was passed, reading as follows:

> Resolved that the Town Board partition the General Assembly of the State of North Carolina to pass a bill enlarging the city limits of the Town of Brookford, making the boundaries read as follows:
>
> Beginning at a white oak tree, the original corner of the boundary of the Town of Brookford as contained in Chapter 230, Section 2 of the Private laws of 1907, and running thence a southeastern direction to a stone at a point 200 feet east of the store building occupied by Sherrill and Company, thence south to the river, thence down the river as it meanders to the mouth of Falling Creek, thence up the creek as it meanders to the mouth of a branch entering from the north side, thence North $4\frac{1}{2}$ degrees east 1300 feet more or less to the southeast corner of the school property and a corner of the boundary as contained in Public-Local and Private Laws of 1925 relating to the Town of Brookford boundaries, Chapter 121, Section 1, thence with this boundary to the Browder line, thence with the Browder line North $4\frac{1}{2}$ degrees East 650 feet more or less to the original corner of the latter act referred to, thence westwardly 1000 feet more or less to the original beginning as named in the first act as herein referred to.

This act is to include any and all land between the East and West boundaries of all of the original acts relating to the boundaries of the Town of Brookford.

Mayor: M. A. Bolick
Clerk: G. B. Flowers
Aldermen: L. R. Beaman
B. B. Bishop
T. M. Cloninger

## CONTRACT

This AGREEMENT, Made and entered into by and between A. D. JUILLIARD & CO., INC., BROOKFORD MILLS DIVISION, hereinafter known as the party of the first part, and J. B. FRYE, SAM E. HEFNER and OTTIE GREGG, hereinafter known as the parties of the second part,

### WITNESSETH:

The party of the first part has agreed to furnish all the paint necessary to paint one coat on the outside of seventy (70) mill village houses, containing 316 rooms, also to furnish the paint for one coat, outside and inside, of one house containing 13 rooms; all these houses located in the Brookford mill village.

The parties of the second part agree to put one coat of paint on the outside of said seventy (70) houses and one coat outside and inside of the one house mentioned, also to furnish all of the paint brushes, ladders and other equipment necessary to do the work as outlined. Also, to protect the party of the first part against any damages for injury to themselves or any other person working for them on the job mentioned.

Parties of the second part also agree to pay any Social Security taxes imposed by the Government for labor performed in fulfilling this contract.

The party of the first part agrees to pay to the parties of the second part a total sum of Eight Hundred and Seventy-Five Dollars ($875.00) for the fulfilment of this contract.

A. D. JUILLIARD & CO., INC.,
BROOKFORD MILLS DIVISION,

*M. A. Bolick*, Agent

Brookford, N. C.,
June 16, 1941.

# Mill House Dream

by Christopher Revis

Frosted windows, bundled faces.
Shuffled out the door we take our places.
Climbing on board not much is said.
We all sit together wishin' we were still in bed.

From the back of the bus in cold morning air,
The girls gossip, the boys just stare.
Cold blank faces but wanting to scream.
Trying to awake from this Mill House Dream.

"What more could you want"
Dad used to groan.
"Clothes on your back and a place of your own"
I would smile and nod as if to agree,
But deep inside I wanted to be free
Of this Mill House Dream.

1 of 8 Mom struggled to feed,
While Dad wastes away from the Millowners greed.
The oldest of 8, next in line.
It was expected of me to be working the twine.
That's what you did when you got on at the Mill,
Either tying up packages or cleaning up spills."

"What more could you want"
Dad used to groan.
"Clothes on your back and a place of your own"
I would smile and nod as if to agree,
But deep inside I wanted to be free
Of this Mill House Dream.

50 years later my body bent and broken.
A pitiful pension and a gold watch token.
Surrounded by boys from the back of the bus,
They clap and shake, stagger and cuss.

We're gonna miss ya, they say, Things won't be the same.
You were our rock, our pillar, the one we could blame.

"What more could you want"
Dad used to groan.
"Clothes on your back and a place of your own"
I would smile and nod as if to agree,
But deep inside I wanted to be free
Of this Mill House Dream.

# Church Brochures

The brochure for the 75th Anniversary of the Faith United Church of Christ and the brochure for the 90th Anniversary of Brookford Baptist Church.

# 75th ANNIVERSARY

OF

## FAITH UNITED CHURCH OF CHRIST
BROOKFORD, N.C.

## MAY 12-16, 1976

### REV. CARL C. KREPS, PASTOR

*Founding Date: May 12, 1901*

# THE 75TH ANNIVERSARY OF FAITH CHURCH

## THE SCHEDULE OF OBSERVANCES

Wednesday Night, May 12, 1976 — Founder's Night Service
    6:30 P.M. Congregational Dinner
    7:30 P.M. Musical Program "God And Country" performed by Corinth Church Choir in honor of Faith Church 75th anniversary and the Bicentennial year of the United States of America
    Speaker:  Dr. James H. Lightbourne, Jr.
                 Conference Minister of the
                 Southern Conference of the
                 United Church Of Christ

Sunday, May 16, 1976 - Anniversary Sunday Services
    11 A.M. Guest Speaker, The Rev. Carl T. Daye
                        Ministerial Son of the congregation
    12:30 P.M. Congregational Picnic Dinner
    2 P.M. Guest Speakers The Rev. Carroll E. Bartholomew
                        Minsterial Son of the congregation
                   Mrs. George J. (Alberta) Miller
                        Ministerial Daughter of the Congregation

# The Old Faith Church

Faith Church as it Appeared
Before the Fire
on December 22, 1944

The Sanctuary of the Old Church
1944

*Chancel Area in the Sanctuary of Faith Church*

# The New Faith Church

*Present Parsonage at 82 - 20th Avenue S. W.
Brookford, N.C.*

fund treasurer, C. D. Daye, J. Raymond Hollar, Gaither C. Hefner, J. Paul Hunt, and A. Wilson Cheek, the pastor.

Church records indicate that in the six year period from 1939 to 1945 church membership grew from 91 active members to 226. The church school enrollment was 250. In those years of World War II, a total of 52 members served in the armed forces of our country.

During the time that the new building was under construction, the congregation worshipped for two years at the Brookford School. Permission was given by the Hickory School Board for Faith Congregation to have Sunday use of the school building. Other meetings and weekly activities were held in the homes of members.

After this two year period of sacrifice and diligent efforts in fund raising, the congregation rejoiced at the placing of the cornerstone in the new building on October 27, 1946. The sermon was delivered by Rev. Joshua L. Levens, President of Southern Synod, and a brochure describing the cornerstone ceremonies tells of the items placed in the cornerstone box for appropriate dedication. By December 31 of 1946, receipts to the building fund totaled $61,031.62 and in early 1947, the building was considered finished at a cost exceeding $65,000.00. Even then some rooms were finished in the rough, to be completed at a later date. (Congregational records indicate, for example, that in January and February of 1949, classrooms on the first and second stories were completed, and some basement rooms at a cost of $5,150.00, the work being done by Elliott Building Company.)

Interestingly, the bell from the bell tower of the old church was not harmed by the fire, and the bell has been placed again in the present tower and continues to be used.

Included in the total building fund was a loan of $10,000.00 from the Board of National Missions of the Evangelical And Reformed Church.

Other sources of help came from the churches of Southern Synod which donated $5,186.76, and once again, the mother church, Corinth, bestowed Faith Church with a $5,000.00 gift, which was used to furnish the new chancel and the chancel area is dedicated to the memory of Dr. J. L. Murphy, the founding pastor, through this gift. Churches of the denomination and other denominational help amounted to $4,184.45. Local industries and businesses donated another $14,752.50. With the congregation's own gifts and sacrifices, the record was accomplished. By May 11, 1947 the building was ready for dedication and a bulletin of that time indicates a week of activities and services commemorating the event. This dedicatory occasion served also as the climax for a recognition of the 46th anniversary of the founding of the church. This was now the third building the congregation would occupy. The dedication sermon that Sunday of May 11th was delivered by Dr. Ralph S. Weiler, Field Secretary of the Board of National Missions of the Evangelical and Reformed Church.

We note with pride that the picture of the newly built Faith Church appeared on the weekly bulletin cover for the entire denomination on Sunday of October 19, 1947. That weekly bulletin was stressing the occasion of National Missions Sunday and used the picture of Faith Church to highlight the theme.

The congregational records indicate that, earlier, a 45th anniversary celebration was duly observed on May 12 of 1946, when a Homecoming occasion was held, and guest speakers were W. W. Rowe and C. C. Wagoner in an all day activity.

Rev. Cheek enjoyed a fruitful pastorate until November 30, 1947, when he became Director of Youth Work for the denomination. And it was with sad hearts, the congregation learned of the death of Rev. A. Wilson Cheek on March 6, 1971 at Atlanta, Georgia. An appropriate memorial was immediately planned by Faith Church. On Sunday, December 26, 1971, a new brass altar cross and bronze plaque with appropriate inscription was placed in the chancel area in memory of this beloved pastor and the work he accomplished during his pastorate.

Dr. H. D. Althouse and Dr. Shuford Peeler were the next supply pastors until a call was given to Rev. Richard Rubright, and he became pastor on January 2, 1949. Under his spiritual guidance, the work of Faith Church continued. He was particularly noted for his educational approach to the presentation of the gospel, and for his keen interest in community social work.

The 50th anniversary of Faith Church was recognized during the week of May 6-13, 1951 with special services held each night, with a different guest speaker each night.

Rev. Rubright resigned on April 15, 1951, to become pastor of St. Matthew's Chapel in Charlotte, N.C., but in a very short time was then appointed as educational missionary to Japan. Rev. Roy Leinbach supplied next until another regular pastor could be called. In the summer of 1952, Banks Shepherd, served as a student supply and accepted a call as full time pastor when schooling was finished. He was installed on June 14, 1953.

During the pastorate of Rev. Shepherd a mortgage burning service was held on August 19, 1956, acknowledging the release of the church from debt, when on April 9, 1956, the $10,000.00 loan from the Board of National Missions was repaid ahead of schedule. Again, Dr. Ralph S. Weiler, from the Board of National Missions was the speaker at this note-burning occasion.

During the time Rev. Shepherd was pastor, the church also purchased the present parsonage and property at a cost of $8,000.00, according to the Consistory records of December 9, 1956. It was Rev. Shepherd's privilege to receive as new members, 90 additions during his 5 year pastorate as the church continued to grow. On January 1, 1956, Faith Church ceased to be a mission church and discontinued asking financial support from the Board of National Missions. The church was now truly maturing into its own right.

In 1958, on August 18th, opportunity was presented and accepted by the congregation to purchase an additional piece of land at the rear of the then existing property. This was the John Holder property which was purchased for $1,600, which now makes up the total property owned by the church.

On November 8, 1958, Rev. Shepherd resigned from the charge, and the next full time pastor was Rev. Bobby Bonds who came to Faith Church on June 15, 1959.

Consistory minutes of this period of time takes note that the present Baldwin Electric Organ was purchased on November 1, 1959 at a cost of $1,900.00 plus the old organ.

On June 25, 1961, Faith Church was privileged to commission the first full time Christian Education worker from out of the ranks of the congregation. She was Alberta Melton, daughter of Mr. and Mrs. Lee Melton of Brookford, and married to the Rev. George J.

*Service of Worship during the Cornerstone Service on October 27, 1946*

Miller on June 18, just one week before her commissioning. Together they have served congregations in the Pennsylvania area.

Along with Alberta, the Rev. Carl Daye and the Rev. Carroll Bartholomew are the ministerial sons and daughters of the congregation over the 75 years of history. Rev. Daye is the son of the late Mr. and Mrs. C. D. Daye, and he began his ministerial career upon seminary graduation in 1946. Rev. Carroll Bartholomew is the son of Mr. and Mrs. Gerald Bartholomew, and he began his ministry in 1963 following his seminary education.

During Rev. Bonds' pastorate, the Macedonia Church was deemed best to be closed, and a relocation made elsewhere in Hickory. Thus Macedonia was dissolved on December 31, 1962, and Rev. Bonds became the first full time pastor of Faith Church in her history. During his tenure, 67 additions of members were made to the church roll.

Following pastors have been Rev. Cedric Hepler in 1964-1965 and Rev. Chester Byerly in 1966-1968. Other supply pastors have been Dr. Donald Selby in 1958 between the pastorates of Rev. Shepherd and Rev. Bonds. Dr. Harvey A. Fesperman supplied in 1963 until Rev. Hepler became the regular pastor. Again Dr. Selby from Catawba College supplied the church after the pastorate of Rev. Chester Byerly until Rev. Carl Kreps became pastor. We note in the records that Rev. Byerly received 51 additions to the church during his pastorate. During that time, the congregation began to see the need for further renovations and improvements to the church property.

This came to fruition in the pastorate of Rev. Carl C. Kreps, beginning January 1, 1969. The parsonage interior was painted, with the kitchen and bath being remodeled at a cost of about $3,000.00. In the fall of 1969, the congregation voted to air condition the sanctuary at a cost of $2,247.72. Next, the exterior of the church was painted, a new roof installed, and siding applied to the gable ends of the building at a cost of $9,588.00 by Hickory Construction Company. The exterior of the parsonage was painted at this time, also. This work was done in the fall of 1970 and into the spring of 1971. Later the sanctuary interior was painted for a cost of over $2,000.00.

Members of the church helped paint all the Sunday School classrooms, drapes were made and hung, carpet installed in several rooms, and many other minor improvements have been made. A new roof was installed on the parsonage in 1972.

The most recent project has been grading the vacant lot behind the church into a parking lot and picnic area. This has been completed in the 1975-1976 period of time.

Thoughts for future projects now center on the need for a better parsonage. A parsonage fund has just been created in 1976 to store monies in anticipation for a new parsonage some day.

Thus, over the 75 years, Faith Church has worked hard and accomplished much in the village of Brookford. The church has known joys and times of crisis. It has survived two natural disasters of fire. The village of Brookford also went through some major social changes when the Brookford mill closed for a number of years in the late 1940's and early 1950's. This resulted in community changes with people seeking other jobs and housing in the Greater Hickory area. Now in the decade of the 70's major changes are again happening to the community as a highway building program for Interstate Route 40 came through the Brookford-Hickory area. Through all these experiences, as the church faces them constructively, the church learns and grows in grace and favor with God and man.

Faith Church has been known over the years for its programs of Christian Education, music ministry, and programs for men, women, and youth. The church has broad outreach for community service through participation in the Co-operative Christian Ministry of the Greater Hickory Area. Additions to the church have numbered 64 thus far in the pastorate of Rev. Kreps. The membership of Faith Church presently stands at 285 on January 1, 1976.

May we march triumphantly into the future as we work and labor together as a congregation united in witness for our Lord.

*Note burning at Faith Church*
*Left to right: Rev. Banks Shepherd,*
*Mr. J. Paul Hunt, Mr. Clifford E. Warren.*

Sources for this history:

"Historic Sketch of the Reformed Church in N.C."
J. C. Clapp, Editory and J. C. Leonard, Assistant Editor  1908
Pages 320 & 321

"History Of The Southern Synod"
J. C. Leonard, Editory  1940
Pages 364 & 365

"A Story Of The Southern Synod Of The Evangelical and Reformed Church"
Banks J. Peeler, D. D., Editory  1968
Pages 218 & 219

Various books of Consistory minutes, church rolls, programs and booklets which are the property of Faith Church.

# The Pastors Who Have Served Faith Church For 75 Years

Rev. Joseph L. Murphy, D. D.
1901 - 1917

Rev. Walter W. Rowe, D. D.
1918 - 1921

Rev. O. Bain Michael
Summer Supply - 1919

Rev. Banks J. Peeler, D. D.
Summer Supply - 1920

Rev. Felix B. Peck, D. D.
Summer Supply - 1921

Rev. William H. McNairy, D. D.
1921 - 1923

Rev. Harvey W. Black, D. D.
Summer Supply - 1923

Rev. Dobbs F. Ehlman
Summer Supply - 1924 - 1925

Rev. William R. Shaffer, D. D.
1926-1929

Rev. C. Columbus Wagoner
1930 - 1938

Rev. Harry D. Althouse, D. D.
1938 - 1939
1947 - 1948
Supply Pastor

Rev. A. Wilson Cheek, D.D.
1939 - 1947

Rev. Shuford Peeler, D. D.
Supply Pastor
1948

Rev. Richard W. Rubright
1948 - 1951

Rev. Roy E. Leinbach, Jr., D. D.
Supply Pastor
1951 - 1953

Rev. Banks D. Shepherd
1953 - 1958

Rev. Donald J. Selby, Ph. D.
Supply Pastor
1958

Rev. Bobby R. Bonds
1959 - 1963

Rev. Harvey A. Fesperman, D. D.
Supply Pastor
1963 - 1964
1966

Rev. Cedric L. Hepler
1964 - 1965

Rev. Chester W. Byerly
1966 - 1968

Rev. Carl C. Kreps
Present Pastor
1969 -

# Members from Faith Church in Christian Vocational Careers

Rev. Carl T. Daye     Mrs. George J. (Alberta Melton) Miller     Carroll E. Bartholomew

Construction of Faith Church

# Miscellaneous

**Brookford Reformed Church Sunday School**

**Christmas Service**

Recreation Hall, Dec. 23, 1910

### PROGRAMME

| | |
|---|---|
| OPENING CHORUS—"Join the Triumphal Celestial" | School |
| RECITATION | Carrie May Cryder |
| RECITATION | "Bill" Hefner |
| SONG—"Little Christmas Pictures" | Primary Girls |
| RECITATION | Essie May Huffman |
| RECITATION | Edwin Warren |
| SONG—"Under the Mistletoe" | Mixed Voices |
| RECITATION | Russell Lail |
| DIALOGUE | Ruth Whitener and Bertha Travis |
| SONG—"My Old Kentucky Home" | Quartette |
| RECITATION | Jennie McIver |
| DIALOGUE | Eight Boys |
| SONG—"Sing a Song of Christmas" | Junior Girls |
| RECITATION | John Mathis |
| DIALOGUE | Twelve Little Girls |
| SONG—"Lo, What Starry Banner" | School |
| RECITATION | Sally McIver |
| RECITATION | Earl Holler |
| SONG—"Better be Good" | Junior Girls and Boys |
| RECITATION | Raymon Warren |
| DIALOGUE | Mayburn Martin and Cricket Davis |
| SONG—"Hark! The Sound of Angel Voices" | Senior Girls |
| RECITATION | Harold Warren |
| RECITATION | Monroe Mathis |
| SONG—"Why Don't the Clock Go Faster" | Junior Boys |
| DIALOGUE | Six Little Girls |
| RECITATION | Loyd Hefner |
| RECITATION | Clarence Warren |
| SONG—"Good Tidings of Great Joy" | Senior Girls |
| RECITATION | Mollie Fry |
| DIALOGUE | Roy Killian and Pate Mathis |
| SONG—"Sugar Moon" | Mr. Sam Lovelace |
| RECITATION | Martha Hefner |
| RECITATION | Ed Mathis |
| SONG—"O Dear Little Baby" | Seven Girls |
| RECITATION | Fannie Pitts |
| RECITATION | Herman Warren |
| DIALOGUE | Five Little Girls |
| RECITATION | Forest Simpson |
| SONG—"The Heavenly Chorus" | School |
| REMARKS | |

SANTA CLAUS

GOOD NIGHT: COME AGAIN NEXT XMAS.

Clay Ptg. Co., Hickory

## An Old Program

# The First Church Roll

Brookford NC
Jan. 29. 1905

At a church meeting held at Faith Reformed Church at the village of Brookford. NC on the 29 day of Jan. 1905 it was resolved that a congregation be arranged at said church. Rev. J. L. Murphey D.D. To serve as Pastor and the following persons was elected to serve as Subordinate Officers of the Congregation as follows

Elder - Labon Reese
Deacon - John Jones
Capt. H. J. Holbrook to take charge of the Collection and T. J. Leonard was elected Sec. & Treasurer

Following is a list of the members

**Males**
1. S. A. Peterson
2. M. H. Sinford
3. Earl Ramsour
4. Labon Reese
5. A. T. Frye
6. Rufus Huffman
7. John Jones
8. John Holler
9. E. M. Huffman
10. Macon Huffman
11. C. B. Huffman
12. Thomas Huffman
13. Charles Huffman
14. Henry Rush
15. P. L. Eaves
16. George D. Rush
17. Edward C. Fail
18. Edgar Shell

**Females**
1. Mary Reese
2. Mary Huffman
3. Minnie Simpson Hewitt
4. Lillian Simpson
5. Aquila Holler Rinehardt
6. Laura E. Coulter
7. C. Jane Eaves
8. Mary A. Eaves
9. Mintie Holler
10. Ella Holler
11. Fannie Holler
12. C. Simpson Paxton
13. Florence Holler
14. Ida Rush
15. Maggie Rush
16. Laura Jones
17. Myrtle Huffman
18. Lillie Reese

{List of Members. Continued}

**Males**
19. Lafayette Moore
20. George W. Sigman
21. J. P. Downey
22. Jesse Barger
23. Henry Pitts
24. J. P. Killian
25. Chas. A. Frye

**Females**
19. Carrie May Shook
20. Louanna Sigman
21. Nattie Simpson
22. Bessie Pope
23. — Barger
24. Ella Pitts
25. Lula Pitts
26. E. C. Killian
27. Annie Killian
28. Annie Hefner
29. Ora Warren
30. Carrie Warren
31. Alice Pope
32. Carrie Travis
33. Essie May Huffman
34. Janie Huffman
35. Bessie Pitts
36. Lou Ella Martin
37. Ora Lee Huffman
38. A. T. Nuttall
39. Lula Travis

*Rev. A. Wilson Cheek at the Door of the New Church.*

# BROOKFORD BAPTIST CHURCH
## APRIL 25, 1907 - APRIL 27, 1997

## "YESTERDAY, TODAY, AND FOREVER"

# THIS BOOK IS DEDICATED TO ALL OUR MEMBERS; PAST, PRESENT AND FUTURE.

*The Founder's Day Commitee
would like to thank
all the members of Brookford Baptist
for their help with locating pictures and facts for this book.
We would like to espcially thank the Senior Adult Members
for their contributions, not only to this book
but for their wonderful Christian example.*

*Brookford Baptist Church has a long history filled with many wonderful memories of "Days Gone By". Please join us as we take a look back over the past ninety years and begin looking towards our future. A future dedicated to serving the Lord in the Brookford Community and beyond.*

*It all began in 1907. The First Baptist Church in Hickory decided to sponsor a mission church in the Brookford Community. On April 25, 1907 the founding document of Brookford Baptist Church was signed.*

*The following is a partial list of the founding members. These few men and women were the beginning of a great tradition of dedicated people who would serve the Brookford Community for many years.*

| | |
|---|---|
| *C.M. Bright* | *Mrs. Mary Lisk* |
| *Dora Bright* | *Maude Bright* |
| *Jessie Burch* | *C.M. Childress* |
| *Alice Childress* | *Mrs. Laverne Foster* |
| *Mrs. Martha Janes* | *M.L. Sherrill* |
| *Mrs. Maggie Sherrill* | *Mrs. Mary Steel* |

*Our first pastor was C.M. Robinson. E.M. Childress and M.L. Sherrill were the first deacons of Brookford Baptist.*

*On August 5, 1914 during the regular business meeting a committee was formed to look after delinquent members to find out why they were not coming to church. The committee would visit these delinquent members and if "no good reason" could be given for their absence, they would be "turned out" for several reasons such as drinking, gossiping, not paying tithes, or for not attending services. Once the committee met with you, you would be given the opportunity to be "restored" to fellowship of the church. The only way you could be "restored" however, was to confess your transgression before the church and ask forgiveness. If you did not confess your name would be stricken from the record book.*

*On June 12, 1916 in another business meeting all offices were declared vacant including the pastor. No one is sure why, but during this meeting the pastor and deacons were reinstated along with all the other officers of the church.*

*Sometime in 1922 the Baraca Class appointed a committee to build a new addition to the church for Sunday School classes. This addition was completed in 1927.*

*Occasionally, something unusual would happen during morning worship. One such experience was when the KKK came to visit. They marched silently down the aisle until the leader reached the pulpit. Once there, he presented Pastor Boggs with a letter and packet. Pastor Boggs read the letter then opened the packet to find $50.00. After he "thanked them fully" they marched out as quietly as they had entered.*

*It is important to remember this bit of history because in 1928 Rev. W.C. Laney would arrive and just ten short years later would begin having inter-racial fellowship meetings here at Brookford Baptist.*

*W.C. Laney became pastor here in 1928 and served until his death in 1976. During these years at Brookford, members were taught many things but the two things most remembered were that all races were equal in God's sight and missions should be our top priority.*

*Rev. Laney would practice exactly what he preached, sometimes not taking a salary so that his pay could go towards missions. Even during the Depression the members of Brookford Baptist were told to give. If they purchased a "Dope" they should give the nickel it cost to missions. His philosophy would make Brookford Baptist known as one of the most mission minded churches in North Carolina. The Biblical Recorder published an article in 1972 where it stated that Brookford Baptist gave more per member to missions than any other church in North Carolina.*

*Probably one of the more controversial things Rev. Laney taught was that all races were equal. After a visit to Lincolnton, he began talking to Herbert Baucom about having a study course and inviting Blacks and Indians. Each year there would be minister's conferences in which several pastors from all over the area would get together to pray and study. Things went slow at first but Mr. Laney did not give up and before long Blacks and Indians began coming to Brookford Baptist for services as well.*

*All during the 1930's there would be great revivals. During which it would not be uncommon for 30 to 40 people to come to know the Lord. Due to the sheer number most people would be baptized all at once. On one of these occasions there were 98 baptized in one day. Some of these baptized that day are listed below:*

| | | |
|---|---|---|
| Fred Copas | Rosa Lee Copas | Homer Deese |
| Gaine L. Deese | L.M. Funderburke | Buelah Fox |
| Sudie Gurley | Alice Hollar | Lillian Isenhour |
| Shelly Johnson | Bonnie Keller | Melvin Lowman |
| Ethel Mitchell | Margie Price | Hugh Pope |
| Lillian Pope | Sue Reese | Ed Reinhardt |
| Archie Simpson | Ernest Spenser | Jim Thompson |
| Mrs. Jim Thompson | Elmer Waters | Henry Wilson |
| Margie Zimmerman | | |

*On July 18, 1936 it was suggested that we change the way we receive offering from passing around baskets to the more biblical way of bringing them to the altar. We continue to collect the offerings this way today.*

*During a business meeting on November 11, 1944, R.S. Bolick suggested we begin bringing material offerings on Sunday and Wednesday nights for whatever use the church may have. This was seconded by H.F. Wallace. Material offerings are still given today.*

*On March 17, 1945, R.S. Bolick made a motion that we form a committee to build a new pulpit and baptismal pool.*

*July 26, 1947 was the day B.B. Bishop made the motion that J.W. Laney be granted a license to preach.*

*In a regular business meeting on August 18, 1954, R.S. Bolick made a motion that we purchase 55 acres of land in Catawba. Mrs. H.F. Wallace seconded the motion. The church hopes to sell this property with proceeds going towards the purchase of new facilities.*

*During all this, Rev. Laney continued to preach about race relations. On the next few pages you will see photos of the fellowship meals everyone enjoyed.*

W.C. LANEY AND HIS WORK

MINISTER'S CONFERENCE

Names of some of those pictured:
- Mr. Wilson
- Mr. Brown
- J.J. Alexander
- Luis Ludland
- Dr. Wesley Grant
- Ben Bushy Head
- Mrs. W.C. Laney
- Sam Townsend
- Rev. Laney
- Rev. F.D. Battle
- Marion Parker
- Walking Stick
- East Side George
- Dr. McGee

# BROOKFORD BAPTIST CHURCH

## SUNDAY, MARCH 8, 1953

# Myrtle Hunt Scrapbook

## Killed

CLIFFORD ROSCOE HEFFNER

# SOLDIER IS HIT BY PROPELLER OF WARPLANE

### Local Mechanic Has Accident At Ark. Air Base

Private Clifford Roscoe Heffner, thirty-two, formerly of Brookford, was struck and fatally injured by a propeller of a plane on which he was working Tuesday at the Newport, Ark., air base.

He is survived by his wife, Mrs. Maude Simpson Heffner of Brookford; his parents, Mr. and Mrs. Clayton Heffner of Hillsboro; two sisters, Hazel and Ruth Heffner of Hillsboro; and four brothers, Adolphus Heffner, who is in the Marines, and James, Harley and Butler Heffner of Hillsboro.

Heffner, a mechanic, had been in the army four months. After spending three months at the Army Flying school in Columbus, Miss., he was transferred to the Newport base a month ago.

Funeral arrangements were incomplete today pending arrival of the body. Mrs. Heffner was notified of her husband's death Tuesday night in a telegram from the War department.

## Instructor

R. W. CARTIER

# BAND DIRECTOR CALLED TO U. S. GLIDER SCHOOL

### Given Leave For Duration; Goes To Arizona

R. W. Cartier, director of the Hickory School Band for the past two years, has been ordered to report as an instructor at the U. S. Army Glider School, at Wickenburg, Ariz.

Mr. Cartier, who holds a commission as a First Lieutenant in the Civilian Air Patrol, will leave Wednesday by automobile, and is due to report in Arizona on Sunday.

The Hickory school board has granted Director Cartier a leave for the duration of the war, and it has been decided that arrangements will be made to keep the band functioning under a temporary director.

Mrs. Cartier, who is a teacher in the Granite Falls schools, will remain here for the coming four months, before joining her husband.

Director Cartier came to Hickory in the Summer of 1940, and organized the local school band that Fall. Since that time the musical organization has won considerable Statewide fame and scores of boys and girls have received instructions as members.

Mr. Cartier was a charter member of the Civilian Air Patrol which was organized here in the Fall of 1941. He was made a Lieutenant last August.

# Open Forum

Contributions to this column must be signed with the full name of the author, concern matters of public interest and be limited to not more than 800 words.

## PRIVATE'S LAST LETTER

EDITOR'S NOTE: The following letter, re-copied and brought to The Record by A. O. Hefner, superintendent at the Brookford Mills, was written by the late Private Roscoe Hefner shortly before he volunteered for the army four months ago. Hefner, thirty-two, was struck by an airplane propeller and killed at the Army Air Base, Newport, Ark., Feb. 9.

"Maud Simpson Hefner,
"Brookford, N. C.
"U. S. A.
"To my friends—

"I am fully determined to join the army. There is nothing else for me to do. My mind is made up and I will not change it. Just as well be me as some one else.

"I have so much at home to love. A wonderful, dear wife—the sweetest woman I have known or ever will know. A lovely and cozy home and the very best of friends and loved ones. God has blessed me so much in my life, I have all these blessings in life. Yes, you see I don't want to go but that is selfish of me. All this is my reason for going. I want to do my bit so others tomorow can live happy American lives as I have lived. If I have all this to live for, I have this to fight for. I will try to be a good soldier as you all have been good friends to me. May we all strive to be worthy of this blessed country that God has blessed us with.

"We all have gotten along so wonderfully together. Oh! Sometimes I as well as you have growled or grumbled just a little. Always, though, you have forgiven me. I admire and love all for the pleasant days we have been together, with regret in our hearts for having to fight other human beings. Yet we know we must fight with all the strength we have in order to hold our freedom. To grumble, dispute, express our opinion, go where we please, and obey laws which are not hard for a good man to obey; and, last but first, go to church where we please and worship God as we please. But it seems most of us are not pleased so much in worshiping God. We are all expecting too much in this life that has been blessed by our wonderful Master without so much as giving Him a thought even though our knees should bend down in prayer. "My knees, where they are supposed to bend down, are just a little rusty. Are yours?

"What our blessed country stands for is right. Let's all do right and fight and work for the rights our ancestors didn't have given to them on a silver platter.

"So long, I hope to see you all soon

—"C. R. HEFNER."

## Graduates

Corporal Homer Sumter, above, former Hickory policeman, has graduated from the army's amphibious vehicle training school at the Charleston port of embarkation, Moultrieville, S. C. Mrs. Sumter, who is continuing to make her home here, attended the graduation, the program for which was as follows: Review of troops by Brigadier General James T. Duke; remarks by Colonel Theodore L. Dunn; introduction of General Duke by Colonel Dunn; remarks by General Duke; an inspection of the school facilities by Colonel Dunn, accompanied by General Duke and party; entry march at pavillion; "National Emblem" by band; address by Major W. E. Schoenfeld; "Star Spangled Banner" by band; and presentation of certificates of graduation by First Lieutenant T. R. Wilkinson.

## Ski Soldier

Pfc. John F. Starnes, U. S. Army ski troops, stationed at Camp Hale, Colo., doesn't mind telling the world that he thinks his job is swell. He is now on a furlough with his parents, Mr. and Mrs. G. F. Starnes of Hickory, Route One, and his wife. When he returns to his post shortly he expects to find the ground covered with snow. Then it will be skiing time again for him. Pfc. Starnes has been in the service for thirty months. Last Winter a Hollywood studio made a short subject at Camp Hale, "Mountain Fighters," in which his company had a part, he said.

## Leave Ends

Private First Class Calvin G. Kirby, above, has returned to duty after spending a ten-day furlough in Hickory with his wife and with friends. He has been in service for eleven months.

## 4 Sons, 6 Brothers In Service

MRS. C. W. WARREN

SGT. AARON WARREN

OFFICER PRESTON WARREN

SEAMAN DEWEY WARREN

PARATROOPER CARL WARREN

### MILL EMPLOYE AT BROOKFORD GOING ALL-OUT

#### Brother Killed In Jap Sneak Attack On Pearl Harbor

Mrs. C. W. Warren, forty-two, of Brookford, oldest sister of Wilson W. Hilton, Catawba county youth who lost his life in the treacherous Jap attack on Pearl Harbor December 7, 1941, has four sons, five other brothers, and one son-in-law in the armed forces of the United States.

Her sons are: Sergeant Aaron (Dock) Warren, 22, with the army somewhere in England; Second Class Petty Officer Preston E. Warren, twenty-six, in the navy's school at Navy Yard, S. C.; First Class Seaman Dewey W. Warren, sixteen, now on sea duty with the navy; and Carl W. War-

### Sheridan

Private Roy P. (Duck) Lafon, above, stationed at Fort Sheridan, Ill., is the son of Mr. and Mrs. Pink Lafon, of the Springs Road section. His address is Hq. Btry. 2nd Bn., 516 C.A. (A.A.) Bldg. 644 Fort Sheridan, Ill. He asks his many friends to write to him.

### Aberdeen

Pvt. Terrell C. Stepp, above, of Brookford, is taking a technical course now at Aberdeen Proving Grounds, Md. A son of Mr. and Mrs. J. J. Stepp of Brookford, he has been in the army for three months and recently completed his basic training.

### Missing

LT. GLENN ZERDEN

## PARENTS GET GRIM MESSAGE FROM WAR DEPT.

### Son Lost In Action Off U.S. Coast February 2

Lieutenant Glenn Zerden, twenty-four, has been reported missing in action off the North American coast since February 2, the War department notified his parents, Mr. and Mrs. L. E. Zerden of Hickory, today.

No further details were given in today's grim message but it was stated that additional information would be relayed to the family when received by the War department.

The officer, who visited here about three weeks ago, had been stationed near Boston, Mass.

Young Zerden graduated from Hickory High school in 1934, attended Lenoir Rhyne college here for a year, and then took several special courses at the University of North Carolina at Chapel Hill. Shortly before he went into the army, he took a course in aircraft inspection at State college in Raleigh.

He entered the army a year ago last January 27 and received his second lieutenant's commission in Miami, Fla., last October. A brother, Marvin, went to the army three weeks ago and is now stationed at Camp Edwards, Mass.

Lieutenant Zerden's father is one of the pioneer merchants of Hickory and while not in school the youth worked in the store, which is on Union Square. He was aggressive and had made a reputation for himself as a very promising young merchant.

### In Africa

Pvt. Doyle Fox, U. S. Army, above, son of Mrs. L. N. Fox of Brookford, now is in North Africa, according to information received by his mother. In his letter home, Pvt. Fox remarked that he was in "pretty country" and that he liked it a lot better than Ireland, England and Scotland, where he has been in past months. Pvt. Fox has a brother, Pvt. Sheridan Fox, U.S. Army, who is stationed at Camp Gordon, Ga.

### Alaska

Telis Burley Fox, seaman second class, son of Mr. and Mrs. B. A. Fox, Route Three Hickory, has been transferred to Dutch Harbor, Alaska, from Bremerton, Wash. He is in training for submarine duty, and has been in service since September, 1942.

## SAILOR AIDING NORTH AFRICA DRIVE IS HOME

### Has One Suit Saved From Davy Jones' Locker

Howard O'Neill Glass, eighteen, one of three Brookford brothers in the U. S. Navy, has arrived home from the North Africa campaign wearing the only suit he managed to save from Davy Jones' locker.

The youth did not suffer a scratch in the big four-day drive ashore on the North African coast but he had a close shave while at mess one day.

He's none the worse for his experience, however, and is ready for more action.

"I really like the navy now," he commented with a broad smile of boyish enthusiasm.

His brothers in the navy are: William, air squadron, Quonset Point, R. I., and Joseph, who has not been heard from in the last four weeks.

**Mother Would Like To Go**

"We're just a navy family," declared their mother, Mrs. Livie Glass of Brookford. "I'd be in there, too, if I could, and so would my other three sons and one daughter."

Her oldest son, Leon O. Glass, is married and in defense work in Atlanta, Ga., and the other two are too young yet for service, she explained. John D. is fifteen and Rudolph is thirteen.

Rudolph, who like his older brothers can swim a mile in the Brookford Mills' pond with ease, according to his mother, has vowed to enlist in the navy at the first and earliest opportunity.

**"Always Paddleducks"**

"All of them including my daughter, Mrs. Mildred Brogdon of Lexington, have always been pad-
(Continued on Page 2)

dleducks," Mrs. Glass commented proudly.

"Their hobby is swimming."

Mrs. Brogdon, who married a former sailor, doesn't think its fair at all that she can't enlist in the navy and serve with her brothers, the Brookford woman said.

"Being the only daughter in the family, she has just been one of the boys all her life and naturally wishes she could be with them in the navy," Mrs. Glass explained.

Mrs. Brogdon's husband has been trying to return to service, it is said, but has been unable to do so as yet because he lost a toe while in the navy before.

**"Got Pretty Hot"**

Asked about the action in North Africa, Howard, who looks at least three years younger than eighteen, replied, "It got pretty hot over there, you know."

He entered service last July 4 and the trip to North Africa was his first voyage on the high seas. He's a second class seaman now but hopes to be promoted to first when his thirty-day furlough is up.

"The whole crew of our ship got thirty-day furloughs, that is, what part got to come back," he said.

Incidentally, Howard was on the same ship as V. B. Gallemore, Jr., twenty-year-old Hickory youth who arrived home Sunday to spend a thirty-day furlough.

## Sixth

Norman Hilton, above, is the sixth son of Mr. and Mrs. A. W. Hilton of Vale and Banoak section to enter the armed forces. He volunteered for service in the U. S. Navy the first of October and completed his boot training in Norfolk, Va., November 1. Following an eight-day furlough spent with his parents he returned to Norfolk and at present is on sea duty. One of the Hilton brothers, Wilson, was killed at Pearl Harbor last December 7. The other four in service are: Private First Class Boyce Shuford Hilton, Battery D, 603rd. C.A. (AA), Burbank, Calif.; Staff Sergeant Amos D. Hilton, Goodfellow Field, 70th. Service squadron, San Angelo, Texas; Corporal Paul W. Hilton, Utilities Detachment, Engineers service, APO 845, care postmaster New York City; and Russell Hilton of the U. S. Coast Guard. Norman's address is Tenth division...

## Returns

Private Stewart Leonard, above, son of Mr. and Mrs. B. P. Leonard of Brookford, has returned to the Curtis-Wright Service school, Buffalo, N. Y., after spending a five-day furlough with his parents and wife, the former Miss Helen Simpson of Brookford. He has been in the army seven and one-half months.

## Furlough

John Cecil Stepp, above, of Brookford has been spending an eight-day furlough with his wife and mother, Mrs. Beula Stepp, after completing his "boot" training at Great Lakes, Ill.

## Wounded

Corporal Williard C. Hendrix, above, United States marine from Rhodhiss, has been reported wounded "somewhere in the Pacific," by the Navy department. Young Hendrix, a son of Mr. and Mrs. Luther T. Hendrix of Rhodhiss, has been in service for about two years. He was first sent to Parris Island, S. C., then to Cuba, and from there back to New River, N. C., Marine base. After a furlough last May, he was sent to duty "somewhere in the Pacific," according to his father.

## Soldier, Sailor Brothers

**JACK V. FRYE**    **TELLAS FRYE**

Mr. and Mrs. D. K. Frye of 2901 Ninth avenue, Hickory, have two sons in the armed forces. Jack is a second class petty officer in the U. S. Navy and Tellas is a private in the U. S. Army. Jack recently arrived home on a ten-day leave after participating in the French Morocco campaign. Upon his return to duty, he will be a diesel engine instructor in Norfolk, Va. Tellas is in the Seventy-eighth Quartermaster company at Camp Butner, Durham.

## Lieutenant

First Lieutenant Joe H. Freeman, above, of the air corps, is stationed at Westover Field, Mass., where he is flight commander in a fighter squadron. Lieut. Freeman has many friends in the Hickory area inasmuch as he was paymaster at the Brookford Mills when he joined the colors in September, 1941. He is a very popular and capable young man, according to M. A. Bolick, who was his boss at the mills. Joe, who is the son of Mr. and Mrs. Bert Freeman, of Weatherford, Texas, came here in 1939 to visit his aunt, Mrs. J. J. Stepp, and secured the Brookford job. Mrs. Stepp is a sister of Joe's father and had visited in Texas previous to the decision of her nephew to try his fortunes in Hick-

## Promoted

Elmer H. Bowman, above, who is stationed at the Naval Base Air Station at Jacksonville, Fla., was recently promoted to Aviation Ordnance Mate, third class. Petty Officer Bowman has been in the Navy eight months. He is a son of Mr. and Mrs. George Bowman, and is married to the former Miss Alice Hyder, of Hickory. He is a brother of Lieut. Charles Bowman, an American aviator who has distinguished himself in service in the Philippines and the South Pacific.

## Great Lakes

Seaman Second Class Clarence Sparks, above, has returned to Great Lakes, Ill., after a brief visit with his family on Ninth avenue. He wants his friends here to write him. The son of Mrs. Cora Sparks of Hickory, he has this address: O.G.U., S.S.S., Co. 1678, Camp Bronson, U.S.N.T.S., Great Lakes, Ill.

## Corporal

Corporal Malcolm Keever, above, recently was promoted to the rank of corporal in the army air corps at Selman Field, Monroe, La. He is the son of Mr. and Mrs. T. S. Keever of Fifteenth street.

## Hickory Men In Wyoming

The five soldiers pictured above are Hickory men enjoying a reunion at Fort Francis Warren at Cheyenne, Wyoming, where they were all stationed for a while. Left to right, they are: Tellas Frye, Harry Bowman, Louis Lavitt, and Efird Yoder, standing, and Jimmie Wentz, kneeling. All were sent to Wyoming about the same time, a couple of months ago, but only three are still there, according to information given The Record today. Wentz was transferred this week to Fort Lewis, Washington, and Frye is now at Camp Butner, Durham.

## McCoy

Private Thomas Workman, above, son of D. V. Workman, Brookford, is stationed with Company G, Ninth Infantry, Camp McCoy, Wis. He has been in the army since September 26.

## Colorado

John F. Starnes, above, has returned to his post at Fort Bragg after spending a ten-day furlough here with Mrs. Starnes. Attached to the 601st Field Artillery, he expects to be transferred this week to Colorado Springs, Colo., for special training in mountain fighting. He was graduated last Fall with a Senior diploma from the veterinary school for enlisted men at Washington, D. C. His parents are Mr. and Mrs. G. F. Starnes of Hickory.

## Only 15

Leroy Miller, Jr., above, fifteen-year-old Hickory boy, has just completed his boot training at the U. S. Navy Training Base at Great Lakes, Ill. He gave his age as seventeen when he enlisted five weeks ago. Charles Travis of Hickory, now in naval training in Norfolk, Va., is said to be only fourteen years old.

## Pacific

Winfred T. Lowman, above, former employe of the Brookford Mill, now in the navy, has been transferred from Norfolk to a Pacific port. His address is: "Winfred T. Lowman, Seaman second class, Navy 8170, Fleet Postoffice, San Francisco." He recently spent a five-day leave at Brookford with Mrs. Lowman and their two children.

## Wounded

Private First Class Milford L. Deitz, above, has been wounded in action overseas, according to a message which his wife, the former Miss Margaret Winstead, has just received. The government message stated that Private Deitz had been injured in the performance of duty in the service of his country and requested that the name of his ship and his station be kept secret. In the U. S. Marine corps for the past three years, Deitz is a son of Mr. and Mrs. Fred Deitz of Hickory. His wife is now residing with her mother in Brookford.

## 3 Brookford Brothers In Navy

HOWARD O'NEILL GLASS     WILLIAM GLASS     JOSEPH GLASS

## Pals

Here's an unusual photograph of three Hickory area service men who happened to come home on leave at the same time. Charles Adams, lower left, son of T. C. Adams, spent an eight day leave with his wife and family while Leroy Donkle, lower right, son of Mrs. Flora Donkle, spent eight days with his mother and friends. Charles and Leroy joined the navy in September and were first trained at Great Lakes, Ill. They have been transferred to San Francisco, Calif. Clyde Hefner, standing behind them in the picture, is a soldier at Fort Bragg. He is the son of Mr. and Mrs. L. M. Hefner.

## At Norfolk

Everette Pruitt, son of Mr. and Mrs. S. P. Pruitt of Brookford, is stationed at Norfolk, Va. He enlisted in the navy in September.

## At Norfolk

James Cloninger, above, has returned to Norfolk, Va., after spending a brief leave with his wife, children, and parents, Mr. and Mrs. T. M. Cloninger of Brookford. He joined the navy about six weeks ago.

## Brothers In Navy

**CARL SCRONCE**     **EARL SCRONCE**

Carl and Earl Scronce, sons of Mr. and Mrs. Mike Scronce of Brookford, recently spent furloughs at home with their wives. Both joined the navy at the same time, about six weeks ago, and both are stationed at Norfolk, Va.

## 3 Brothers In Army; One Overseas

**PAUL PRUITT** — **ROSCOE PRUITT** — **BUCK PRUITT**

Mrs. Zella Pruitt, who lives near Brookford, has three sons in the army, one of them overseas and the others expected to go before long. Buck, thirty-one, is in Ireland; Paul, twenty-two, in California; and Roscoe, thirty-four, has been transferred from Oakland, Calif., to an undisclosed location in the East.

## 2 Sons-In-Law In Service

**HARRY VERVOORT** — **L. P. TUCK**

Pictured above are two sons-in-law of Mrs. John Murphy of Hickory who are serving in their country's armed forces. Private Tuck has been in the army since March 17, 1942, and is stationed at the Sarasota Air base, Sarasota, Fla. Vervoort, whose family lives here, volunteered for Naval service last August 7. He completed his "boot" training at Norfolk, Va., and is now in a school for machinists at Richmond.

## Family Trio In Service

**ALEX PROPST**
Chief Petty Officer Alex Propst, former teacher and coach at the Mountain View High school near Hickory, is pictured above with a brother and a brother-in-law, both of whom are in the service. Mr.

**TOM H. PROPST**
Propst, who was scheduled to be transferred from San Diego, Calif., to Idaho August 22 as company commander to train new recruits, is pictured in the center, Tom H. Propst, his brother, at the left, and Russell Huffman, his brother-in-

**RUSSELL HUFFMAN**
law at the right. Mr. Huffman is thought to have sailed for a foreign field and Tom is at Camp Walters, Texas. Tom and Alex are sons of Mrs. F. L. Propst of the Propst Crossroads community near Hickory.

## Canal Zone

Pfc. Ralph F. Fisher, above, son of Mr. and Mrs. P. G. Fisher of Brookford, enlisted in the army August 20, 1941. He was stationed at Camp Croft, S. C., until December 5, when he sailed for the Panama Canal Zone. Ralph writes that he likes the army fine, although things are different there. His address is Number 34119296 APO 827, c/o Postmaster, New Orleans, La.

Guy Jolley, formerly of Brookford, is in the U. S. Navy radio school at Miami, Fla.

**SERGEANT FRANK STACK**
And His Daughter
**LINDA MARIE STACK**

## Returns

**ELVIN REINHARDT**

After thirteen months at a secret base somewhere in the South Pacific, T-5 Elvin Reinhardt has returned to his home in Hickory.

Elvin, a son of Mrs. R. L. Reinhardt of Hickory, was given a C.D.D. discharge at an army hospital in Temple, Texas, recently and arrived here late Tuesday.

He is unable to name the last place he was stationed with the
(Continued on Page 10)

### RETURNS
(Continued from Page 1)

field artillery in the South Pacific but stated he spent some time in the Fiji Islands, where he found the climate quite agreeable.

Since his induction in the army two years and eight months ago, young Reinhardt has traveled approximately 20,000 miles but found no place more to his liking than North Carolina, especially the Hickory area, he said today.

He received The Record during his stay in the South Pacific and enjoyed it to the utmost, he commented today, although the copies were usually a couple of months old.

"They usually reached me ten and fifteen copies at a time and I wanted to read them all at once," he said today.

He said his companions also liked The Record, particularly a boy from California.

"I want to thank the Hickory people for all the letters and Christmas cards they wrote me while I was away," Elvin told The Record today, adding:

"The main thing the boys appreciate in the war theatres is mail."

Elvin spent some time in a hospital in New Zealand before returning to the States last August 31 and was surprised but delighted to find a copy of The Record in the library there.

## Old Tar

Hugh F. Reinheart, Jr., above, man second class, recently spent a short leave with his mother, Mrs. Hugh Reinheart of Brookford, after completing his boot training at Great Lakes, Ill. He entered the navy July 5, after graduating from Hickory High school in June. His address is: R. S.—P.S.N.Y., Bremerton, Washington.

## In Texas

Jay S. McDaniel, above, Aviation Mechanic's Mate, third class, U.S. N. R., recently spent a ten day leave with his brother, George McDaniel, of Ninth avenue. He took his basic training at Norfolk, Va., last August, and entered Aviation Mechanics school at the Naval Air Technical Training Center at Jacksonville, Fla., last November. He was graduated there in May, 1943, sent to the Naval air station at Corpus Christi, Texas, where he is now stationed, and promoted to first flight engineer.

## Three Brookford Brothers In Service

**HOWARD HEFNER** — **JOE HEFNER** — **CLYDE HEFNER**

Mr. and Mrs. L. M. Hefner of Brookford are the proud parents of the three young men pictured above, all in the service. Howard, who joined the navy last December, is first class fireman on the U.S.S. Osprey. Joe, who also joined the navy in December, is on a submarine, the U.S.S. S-31. Clyde, drafted last March, is in the Eighty-second Division at Camp Claiborne, La. Howard and Clyde have both been home on recent furloughs, but Joe has not come home yet. His parents are hoping to see him soon.

## Fifth — Norfolk

**WILSON W. HILTON**
**LOST IN ACTION AT PEARL HARBOR**

Russell L. Hilton, above, a member of the U. S. Coast Guard, is a fifth son of Mr. and Mrs. A. W. Hilton, of Bandys township, Catawba county, to participate in the present World war. First Class Gunner's Mate Wilson Hilton, on duty aboard the U. S. Battleship Arizona, made the supreme sacrifice at Pearl Harbor. Paul W. Hilton is stationed at Puerto Rico. Amos D. Hilton is stationed at San Angelo, Texas. Shuford Hilton's address is Terminal Island, California. Russell Hilton was a policeman in Baltimore for fourteen years and volunteered in July. He is thirty-nine and his wife was Miss Florence Penner, of Vale. They have two children.

CATAWBA, Sept. 16.—Third Class Petty Officer Osborn Denford Witherspoon, above, returned to Norfolk Sunday after a five-day furlough spent here with his father, Clarence Witherspoon and family on Highway No. 10, West of Catawba. He was graduated from Catawba High school in 1940, and enlisted in the U. S. Navy in December, 1941. He has spent all the time since enlistment at Norfolk, and Cherry Point. He has two sisters, Miss Inez Witherspoon, Catawba and Miss Florence Lee Witherspoon of Thomasville. He is known to his friends as "O. D."

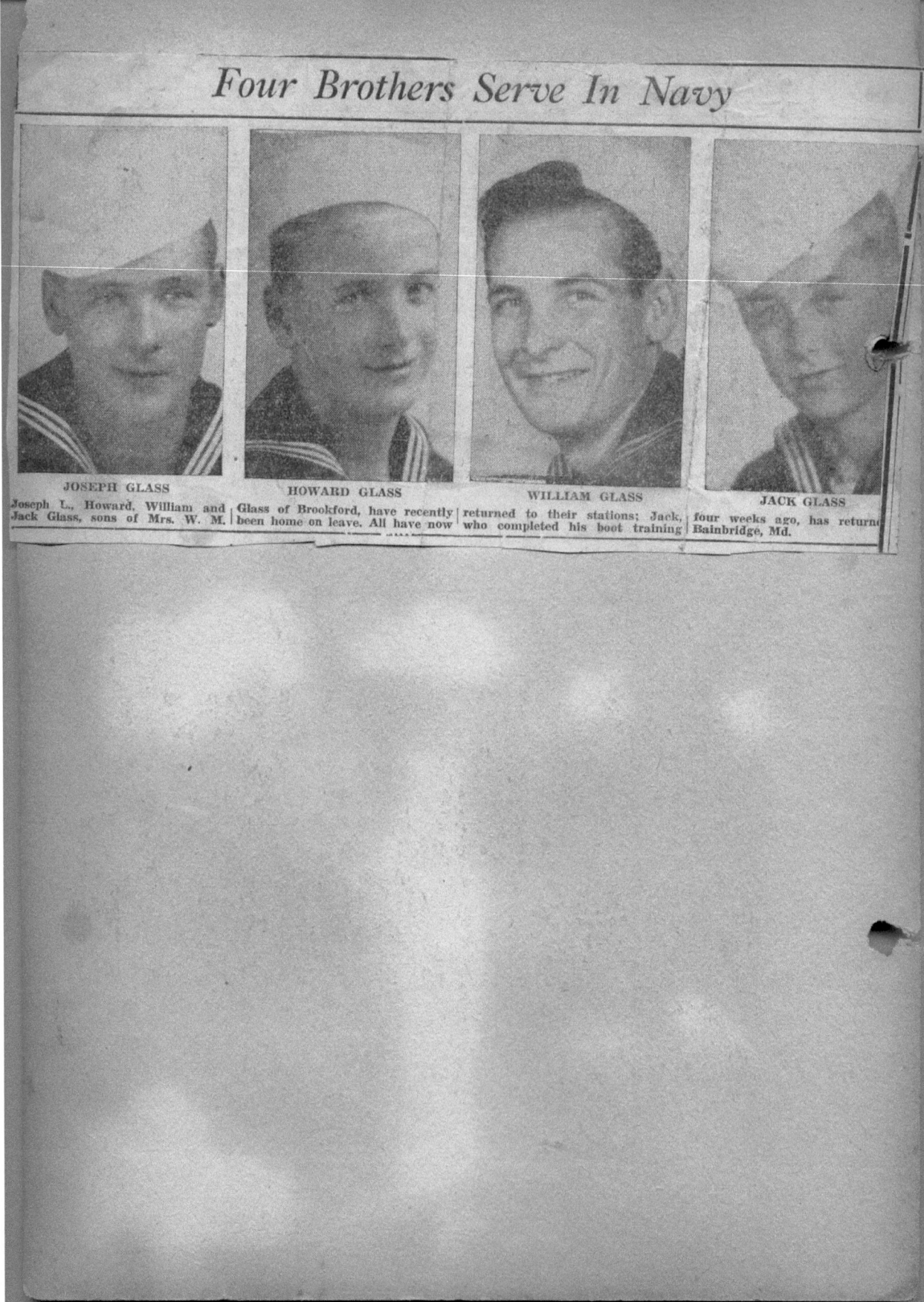

## Four Brothers Serve In Navy

**JOSEPH GLASS** — **HOWARD GLASS** — **WILLIAM GLASS** — **JACK GLASS**

Joseph L., Howard, William and Jack Glass, sons of Mrs. W. M. Glass of Brookford, have recently been home on leave. All have now returned to their stations; Jack, who completed his boot training four weeks ago, has returned Bainbridge, Md.

## On Leave

Morris Lee Newton, above, aviation radioman, third class, in the Navy, is home on leave, after a year and a half of training. A son of Mr. and Mrs. D. W. Newton of Hickory, he is to leave next Monday to report at Seattle, Wash. The young Hickory man, formerly payroll clerk at the Brookford Mills office, has been assigned to a dive bomber squadron, as radioman and gunner. The Newtons have another son in service, Sergeant Robert James Newton, a marine and a veteran of the Guadalcanal campaign. Following the Solomons campaign, he was sent to Australia along with other marines for a recuperation period. Sgt. Newton has been in service for the past two years.

## Local Soldier And Officer Meet At North Africa Base

After almost a year overseas, Joe Donkel, soldier son of Mrs. F. L. Donkel of Hickory, recently met for the first time someone from home, Lieutenant Conway Yost.

Joe wrote that he had gone to a replacement center in North Africa to set up a public address system when he met Lieutenant Yost.

"It was the surprise of my life," Joe told his mother.

"Were we glad to see each other! We didn't lose any time in starting talking about home and swapping what little news we knew."

In the same letter, Joe stated that it was hot as H— at his post and that flies weren't making things any better.

"We can still enjoy the beach most every day, though, thank the Lord.

"Mom, we have exercise every morning before it gets too hot, which, together with swimming, baseball, etc., keeps me in tip-top shape. I have a good sun tan, too.

"Gee, bet you wouldn't even know me. Of course you would; I haven't changed one bit. I haven't weighed since I left the states, but I'd say I weigh about 170. My greatest ambition is to come back home with a healthy body." Joe was an athlete at Hickory High school.

JOE DONKEL

"Just think, August 6 and I will have been overseas one whole year," he said. "Seems like ten to me. Oh well, I expect to be home in another ten months."

## In Utah

Sgt. Thomas B. Walker, above, son of S. M. Walker of Hickory, Route One, has returned to the Army Air Base at Salt Lake City, Utah, after spending a ten day leave here with his wife. Sgt. Walker took his basic training at Keesler Field, Miss., and attended B-24 Airplane Mechanic's Specialist school there. He was transferred to Flexible Gunnery school at Laredo, Texas, and upon his graduation there was assigned to a permanent squadron at Salt Lake City. He has been in service since December 20, 1942.

## Captain

JOHN D. BARRINGER

Chaplain John D. Barringer, former pastor of Zion Lutheran church, South of Hickory, has been promoted to the rank of captain at Keesler Field, Miss.

He was commissioned a lieutenant and attended the army chaplains' school at Harvard university in October, 1942. Since that time he has been stationed at Keesler Field, where the Army Air Forces Technical Training Command is training ground crews to service B-24 Liberator bombers.

Chaplain Barringer, who was graduated from Lenoir Rhyne college six years ago, is the son of Mr. and Mrs. Daniel L. Barringer of Mount Pleasant.

# 3 Of Family Are In North Africa

**JAMES E. KELLER**

**MARSHALL KELLER**

**EARL RANDLE**

The two brothers and their brother-in-law pictured above are all three in Africa. Corporal Marshall Keller was wounded slightly in action in North Africa but is back on duty now, according to a message received by his parents, Mr. and Mrs. M. G. Keller, of Brookford. Pvt. James E. Keller is also in North Africa. The brothers have been in the army for about five years and were at Pearl Harbor, when the Japs attacked there December 7, 1941. They spent about three years in Hawaii and were in the same company during that time. Their father is a veteran of World War No. I, during which he was wounded in France. A younger brother, Marvin G. Keller, Jr., was in the group of eighteen-year-olds called recently for army service. He is at Fort Leonard Wood, Mo. The Kellers have two other sons, Paul and Arthur, but they are too young for army service. Randle is at a naval base in West Africa. He has been in the Navy for several months. His wife is the former Miss Edith Keller.

## Waiting

Staff Sgt. James E. Deese, above, son of Julius E. Deese of Hickory, Route Three, is awaiting ship for service abroad. Sgt. Deese volunteered for army service May 20, 1941, and has been stationed at Camp Croft, S. C., for the last several months. He has three brothers in the army, and visited relatives here recently on a ten-day furlough.

## California

Sergeat Paul S. Daye, above, returned recently to Camp Cooke, Calif., after spending a furlough here with his father, C. D. Daye. Sgt. Daye joined the army last August. His address at present is: U. S. Army, Btry. D 202nd, A.A.A.-AW. Bn., Camp Cooke, Calif, Unit No 2.

## In Texas

Private William H. Herman, above, returned last week to Camp Maxey, Texas., after spending a nine-day furlough here with his wife, their son, Danny, and his parents, Mr. and Mrs. Sam F. Herman. It was his first furlough home since he was inducted into the army last January. He was on desert maneuvers in California before being moved to Camp Maxey.

## Air Corps

Technical Sergeant George E. Beaman, above, returned Sunday to Barksdale Field, Schrevesport, La. after a three-day visit with his father, L. R. Beaman of Brookford Mills. Beaman enlisted as a mechanic in the air corps when he was eighteen years old and has been in service for fifteen months. Sent first to Jackson, Miss, he was ordered to school in Dallas, Texas. From there he was transferred to San Francisco, Calif., and then ordered to report to Fairfield, Ohio.

## Secret Post

Sergeant Joe Donkel, above, son of Mrs. F. L. Donkel of Hickory, has arrived safely at an undisclosed destination, according to the latest message received here.

## Brothers In Service

**WALLACE BEAMON**

**GEORGE BEAMON**

These two young men, sons of Mr. and Mrs. L. R. Beamon of Brookford have had parallel experiences since joining the army June 2, 1941. Both were sent to the Jackson Air Base at Jackson, Miss., for their initial training. For further instruction they were sent to Texas, Wallace to Hix Field at Fort Worth and George to Love Field at Dallas. And now they have both been sent "somewhere on the West coast," their parents have been notified. Wallace received his pilot's license at Lenoir Rhyne college and George had just finished Brookford High school when he entered the service.

## Lieutenant

**ADRIAN SHUFORD, JR.**

NEWTON, July 16.—Adrian Shuford, Jr., Newton manufacturer and president of the Shuford National bank here, was sworn in as a naval reserve lieutenant, junior grade, in Raleigh. He has since returned home and will report for officer training August 9, at Babson Park, Mass.

The officer is a son of Mr. and Mrs. Adrian Shuford, Sr., of Conover. He and his wife have been making their home in Newton for some time.

Mrs. Shuford will remain at Newton while her husband receives his training in the supply corps. He is secretary and general manager of the Conover Knitting company and of the Warlong Glove company, besides being president of the bank.

## Missing

**PVT. TOM H. PROPST**

Mrs. Sallie F. Propst of Hickory, Route One, received a telegram from the U. S. War department today saying her son, Private Tom H. Propst, was lost in the North African area July 13.

The fateful message was received only a few minutes ahead of a V-mail letter written July 7 in which the soldier said he was well.

Pvt. Propst, thirty years old last February, had been in the army since April 14, 1942, and in North Africa since April of this year. A brother, Alex Propst, is a chief petty officer in the navy at Camp Farragut, Idaho, and a brother-in-law, Russell Huffman, is a sergeant in the army in England.

He also has two brothers Ralph and Reid Propst; and two sisters, Mrs. Russell Huffman and Mrs. Cecil Brittain all of Hickory, Route One.

Tom had received his training at Camp Wolters, Texas and Camp Edwards, Mass.

## Leave End

Pvt. Leonard Reinhardt, above, has returned to his base at Columbus, Miss., after spending a ten-day furlough with his wife and relatives. Mrs. Reinhardt will remain in Hickory until her husband is assigned to a new post.

## Home

LT. CHARLES BOWMAN

### LOCAL BOMBER PILOT RETURNS FROM PACIFIC

**Philippines, Australia Action Recalled; Brief Visit**

Lieutenant Charles Bowman, Hickory bomber pilot who flew out of the Philippines only twenty-four hours ahead of the Japs, arrived here Tuesday night to visit his parents, Mr. and Mrs. George W. Bowman.

He arrived in San Francisco several days ago but did not reach Hickory until last evening. This is the first time he has been home since shortly after his graduation from Kelly Field March 14, 1941.

Incidentally, Lieutenant Bowman was on the last plane to leave the Philippines ahead of the Japs in April 1942.

After leaving the Philippines, the Hickory pilot went to Australia and had not been heard from since last October until he telephoned his father from San Francisco
(Continued on Page 10)

With a big smile, he said, "Wonderful."

He said he had seen several Hickory boys but did not disclose more.

A brother of Charles, Elmer Bowman, is a machine gun instructor in the U. S. Navy, stationed at Jacksonville, Fla.

**ROMMEL 'ILLNESS' DOUBTED**

ALLIED HEADQUARTERS IN NORTH AFRICA, Feb. 17.—(AP)—A rumor has circulated on the Tunisian front that Marshal Rommel had become ill and had returned to Germany but competent officers at Allied headquarters viewed the report today with the greatest skepticism. They pointed out that it might have been planted by the Axis.

## Brothers In Service

RALPH J. FISHER

Mr. and Mrs. P. G. Fisher of Brookford have two sons in service, Corporal Ralph J. Fisher and Seaman Second Class Clyde M. Fisher.

Corporal Fisher entered the army August 20, 1941, and has served twenty-one months in the Panama Canal Zone. His address is: 34119296, APO 828, care of Postmaster, New

CLYDE M. FISHER

Orleans, La.

Clyde enlisted in the navy April 19, 1943, and has received his "boot" training at Bainbridge, Md. He was transferred to Boston and later to New York. His present address is Care Fleet Postmaster, New York, N. Y.

## In Utah

Cpl. Ernest Pope, thirty-two, U. S. Army, above, has returned to his base at Rendova Field, Utah, following a furlough spent at Brookford with his wife and family. He entered the armed forces ten months ago and is now serving as a gunnery instructor at the base. Cpl. Pope is a son of Mrs. W. P. Pope of Brookford.

## In Tenn.

Corporal Henry Ransom Reinhardt, above, son of Mr. and Mrs. W. D. Reinhardt of Hickory, Route One, is on maneuvers in Tennessee. He entered the Army in November, 1942. In a recent letter to his parents, he said: "I have had some of the best times in my life since I have been in the Army."

Private First Class Gordon W. Kanupp, above, has returned to Fort Jackson, S. C., after spending a seven-day furlough with his parents, Mr. and Mrs. E. W. Kanupp, Newton, Route Two.

## Oldest

Fred Warren, above, forty-four-year-old Hickory man, who has a son in Army service in Honolulu, has been drafted for military service. Mr. Warren, married for twenty-seven years, is reportedly the oldest man to be drafted so far from Hickory. He was given a ten-day furlough following his induction so he could put his business affairs in order.

## In Pacific

Corporal Adolphus Hefner, above, of Brookford and Hildebran, has seen service with the marines at Pearl Harbor, Midway and Johnson Island, and is still on duty "somewhere in the Pacific."

## Returns

Luke Heavner, above, has returned to Baltimore, Md., to resume his duties with the U. S. Navy after spending a furlough in Longview with his parents, Mr. and Mrs. H. A. Heavner. This is the young man's fifth year in the Navy. He re-enlisted after World War II broke out.

## In Africa

Pfc. Lee Roy Whitner, above, son of John E. Whitener, of Hickory, Route One, has been in the army about a year and a half and is now with Uncle Sam's expeditionary forces in North Africa. He has written home that he would like for his friends here to write him.

## Two Sons In Service

**TROY BARGER**     **CECIL BARGER**

The two sons of Mr. and Mrs. C. H. Barger of Hickory are now in the Army. Corporal Troy O. Barger is stationed at Camp Howze, Texas, and Private Cecil Barger is somewhere in the South Pacific. Corporal Troy will have been in service two years April 5, while Cecil was inducted in February, 1942. Troy's wife, the former Mrs. Arlie Bowman Wheeler of Hickory, is cashier and bookkeeper in the service club cafeteria at Camp Howze.

## Air Corps

Private Ralph Reinhardt, above, has been in the U. S. Army Air Corps since November 5, 1942. He is the son of Mr. and Mrs. Joe Reinhardt of Brookford. His address is: 20th Base Hq., AB Sq., Barracks 311, AAB, Salt Lake City, Utah.

## In Africa

Sgt. Vance Goode Smith, above, son of Mrs. A. B. Smith, of Brookford, and husband of the former Miss Ella Mae Moore, is with U. S. Expeditionary forces in North Africa. In the army for twenty-one months, he was stationed at one time in Los Angeles, Calif. He arrived in North Africa last Christmas.

## California

Private Albert J. Pope, above, son of Mrs. T. M. Pope of Hickory, has returned to Camp Cooke, Calif., after spending a ten-day furlough in Hickory. He has been in the Army since last October.

## Three Buddies In Marines

**PFC. O. M. YODER**

**PFC. C. F. WEAVER**

**PVT. TELLIS JARRETT**

Pfc. Orin M. Yoder, son of Mr. and Mrs. Guy Yoder, Hickory, Route One, and Pfc. Claude F. Weaver, son of Mr. and Mrs. Russell Weaver, also of Hickory, Route One, recently were at home on an eight-day furlough visiting their parents and friends. They left for Camp Lejeune Tuesday and expect to be transferred to some other camp soon. While the two New River Marines were home, they met one of their former buddies at Mountain View High school, Pvt. Tellis Jarrett, U.S.M.C., who is now on thirty-day furlough after being wounded in the Battle of the Solomons. Jarrett, son of Mr. and Mrs. B. M. Jarrett of Hickory, Route One, will later report to New River. Yoder and Weaver have just completed a twelve weeks' course in the Motor Transport School, consisting of automotive mechanics, at Training Center, Camp Lejeune, New River, where they received their promotion to private first class. Pfcs. Yoder and Weaver volunteered for service in the Marine Corps early last Fall and were sent to Parris Island, S. C., for their boot training. From there they went to New River. Their present address is 9th Mechan___ ___ ___ ___ racks ___ ___ River.

## Trip Ends

Forrest Gaines, above, petty officer, second class, U. S. Naval Reserve, returned recently from a voyage to Africa. A machinist's mate, he has been in the navy for ten months. He visited his wife, who lives on Ninth street, Hickory, and his parents, Mr. and Mrs. J. H. Gaines of Brookford, a few weeks ago.

## Leave Ends

Private Claude Reinhardt, U. S. Army, above, has returned to Chanute Field, Rantoul, Ill., after spending a furlough with friends and relatives here. He has been in the Army for the past seven months.

## In Cuba

Sgt. Edward F. Herman, above, of the U. S. Marine Corps, has been transferred from the Great Exuma, Bahamas, to Cuba. He was recently promoted to sergeant. A son of Mr. and Mrs. Sam F. Herman of Hickory, he had been in the marines for three years last January. His wife, the former Miss Viola Costner, is making her home in Gastonia with her parents. A brother, Pvt. William H. Herman, has been serving in the U. S. Army since January and is now on desert maneuvers in California. Sgt. Herman's parents also have a son-in-law, two brothers, and four nephews in the armed forces.

## Africa

Pfc. James David Lutz, above, has been in the army for nineteen months and is now located somewhere in Africa. He is a son of Mr. and Mrs. Abel Lutz, of Hickory. Beginning his training at Ft. Belvoir, Va., he was later transferred to Ft. Jackson, S. C. His parents and his wife, Mrs. Ruby Lutz, received word recently that he was well and likes it all right. Pfc. Lutz has two brothers in the service, also. Corp. Marvin Lutz is at Ft. Jackson, and has been in the army for twenty-two months. Private Abel T. Lutz is at Camp Shelby, Miss., having been transferred there from a Texas camp. He has been in the service five months.

## Seaman

Charles Bollinger, above, of Highland left last Tuesday to return to his base at Norfolk, Va., after spending an eight-day furlough with his wife here. Bollinger who has just completed his "boot training" likes the Navy fine according to his wife. Before enlisting in the services, he was employed by the Brookford Mills. He is the eldest son of Mr. and Mrs. P. E. Bollinger of Brookford.

## At Last

ALBERT W. DEESE

## Likes It

Neven Harold Hunt, above, has returned to his naval post at Norfolk, Va., after spending an eight-day furlough visiting his wife and other relatives and friends. He is a son of Mr. and Mrs. O. H. Hunt, of Brookford. He volunteered for service in September of this year.

## New Guinea

SGT. VERNON RAY KAYLOR

## In Maine

Richard F. Overcash, above, son of Mr. and Mrs. J. B. Overcash of Granite Falls, recently spent an eight-day leave with his wife, Alice, and young son, Stuart. He enlisted September 1, took his boot training at Norfolk, Va., and now is stationed at Casco Bay, Portland, Maine.

1942

More Brookford Photos

Ruth Melton and Ray Pope.

Bill Crump

Hubie Pope and George Flowers

Aileen, Buna, and Pauline Lowman

Len Workman, Myrtle Hunt, and Granny Little

Clockwise from top left: Bee Adams and Ada Scronce with unidentified woman.

W.J. "Jerm" Foster in front of his garage.

Mrs. Steelman's 6th Grade Hobo Party

L to r: Wade Warren, Forest Gaines, Shyke Traves, and David Foster

Brookford Memories · More Brookford Photos

Clockwise from top left: Mark Bolick presenting washing machine to Mrs. Clinard, Ruth Hollar PTA President looks on.

Dewey and Doly Austin.

Hal Simpson with Becky Austin, Maude Hefner in the background.

Ada Miller

Bee Adams

Brookford Memories · More Brookford Photos

Printed by Libri Plureos GmbH in Hamburg,
Germany